# Islamic Economic Systems

**STUDIES IN ISLAMIC SOCIETY**

Islam is now taken as the fundamental social, political and economic reference point in many societies. This new series examines the elements that have gone into making such a claim possible, assessing and explaining the distinctive features of Islam as a social model, both in theory and practice.

*Forthcoming in the series:*

ALI RAHNEMA (EDITOR)

PIONEERS OF ISLAMIC REVIVAL

# Islamic Economic Systems

Farhad Nomani and
Ali Rahnema

Zed Books Ltd
London & New Jersey

*Islamic Economic Systems*
was first published by Zed Books Ltd, 7 Cynthia Street,
London N1 9JF, UK, and 165 First Avenue, Atlantic Highlands,
New Jersey 07716, USA, in 1994.



Cover designed by Andrew Corbett.
Typeset by Ray Davies.
Printed and bound in the United Kingdom
by Biddles Ltd., Guildford and King's Lynn.



A catalogue record for this book is available from the British Library

US CIP is available from the Library of Congress

ISBN Hb 1 85649 057 2
ISBN Pb 1 85649 058 0

# Contents

# Acknowledgements

This book is the outcome of a course called "Models of Islamic Economics" that we developed three years ago at the American University of Paris. We would like to thank the International Economics department for allowing us to offer the course and thereby combine our research with our teaching.

In class, our students pressed us for clarity, precision and a systematic presentation of ideas. Teaching such a course to students coming from different nationalities, convictions, family and educational backgrounds is both challenging and enlightening. We all have our biases, which economists like to call preferences; our students had theirs too. Their presence in such an exotic class signified their curiosity about the two topics that preoccupied us as well. Based on our common interests, economics and Islam, we sought to learn enough about Islam in order to apply it to economics and to see whether we could derive from it specific theories and systems. We wish to thank our students for their participation, interest and enthusiasm in this project.

We wish to thank all those who helped and encouraged us to finish this book. Mike Pallis of Zed Books gave us the go-ahead with this project and Anne Rodford was unfailingly supportive. Professors Sohrab Behdad of Denison University, Charles Tripp of the School of Oriental and African Studies and A.S. Fatemi of the American University of Paris read the earlier draft of this book. We are grateful to them for the issues they raised and the useful comments they made. Valuable research material was provided by the Center for Iranian Documentation and Research in Paris.

Clearly the opinions and shortcomings are ours.

Farhad Nomani and Ali Rahnema
The American University of Paris

# Introduction

In the tradition of comparative economic analysis, the object of this book is to construct an ideal Islamic economic system, or the Islamic economic system as it "ought to be", and then proceed to demonstrate the experience of four self-proclaimed Islamic countries. We, therefore, seek to present and analyse the ideal and the real. The degree to which actually existing Islamic economic systems differ from or resemble the ideal becomes apparent after the study of part one, which explains how "it should be" and part two, which demonstrates how "it is".

To present the ideal model and its theoretical economic implications, a number of problems were encountered and, we hope, surmounted. First, the identification of the Islamic economic system is impossible without some familiarity with the *Shari'a* or the legal basis on which it is based and from which it is deduced; hence the necessity of engaging the reader in an introductory understanding of the legal sources of Islam, as presented in Chapter One. We feel that without this chapter it would have been impossible to understand the Islamic economic jargon. Furthermore, readers would have been unable to grasp the reasons and the procedures by which different Islamic economic systems can be derived from a single legal source which is acceptable to all Moslems.

Second, readers need to be exposed to the "belief system" that shapes and defines Islam's conception of the Ideal Man, life and society. The Islamic economic system as an aspect of the Islamic system seeks to promote, develop and create these ideal categories. The intricate and irrefutable relation between the Islamic economic system, and the essentially value-judgemental Islamic economic philosophy, is established through the examination of the Islamic Man in Chapter Two.

Third, the Islamic Man is partially human and partially divine. If his behaviour was totally prescriptive and therefore completely predictable, we would have had no problems with the determination of his expected reactions and behaviour in Chapter Four, where we deal with economic behaviour of the Islamic consumer and firm. The fact that makes the Islamic Man a difficult being to come to terms with is his duality, partly induced by rationality and partly driven by divine revelations.

Fourth, this dual nature of the Islamic Man can create further problems. Is Islamic economic theory a contradiction in terms, since it hinges upon a tautology? In other words, since the behaviour of Islamic economic actors is predetermined by the prescriptive nature of the Islamic Man, a theory would merely establish a pre-defined condition. One could ask, what would be the point of seeking to establish a causal relation on the basis of a self-fulfilling hypothesis? All empirical tests of our hypotheses under such conditions would have perfect predictive accuracy and prove "unfalsifiable". An odd combination! The issue, however, becomes much more complex and far less mundane, when the dual nature of the Islamic Man enters into our calculations. We enter into the realm of economic theory because economic decisions pit the rationality of the Islamic Man against his prescriptive economic philosophy.

Fifth, in the process of constructing an ideal Islamic economic system in Chapter Three, we discovered that on the basis of different and even opposing, yet equally justifiable, Islamic interpretations it would be possible to construct three different Islamic economic systems. The detailed and intricate procedure of arriving at that conclusion would have been impossible without the groundwork laid out in the first two chapters.

Sixth, it is generally accepted that the smooth operation of the market system depends on the efficient operation of price signals and the generally predictable reaction of household and firms to them. How, we must ask, could, should and finally does the Islamic Man react to these signals? To provide a reasonable response to this question, we develop, in Chapter Four, what could be called the Islamic consumers' and the Islamic firms' market behaviour. The clash between the prescriptive half with the rational half of the economic agents is the subject of how an Islamic market economy may function and the problems that it may encounter. In this chapter we will demonstrate the possible results of this unpredictable battle in micro-macro cases. The ensuing theoretical problems have even led a large number of Islamic economists to replace the Islamic Man with the Economic Man, thereby undermining the whole *raison d'être* of an Islamic economic system.

Our objective in part two has been: to review the role of Islamic ideology in the politico-economic development of Pakistan, Saudi Arabia, Iran and Libya; to show the main characteristics of their economic systems; and to reveal the difficulty of implementing their version of Islam, which indirectly demonstrates the deviation of these concrete economic forms from the ideal models constructed in part one. The countries selected as case studies claim to follow the Islamic path and are officially committed to the implementation of Islam. However, the politically dominant Islamic ideology in each country differs from the other with respect to political, religious and economic institutions. Therefore any comparative analysis involving the economic systems of these countries cannot result from the study of a homogeneous and universally accepted Islamic ideology. The problem begins with the acknowledgement of the fact that different state Islamic ideologies influence and shape different Islamic economic systems based on different Islamic sub-systems.

In our case studies, ideology in the form of religion provides a framework by the aid of which one can understand individual and social action in relation to economics, social and political matters. Thus, Islamic ideology based on the *Shari'a*, irrespective of how it is interpreted, constitutes the basis of economic and non-economic institutions of an Islamic country. The *Shari'a* should, therefore, be able to explain the kind of economic and political policies and measures adopted in these countries in the name of Islam. In all Moslem countries the dominant traditional *ulama*, despite their differing levels of conservatism or pragmatism, believe that the politico-economic issues and institutions must be deduced from the primary, secondary and tertiary sources. Islamic economies based on the *Shari'a* may lead us to believe in the homogeneity of actually existing Islamic economies. In Chapter One we show that even in the theoretical realm, the *Shari'a* could become the source of divergent opinions and thus systems and policies.

We demonstrate that each Islamic economy will differ from another. In none of our case studies will we come across an incontestable and clearly outlined national Islamic ideology. The existence of a number of opposing Islamic sub-systems between and within each country, along with their individual peculiarities and different religious institutional settings, further accentuates the differences between Islamic economies.

Each country emphasises some aspects of Islamic economic ordinances and ignores or remains mute on others. In Saudi Arabia insurance and stock markets are considered un-Islamic by the *ulama*, while in Iran the Shi'ite *ulama* have approved their Islamic legitimacy. In Iran, discounting of commercial papers and mark-up contracts are practiced with no serious religious opposition, in Pakistan and Saudi Arabia, *Shari'a* Courts disapprove of them. In Iran and Pakistan, on the other hand, Islamic banking with its nomenclature is officially institutionalised in the banking laws, whereas the Saudi Arabian government, fearing Wahhabi *ulama*'s objection to the current official practice of the payment and receipt of interest, prefers to leave the topic in legal abeyance. Although in Saudi Arabia a 2.5% income tax is collected under the title of *zakat* and in Pakistan, aside from other taxes, a 2.5% tax is imposed on bank deposits as *zakat*, the Iranian government has avoided the imposition of *zaka*t and its official institutionalisation in order to avoid polemics on the national tax structure and composition.

The position of the Libyan Islamic economy is different. Qadhafi is of the opinion that *Shari'a*-deduced policies are not sufficient for the construction of a modern and equitable Islamic society based on public ownership of the means of production. According to the declaration on the establishment of "the authority of people", the Qur'an "is the constitution of the Socialist People's Libyan Jamahiriya" (El-Khawas, 1986, p. 192). Qadhafi's claim to *ijtihad* and his advocacy of the application of human reasoning based on the general "principles" laid down in the Holy Book, provides him with considerable room for labelling his policies as Islamic, when he wishes to do so. Thus in Libya, contrary to explicit Islamic ordinances, state banks engage in the payment of interest on savings accounts and the receipt of interest on loans to individuals and state firms. The Libyan government's official adherence to socialism as a means of achieving people's ownership, however, can be Islamically justified, as we will show in Chapter 3.

In addition, the different role played by the *ulama* in each particular country and their relation with the respective governments affects the Islamic content of each national economy. The *ulama* are the interpreters of the *Shari'a* and can be ultimately viewed as legitimisers of Islamic governments and their worldly policies. It therefore seems consistent to assume that Islamic governments should rely on their judgements, opinions and final approval of socio-economic measures.

In Saudi Arabia, Wahhabi *ulama* have always had a subdued reservation about the Islamic nature of the ruling family's economic reforms. They have either mildly opposed, ignored or uneasily adjusted to the demands of the Saudi princes. In Pakistan, the Sunni and Shi'ite ulema have failed to reach a consensus on the application of Islam to the economic system. At times, different governments have ignored their role as the interpreter of the *Shari'a*. In Iran, all legislation, including economic law, has to be approved by the Guardianship Council or a group of Islamic jurists. Even in this *ulama*-dominated state, a clear and uncontested official ideology with a well defined politico-economic orientation is wanting. In Libya, the Sanussi and other Sunni *ulama* have been either suppressed or harnessed and Qadhafi has claimed to be the final arbitrator on religious issues. Recently, however, Qadhafi's Islamic interpretations have been increasingly challenged by rival Libyan Islamic movements, which explains his continuous justification of his policies by reference to Islam.

The politico-economic development of our case studies within an Islamic framework necessitates an understanding of the changing content and role of the Islamic ideology applied in each country. The inter-temporal approach used in this study allows us to demonstrate the process of political and economic Islamisation of these countries through the ongoing debates between different Islamic sub-systems and interpretations.

Given the above considerations, we can outline the main characteristics of the economic system of our four case studies. Despite their major religious and institutional differences, Iran, Saudi Arabia and Pakistan cluster around the Islamic market system. Libya's economic system can be considered as a variant of the Islamic plan economy. In the first group of countries, private ownership of the means of production is dominant and Islamically legitimate. Private production and trade prevail and are encouraged by a great majority of religious authorities. Profit and rent are officially legal, whereas interest has a dual existence — illegal officially but charged and received unofficially or under a different name. The production, distribution and consumption of religiously forbidden goods are prohibited. The market is the basic economic institution for the provision of needs and information. Economic decision-making is relatively decentralised. Distribution of income is based on private and material incentive systems, with private property income playing an important role in the economy. However, as is typical of all developing countries, especially those which own valuable natural resources, these countries are characterised by a considerable degree of state intervention in the market system. Indicative planning plays an important role in these economies: regulating the economy; producing and distributing goods and services; controlling certain prices, foreign trade and foreign exchange. However, recent developments in these countries indicate a further movement towards private initiatives, privatisation of nationalised or state industries, deregulation of financial markets and a more market-induced mixed economy.

In Libya, despite deviations from a planned economy on a day-to-day basis, the basic characteristics of a planned economy are in place. Planning is the guiding force of the national economy. Private ownership of the means of production is replaced by state and the so-called "collective partnerships" in all economic sectors. Private and individual proprietorship can legally exist only on the condition that wage labour is not hired. Major economic decisions are made in a centralised manner and the information mechanism is based on administrative and market signals. Despite substantial propaganda efforts to inculcate the labour force with the idea of partnership in the economy and the superiority and advantages of social goods over private goods, differential material incentives prevail. Recently, Libya has also been subjected to economic restructuring and the transition towards greater market orientation. The Libyan economic reforms include partial privatisation of retail trade, small-scale production, professional services and foreign trade. The justification provided is that, since the highly planned economy has been successful in the provision of basic needs for the whole society, the market system and private initiative could be given a greater role.

On the basis of our case studies we could generalise that, despite the relatively privileged position of all these countries, except Pakistan, due to their oil revenues, they are still grappling with the common problems of developing countries, characterised by social and economic dualism. Our study demonstrates that the economic system of these countries does not necessarily fit into any of the ideal models we have constructed on the basis of the *Shari'a*. If a close fit of the actually existing system to the ideal model characterises the successful implementation of an Islamic economy, one could conclude that on the basis of our ideal models the actually existing Islamic states have been unsuccessful in establishing any pure variant of the Islamic economic system.

The prevalence of official state policies and private practices in Islamic countries, aimed at the circumvention or ignoring of primary ordinances and the distinguishing ethical and value-judgemental invocations of the *Shari'a*, could lead to the observation that a pure or ideal Islamic economic system is incompatible with the existing international and integrated world capitalist economy. In the absence of empirical studies to prove this contention, we are forced to present our argument on the basis of the above observation.

The implementation of an Islamic economic system and its appropriate economic policies is further exasperated by the existence of different and often opposing views of what constitutes an Islamic economic system among the *ulama* and Islamic social scientists. The existence of competing Islamic subsystems in these countries is both a blessing and a curse. It is a blessing since it constitutes an in-built automatic and flexible mechanism for the adaptation and adjustment of the economic system to new national and international conditions, without a nominal change in the system. It is a curse in those countries where one Islamic subsystem has not established its hegemony and thus economic policies are subject to periodical change, thereby creating an economic atmosphere of uncertainty and instability.

Finally the successful establishment of an Islamic economic system hinges on the creation of the Islamic Man. The history of economic systems has always witnessed the necessity of creating a New Man. In the 20th Century, this pure spirit was usually assumed to be the legitimate child of a revolution against past evils. After victory, revolutionary governments attempted to institutionalise and eternalise the special and unique spirit of collectivity, fraternity, sacrifice, compassion, equality and the pursuit of social good, which prevailed during the hours, days and years of common struggle against a common enemy. This pure spirit was subsequently codified into what the New Man ought to be if the revolution against the status quo was to succeed. Islam's New Man, in the form of the ideal Islamic Man, has been with us for centuries. If the realisation of the Islamic economic system is unsuccessful, one may also have to question the tenability of the concept of Islamic Man as a realistic reflection of human nature.

We have to conclude with an observation. Our study, which was intended to be an exercise in the study of an economic system in theory and practice, turned out to be far more inter-disciplinary, requiring the use of different types of discipline-jargons. The book has therefore become a marriage between economics and Islamic studies. We hope that it will induce some cross fertilization.

# 1. *Shari'a*: The Legal Foundation of the Islamic Economy

A firm grasp of the theoretical underpinnings and characteristics of the Islamic economic system is impossible without a clear understanding of the legal parameters that condition and shape it. Economic textbooks do not usually start with a legal exposition of the system under consideration, for such a concern is implicit. In a capitalist economic system, the sanctity of private property and contract that is the basis for the freedom to pursue profit is established by law and taken for granted. The right and obligation to work, and the illegality of the private ownership of the means of production were particular features of the Soviet constitution. Centrally planned economic systems were compelled to function within the limits set by such legal stipulations.

The role of Islamic law in delineating the broad contours of the Islamic economic system is similar to the role of any other legal system in shaping an economic system. However, whereas laws in secular societies are made, modified, altered and annulled by the collective will of individuals in society and are therefore subject to change, laws in Islamic societies are supposedly divinely ordained and hence immutable, eternal, beyond human reach or modification.

The notion of *Towhid* or the singularity of God implies that He alone is the absolute sovereign of the world, His dominion includes all men, all those that He has created and chosen as His own vicegerents [57:5, 67:1].[1] To direct men along the proper path, He revealed to the Prophet, Mohammad, the code of conduct, or the *Shari'a*, the precise application and observance of which guaranteed individuals felicity in this world and salvation in the next. The science of *Shari'a* is known as *fiqh* and he who is knowledgeable about the *Shari'a* is a *faqih* (Mahmasani, 1358, p. 17).[2]

The laws of Islam, co-ordinating an Islamic society, are therefore divinely pre-ordained. The fact that these laws were communicated through revelations implies that they are not subject to human reason and interference. The *Shari'a,* as a comprehensive and coherent body of legal injunctions, is complete. It constitutes the commands and prohibitions of God and is therefore binding and incumbent upon all believers. The *Shari'a* is considered eternally valid and applicable to all times and places. God's omnipotence, omnipresence and omniscience guarantee the righteousness, justice, comprehensiveness and indefinite applicability of His legal framework. Islamic laws precede all social configurations and forms of government, therefore the modality of individual and social behaviour and interaction can not be dependent upon or defined by state or majority decisions. In an Islamic society, therefore, there is very little room for man-made laws. Society cannot promulgate laws that infringe the *'ibadat,* the divine laws concerning religious practices and duties, the *'uqubat,* the laws concerning Islamic punishments, or the *munakehat*, the Islamic civil and family laws. It is only in the field of *mu'amelat*, financial transactions, or those areas in which no clear stipulation has already been made in the Qur'an, that men can legislate, and even then under the strict condition that such laws should not in anyway contradict, oppose or undermine pre-ordained divine laws.

The sovereignty of an Islamic state is therefore conditional upon compliance with the *Shari'a* from which it obtains its legitimacy. It is on this basis that many Islamic theoreticians argue that democracy as a political system in which the majority of men exercise their sovereignty through legislating change is incompatible with the principles of Islam. In an Islamic society, the wisdom of people, the validity of their decisions and their power to implement their aspirations is entirely subjected to the will of God as it is expressed in the *Shari'a*.

Even though human reason and discretion thus have only a limited role in the legislation of an Islamic society, it is important to point out that the Islamic legal system is not considered absolutely rigid and static by all Islamic schools or subsystems. The differences do not concern the basic principles of the *Shari'a*, but subsidiary inclusions or additions to the body of Islamic jurisprudence.

The *Shari'a* not only provides society with a collection of laws and prescriptions which indicate the right path, it also focuses on specific human activities and classifies them according to their degree of desirability from God's perspective. Every activity is therefore either obligatory (*fard* or *wajib*), recommended (*mandub* or *mustahab*), permitted or left legally indeterminate (*ja'iz* or *mubah*), reprobated (*makruh*) or forbidden and prohibited (*haram*) (Muslehuddin, 1986, p. 65; Qadri, 1986, pp. 18–19). The determination of the legality or illegality, permissibility or impermissibility of an act requires the *faqih* or jurisconsult to search for proofs or refutations in the valid sources of Islamic jurisprudence. The sources on which the science of *Shari'a* or *fiqh* is constructed and from which it obtains its legitimacy are called evidences (*adalat*, plural of *adeleh*) and are generally agreed to be fourfold. The process of examining the four sources and deducing from them the particular behaviour that is authentically Islamic is often a complex task, given the enormous variety of individual human activities. The science of the *Shari'a* reflects the result of the process of compilation, authentication, categorisation and arrangement of each and every authoritative judgement of the *fuqaha* (plural of *faqih*) in every conceivable field. The development of different Islamic schools or subsystems, which in turn leads to at times radically different Islamic economic systems and policies, is itself rooted in differences of opinion on what can and should be included and utilised as legitimate sources of Islamic jurisprudence (*usul-e fiqh*).

## The sources of *fiqh*, or Islamic jurisprudence

The four principal Sunni schools of jurisprudence, the Hanafi, Maliki, Shafi'i and Hanbali schools, all accept the validity of the following four sources for the *Shari'a*: the Qur'an or Holy Book; the *Sunna* or tradition of the Prophet;

*ijma'* or consensus; and *qiyas* or analogy. Shi'ites, like Sunnis, uphold the first three sources but they replace *qiyas* or analogy with *'aql* or reason.

## Primary sources

### *The Qur'an*

The Qur'an, which literally means reading and recitation, is the first and most important source of law for all Muslims. All that was revealed to the Prophet through the angel Gabriel in Mecca and then Medina, and subsequently presented in the Qur'an, is the direct word of God. It constitutes a complete and unique text, the exact letter of which is God's design and will. As such, it specifies the moral, philosophical, social, political and economic basis on which an Islamic society should be constructed. The verses revealed in Mecca deal with theological issues: the basis, requirements and practices of the faith and its system of rewards and punishments in the hereafter. The verses revealed in Medina, on the other hand, deal essentially with socio-economic laws governing an Islamic state. During his lifetime, the Prophet did not compile the Qur'an into a single collection. The revelations recited by the Prophet were either memorised or written down disjointedly by his Companions, since the Prophet did not know how to write (Mahmasani, 1358, p. 128). The Qur'an as it is available to us today was compiled during the reign of the third Caliph, Uthman, who ordered the destruction of all previous copies and collections once the compilation was complete.

The Qur'an is believed to be unique and inimitable. Its revelation to the Prophet, Mohammad, and his recitation of its contents, are considered a miracle. It is divided into 114 chapters of different lengths and 6,666 verses, and was revealed over a period of approximately twenty-two years (*ibid.*, p. 126; Doi, 1984, p. 21). The verses in the Qur'an cover three broad areas: the "science of speculative theology", "ethical principles" and "rules of human conduct" (Qadri, 1986, p. 186). Islamic jurisprudence is directly concerned with the third category of verses, revealed in Medina and destined to transform the behaviour of individuals and thus reform society according to divine injunctions (*ibid.*, p. 186).

The Qur'an categorises its own verses into the obvious and the veiled. The meaning of the obvious verses is so clear that the reader will grasp their message and content immediately. The veiled verses are in the form of allegories (*ibid.*, pp. 180–81) and their meaning is not always immediately apparent. While the faithful are commanded to accept the Qur'an in its totality, it is pointed out that only the "men of understanding" will grasp all its messages [3:4, 3:7].

Mahmasani pointed out that the task of interpreting the verses of the Qur'an has led to different and conflicting opinions and judgements. He opined that the most authentic interpretation could be found among the Prophet's companions, who were closest to him and were therefore knowledgeable about the why, where and when of each revealed verse (Mahmasani, 1358, p. 128). Mahmasani's approach might lead one to expect that the interpretations of the four Rightly Guided Caliphs, Abu-Bakr, Omar, Uthman and Ali, would evince a great degree of homogeneity and similarity since their authors were all witnesses to the circumstances of the revelations and learnt the inner meanings of the verses directly from the Prophet (Doi, 1984, p. 25). However, individual interpretations of the Qur'an by the four Caliphs indicate marked differences.

On the issue of wealth and its distribution, the position of the third Caliph, Uthman, conflicts with that of the other three. Uthman is said to have been in favour of the individual pursuit of wealth during his Caliphate, while the other three are said to have been egalitarian and even biased against the wealthy who conspicuously flaunted their riches. During the last days of his life, Omar is reported to have said: "If I continue to be in a position of power and responsibility, I will take away the excess wealth of the rich and divide it among the poor" (Va'ezzadeh Khorasani, 1369, p. 21). Informed that Sa'ad ibn Abi Waqqas, a prominent Islamic figure had built a palace to seclude himself from the public, Omar ordered the palace to be burnt down (Ibn Taymiya, 1983, p. 63). In contrast, Uthman is said to have encouraged individual enrichment without due consideration for the condition of the poor and to have given free reign to those who accumulated wealth (Va'ezzadeh Khorasani, 1369, p. 25).

Hojatoleslam Va'ezzadeh Khorasani argues that such conflicting interpretations and positions could result from reference to different and even contradictory verses in the Qur'an (*ibid.*, p. 23). He concludes that Omar probably based his position on a verse in the Qur'an which states that the wealthy will be punished on the Day of Judgement with the molten gold and silver they accumulated [9:35], while Uthman's interpretation is probably based on another, in which people are invited and encouraged to wear and display their adornments and beautiful clothing [7:31] (Va'ezzadeh Khorasani, 1369, p. 23).

The fact that different verses in the Qur'an could be called upon to support different and at times opposing opinions on a single issue was apparent even to the Rightfully Guided Caliphs. In the directive that Imam Ali, the fourth Caliph, gave to his envoy who was to confront and negotiate with the Khawarij, who had rebelled against their Caliph, he wrote: "Do not argue with them by the Qur'an because the Qur'an has many faces. You would say your own and they would say their own; but agree with them by the *Sunna*, because they cannot find escape from it" (Nahjul Balagha, 1984, p. 567).

### *The Sunna*

The everyday words and utterances of the Prophet, in addition to his acts and his tacit consent or acknowledgement of statements or activities of his companions constitute the *Sunna* or the tradition and custom of the Prophet. The *hadith* are the reports of a saying, an act or an acknowledgement by the Prophet. The *Sunna* is "what was practised" and the *hadith* are "the record of what was practised" (Qadri, 1986, p. 190). The Qur'an invites Muslims to follow the path of the Prophet: "Take what the Messenger gives you, and refrain from what he prohibits you" [59: 7]. The tradition of the Prophet, in its entirety, is regarded by all Islamic schools of law as the most important source of Islamic jurisprudence, second only to the Qur'an. The *Sunna* is "not only explanatory of the text of the Qur'an, but also complementary to it" (Muslehuddin, 1986, p. 68).

The *Sunna*, according to Shi'i jurists, also includes the words, deeds and acknowledgements of the twelve infallible Shi'i Imams. The Shi'ites' broadening of the authoritative sources capable of exploring and explaining the hidden meanings of the Qur'an can lead to a proliferation of positions and paths. Even though positions taken over an issue by individual infallibles are valid by definition, the fact that each is pronounced under different historical, social, political and economic circumstances can lead to a diversity of injunctions and positions by the infallibles over the same issues. The *Sunna* is generally accepted as a supplement to the Qur'an and as such constitutes a fundamental source of Islamic religious law; reference to differing or non-homogeneous pronouncements by different infallibles can lead to multiple legal standards and judgements in the practice of Islamic law. For instance, on the controversial issue of the virtue or vice of the pursuit and accumulation of wealth in Islam, Imam Saddeq says: "request from God, wealth and health in this world, salvation and heaven in the hereafter" (Khoshneviss, n.d., p. 54). In the above *hadith*, the pursuit of wealth is presented as a desirable objective that God bestows upon men as a sign of His grace.

During his lifetime, the Prophet is said to have discouraged his companions from compiling his sayings in a written form; however, he instructed them to disseminate them orally (Mahmasani, 1358, p. 133).[3] The Prophet also encouraged the faithful to follow the Qur'an and his own tradition as the path to salvation. He said: "I leave with you two guides; if you follow them faithfully, you will never go astray: the Qur'an and my practice" (Qadri, 1986, p. 191). Based on the legitimacy, reliability and absolute acceptability of the tradition of the Prophet, the *Sunna* was invoked by the faithful to validate their respective positions in legal disputes. While the Prophet was alive, the authenticity of his sayings could be verified. After his death, however, the absence of a rigorously documented collection of his sayings and acts gave rise to legal problems as well as to some confusion over proper Islamic conduct in the community. Words and acts fabricated by individual opportunists for private interests, and unreliable sayings attributed to the Prophet, were in circulation and used to support individual positions.

To distinguish and select the authentic traditions, a *hadith* had to be checked by following the chain of transmission of the *hadith* to the Prophet himself. It was therefore incumbent upon the narrators of a tradition to cite their reference and the reference of their source all the way back to the Prophet. All those referred to in the chain as narrators of the *hadith* had to be honest and authoritative individuals possessing a good retentive memory, on whose good reputation a consensus existed. The criteria of assessment of the trustworthiness or authenticity of a *hadith* came to be based on, first, its well established line of continuity and lineage to the Prophet, and second, the reputation of the narrators. In general, three classifications of *hadith* can be identified. First, there is the indubitable (*mutawatir*) or firmly established *hadith*, which has the greatest degree of acceptability since it is based on the fact that the act or word reported is very widely known and backed by numerous reports or references. Second, there is the widespread (*mashhur*) or known *hadith*, based on the original report of a few individuals, but later used and narrated by too many people for it to be considered misinformation. Third, there is the isolated (*wahid*) or discontinuous (*mursal*) *hadith*, based on the report of one or a few sources.

Even though the *Sunna* is accepted as a primary source of Islamic jurisprudence by all Islamic schools, all existing *hadiths* do not necessarily constitute acceptable sources of law for the different Islamic schools of law. The Shi'i school accepts and uses those *hadiths* which can be traced to members of the Holy Family — the infallible Shi'i Imams. They call these hadiths *akhbar* or reports (Mahmasani, 1358, p. 66).

Abu-Hanifa (d.767), the founder of the Hanafi school and a contemporary of some of the Prophet's Companions, is reported to have been extremely selective in accepting the authenticity and validity of traditions (Mahmasani, 1358, p. 38; Qadri, 1986, p. 93). It is said that he accepted the authenticity of only seventeen *hadiths* (Mashkour, 1989, p. 170).[4]

Imam Malik ibn-Anas (d.796), founder of the Maliki school, accepted and relied on several traditions which he deemed authentic, even though they were isolated *hadiths* reported by only one narrator (Mahmasani, 1358, p. 47). In his selection of traditions, it is reported that Malik rejected those which reported an act or an account which went against the established tradition and practice of the city of Medina (Qadri, 1986, p. 114; Coulson, 1990, p. 47).

Although both the Qur'an and the *Sunna* are considered as primary sources of Islamic jurisprudence, the primacy of the Qur'an over the *Sunna* is widely accepted by most Islamic jurists. However, for Imam Shafi'i (d.820), the founder of the Shafi'i school of Sunni jurisprudence, the *Sunna* constitutes a legal source as important as the Qur'an. He is reported to have maintained that both the Qur'an and the *Sunna* "are from God though the reason for their revelations differ" (Qadri, 1986, p. 128). In cases of difference between the injunctions of the Qur'an and those of the *Sunna*, Imam Shafi'i argues that the Qur'an cannot abrogate a tradition; that has to be done by another tradition (*ibid.*, p. 128).

For Ahmad-ibn Hanbal (d.857), the founder of the Hanbali school, research into the *Sunna* provides the most solid approach to the achievement of a sound legal solution. His verdicts, therefore, were primarily based on the tradition of the Prophet. Imam Hanbal accepted and collected more than forty thousand *hadiths* in his book *Masnad al-Imam Ahmad.* The Imam is said to have accepted and relied on discontinuous (*mursal*) and weak *hadiths* (*ibid.*, p. 141). A discontinuous *hadith* is one where the narrator reports an act or a word of the Prophet without quoting the source of his information (Mahmasani, 1358, p. 138). If the tradition of the Prophet did not provide solutions for the problem that had been brought to his attention, Hanbal sought the legal opinion of the Companions of the Prophet. He is reported to have said that, "Anyone who rejects the Traditions of the Prophet brings himself to the verge of death" (Qadri, 1986, p. 139). Hanbal is known as the father of the *ahl-e hadith*, those jurists who place heavy emphasis on the *hadith* and reject any application of human reason as a source of law. Shi'i jurists who, like Hanbal, place a great emphasis on *hadiths* and base their interpretations and their subsequent judgements on it are called the *Akhbariyoun.*[5]

## Secondary and tertiary sources

### *Ijma'*

*'Ijma''* or consensus among Muslim jurists on a particular legal issue, during a specific period of time, constitutes the third source for the *Shari'a*. The proof of *ijma''*s legitimacy as a source of legislation equivalent to the Qur'an and the *Sunna* is sought in the Qur'an and the *Sunna*. Several verses in the Qur'an are presented as evidence of the fact that consensus and agreement among Muslims on a particular issue constitutes a valid legal basis, acceptable to God and subsequently binding on all Muslims.[6] Furthermore, *hadiths* from the Prophet are invoked as a confirmation of the validity of *ijma'* as a source of legislation. The most important of these *hadiths* is: "My followers will not agree upon an error or what is wrong" (Muslehuddin, 1986, p. 146).[7]

As long as the Prophet was alive, his decisions and judgements were sufficient proof of the validity or invalidity, legality or illegality of an act. The importance of arriving at a uniform view and expressing a single unified judgement as the correct Islamic solution among the Companions emerged as soon as the Prophet passed away. The principle of *ijma'*, or general agreement among the Companions, was successfully applied for the first time in the election of Abu-Bakr as the first Caliph (*ibid.*, p. 146). The event, however, brought the crucial issue of the exact meaning of consensus to the foreground.

Different Islamic schools of jurisprudence offer different interpretations of who is eligible and qualified to participate in the process of reaching an agreement, and of how consensus is to be reached. The Hanafi school of jurisprudence accepts *ijma'* as a legal proof. It maintains that consensus can be reached by the public agreement of jurists or through the silence of other jurists once the legal opinion or judgement of one Islamic jurist has become public knowledge (Mahmasani, 1358, p. 145). According to the Hanafis, therefore, an agreement is valid only through the participation of Islamic jurists and not the public at large. The Maliki school maintains that *ijma'* is only valid if it is reached by the residents of the city of Medina. The Malikis provide evidence for their position by referring to a tradition of the Prophet according to which he said: "Medina expels bad people like the blacksmith's furnace expels impurities from the iron" (Imam Malik ibn Anas, 1989, p. 375). The three other schools of Sunni jurisprudence all reject the rigidity of the Maliki position. The Shafi'i school also rejects the Hanafi method of ascertaining the validity of a judgement through the silence of other jurists (Mahmasani, 1358, p. 145). Imam Shafi'i is reported to have accepted consensus as a proof only when it applied to "the principles of duties established through a definitive text or through well established traditions" (al-Rafi'i, 1987, p. 60). For Shafi'i, consensus did not imply the agreement of a select few, but that of the "public" or the "entire community" (Shafi'i, 1987, pp. 286–7). Shafi'i's emphasis on the legitimacy of the decision of the community is based on three considerations. First, the public is knowledgeable about the *Sunnas* of the Prophet on various issues; second, the authority of the public has to be obeyed since the community cannot agree on an error; and third, the public cannot agree on anything contrary to the *Sunna* of the Prophet (*ibid*., p. 286). In this context, the Shafi'i view of consensus could be construed as a public confirmation of what had already been established through the Qur'an and the *Sunna,* thus leaving no room for agreements without precedent in the primary sources. Whereas according to Malik consensus was limited to the citizens of Medina, Imam Hanbal limited the validity of consensus only to the practice of the Prophet's Companions (Mahmasani, 1358, p. 144). Certain Hanbali jurists further limit the application of *ijma'* by reducing it to the agreement of the four Rightly Guided (*Rashedin*) Caliphs, namely: Abu-Bakr, Omar, Uthman and Ali (Doi, 1984, p. 68). The Hanbalis' rigid conditions for a general agreement effectively foreclosed the possibility of legislation through consensus by generations later than the Companions.

Certain modern Islamic jurists, however, hold that *ijma'* provides the mechanism for the adaptation of Islamic law to evolving circumstances and changing conditions. The ability of the jurists to agree on an emerging contemporary issue based on the primary sources is viewed as the introduction of a dynamic factor which allows the *Shari'a* to remain eternally applicable without undermining its fundamental divine basis (Qadri, 1986, p. 206). Even in this case, since *ijma'* cannot abrogate the provisions laid down by the Qur'an and the *Sunna*, it can only act as a complementary problem-solving tool for Islamic jurists (Doi, 1984, p. 68).

The extent to which *ijma'* can be considered as a dynamic factor depends on its definition according to the founders of different schools of jurisprudence. Various constraints placed upon the exercise of *ijma'* by different Sunni schools limit and in certain cases prohibit the free application of consensus to the resolution of contemporary legal problems. On the sensitive issue of whose agreement is necessary for a binding consensus, Doi argues that different issues require the consensus of different groups in society. He argues that "any *ijma'* that has to do with some marginal issue concerning *'Ibadah* (religious worship) must be ratified by every member of the community that is concerned". Consensus on issues related to economic concerns or financial transactions (*Mu'amelat*), however, is said to need "thorough reasoning" and therefore requires the opinion of the jurists rather than that of the laity (Doi, 1984, pp. 67–8).

The Shi'i school of jurisprudence defines consensus as the agreement of Shi'i jurists on an injunction (Daftar-e Hamkariy-e Howzeh va Daneshgah, hereafter D.H.H.v.D., 1363, p. 59). However, unlike the Sunnis, the Shi'ites do not consider consensus as a source of legislation equivalent in importance to the primary sources of the Qur'an and the *Sunna*. Even though they accept *ijma'* as one of the four sources of legislation, it is clearly relegated to a position of secondary importance. They argue that the judgement of Shi'i jurists and the resulting *ijma'* are not free of the possibility of error. The question of the Prophet's succession provided the Shi'ites with sufficient cause for concern over the concept and applicability of *ijma'*. While the Sunnis take the election of Abu-Bakr as proof of the practicality and effectiveness of consensus in reaching a settlement over issues not addressed by the primary sources, the Shi'ites question the validity of the consensus reached on the election of Abu-Bakr as the first Caliph. They view the decision and the procedure used to arrive at it as unjust and usurpatory. It is also pointed out that certain Companions, like Sa'd ibn 'Ubada, never conceded to the election of Abu-Bakr, thus invalidating the claim to a meaningful consensus (al-Rafi'i, 1987, p. 61).

*Qiyas*

The success and expansion of Islam brought it into contact with societies of different cultures, traditions and socio-economic structures such as those of Persia and Rome. Confronted with new socio-economic relations representing different levels of economic development, Islamic jurisprudence had to produce legislation on emerging problems for which there were no clear legal precedents in the primary sources. This task, which had emerged as a social necessity, had to be successfully implemented without losing sight of the divine foundation of the law. The geographical distance between Medina, the hub of Islamic culture, and far-off lands, conquered by the triumphant Islamic army, rendered the centralised dissemination of Islamic injunctions incompatible with the immediate needs of the newly Islamic states on the periphery. The search for and deduction of novel Islamic solutions, based on the primary sources, was by necessity extended to those jurists who resided in the far-off Islamic lands. The incorporation of analogical deduction as a means of facilitating the decision-making of far-off jurists meant that the *Shari'a* could be expanded without close supervision of its direction or nature. Faced with the absence of appropriate guidance in the primary sources, the Islamic legal system had to rely, as a last resort, on the rational judgement of its jurists. The use of different guidelines for individual judgement and interpretation, based on different and at times contradictory accounts of the Prophet's Tradition, sowed the seeds of competing Islamic subsystems. *Qiyas* or analogical deduction constitutes the fourth source or proof of Islamic legislation for the Sunni schools of jurisprudence. The Shi'ites, however, reject the validity of analogy as a source of law and replace it with *aql* or human reason. Analogy is a process of legal deduction according to which the jurist, confronted with an unprecedented case, bases his arguments on the logic used in the text of the Qur'an or the *Sunna* and applies the same logic to the case at hand. The authority of analogy cannot be upheld unless reason, applied by the jurist, is also accepted as a source of law. If act *A* is stipulated as deserving punishment *Y*, according to the Qur'an or the *Sunna*, then it can be argued that an act *B*, for which the primary sources have not defined a punishment but which would lead to *A* subsequently, also deserves punishment *Y*. Although evidence and cases are sought in the primary sources, analogy assumes the proper application of reason by jurists. For instance, the consumption of wine is forbidden by primary sources for its intoxicating property; analogical deduction leads to the rule that all drinks which possess an intoxicating quality are ipso facto forbidden, and all non-intoxicating drinks are permissible. The new prescription, in relation to a drink unavailable during the time of the Prophet, is viewed as an extension of the *Shari'a*, since it reflects the reasoning, spirit and legal methodology employed in the primary sources. Legislation on the basis of analogical deduction is, however, generally limited to matters of social and financial affairs (*mu'amelat*).

The analogical deduction used by Imam Ali, in response to Omar's inquiry about the Islamic punishment for wine-drinking provides a clear example of the process utilised in the application and practice of this legal source. Even though the Qur'an does not stipulate the penalty for wine-drinking, it fixes eighty lashes for false accusation or slander. Imam Ali argued that: "We think that you flog him [the wine-drinker] for it with eighty lashes because when he drinks, he becomes intoxicated, and when he becomes intoxicated, he talks confusedly, and when he talks confusedly he tells lies" (Imam Malik ibn Anas, 1989, p. 355). In this case, since the penalty for false accusation, which is a lie, is fixed by the Qur'an, the practice of wine-drinking which would cause the same wrong is deemed to merit the same penalty.

Mahmasani explains the process of *qiyas* in the following words: "The general principle is based on the understanding that every injunction guarantees a beneficial and welfare satisfying objective. The underlying principles of laws are none other than these welfare satisfying conditions. Therefore, if we can deduce the cause of an injunction in the primary sources, we can apply analogical deduction to cases with similar causes and pronounce a valid injunction" (Mahmasani, 1358, p. 146). Two types of analogical deductions emerge on the basis of this definition. First, there are the analogical deductions based on a clear and apparent example in the primary sources, such as the one used by Imam Ali. These are called "strict analogies" (*qiyas tam).* Second, there are analogical deductions based on causes that are not clear and apparent in the primary sources. In these, the jurist relies primarily on his own reason and pronounces an injunction on the basis of the implicit meaning of a primary text. These are called "sound analogies" (*ta'wil*) (Muslehuddin, 1986, pp. 129–30). Islamic jurists have argued that, contrary to the position of many orientalists, "sound analogy" or *ta'wil* does not mean "reliance on one's own (independent) judgement" but rather the attempt to deduce the "inner meaning of the text", with regard to "the word and meaning of the text, its context and the traditions of the Prophet" (*ibid*., p. 131). As a proof that *ta'wil* is not primarily based on the application of human reason and the discretion of the jurist, Muslehuddin presents the controversial case of Omar, the second Caliph, abrogating the text of the Qur'an. In this case, an apparently clear injunction of God is negated by Omar on the basis of his discretion. One of the most important conditions of an acceptable *qiyas* is that the ruling should not contradict the Qur'an or the Tradition of the Prophet, which was not the case in Omar's ruling (Doi, 1984, p. 77).[8] The application of human reason, rooted in and conditioned by the primary sources, thus provides a potent and perpetual instrument for problem-solving and adaptation, in the form of consensus or analogical deduction.

Injunctions based on analogical deductions therefore represent a synthesis of divine revelation, the words and acts of the Prophet and human reason.

Justification of the use of analogical deduction (*qiyas*) as a source or proof of Islamic jurisprudence is based on both the Qur'an and the *Sunna*. The most often cited Qur'anic passage in support of analogical deduction is: "And such are the Parables we set forth for mankind, but only those understand them who have Knowledge" [29:43].[9]

It is argued that those who seek and attain knowledge of the meaning and significance of the complex parables that are found in the Qur'an are capable of applying their knowledge to emerging problems faced by the Islamic Community (*ummah*). Apart from the passages in the Qur'an, the supporters of analogical deduction present a number of cases from the traditions of the Prophet. According to a *hadith,* the Prophet said: "Where there is no revealed injunction, I will judge amongst you according to reason (*ra'y*)" (Mahmasani, 1358, p. 149). Further, the Prophet is said to have extended this right to other Islamic jurists. According to a *hadith*, the Prophet asked his newly appointed judge to Yemen to explain the legal basis on which he would pass judgements. The judge said that he would base his decisions on the Qur'an. In response to the Prophet's question as to how he would proceed if he could not find guidance in the Book, the judge responded that he would refer to the tradition of the Prophet. When the Prophet pursued the matter further and asked what the judge would do if he found no guidance in the *Sunna*, the judge said that he would resort to an opinion or apply his independent judgement and interpretation (*ijtihad*). The Prophet is said to have approved of this response (Qadri, 1986, p. 213. Mahmasani, 1358, p. 150). Furthermore, analogical deduction is said to have received the support of the Companions through a consensus among them (Mahmasani, 1358, p. 150).

After the death of Imam Ali, the fourth Caliph, Mu'awiyyeh, founded the Ummayad dynasty in 661. During the Ummayad dynasty, Islam became an instrument in the hands of the Caliphs for the advancement of their worldly interests. Islamic legal practice under the Ummayads was characterised by the application of unrestricted personal opinion (*ra'y*) of the jurists and judges (Coulson, 1990, p. 30). This practice clearly led to a diversity of rulings which undermined the predictability of the legal system. The Abbasids, who succeeded the Ummayads, tried to bring greater consistency to the legal system by placing it on more strictly defined foundations than personal opinion. Coulson argues that it was at this point that the use and application of *qiyas,* as a stabilising element became more prevalent (*ibid*., p. 40).

From the time of the Abbasids, it became generally accepted that the opinion, or interpretation, of a judge engaging in analogical deduction should not be based on arbitrary judgement, but firmly rooted in the primary sources. Later developments in Islamic jurisprudence reveal a gradual tendency back to the use of personal opinion. This latter type of personal opinion was, however, shrouded in the justification of *qiyas*, employed under different names, by different Islamic schools.

The proponents of *qiyas* argue that emerging problems, especially those related to financial transactions, are numerous and one cannot find a relevant injunction for each and every particular event or problem in the primary sources. "Therefore, since clear and directly pertinent injunctions in the primary sources are limited and events are unlimited, and the unlimited can not be confined to the limited, many problems have remained without appropriate Islamic solutions. This situation necessitates the application and practice of *ijtihad* [an effort by a jurist to deduce the proper Islamic legal solution from the primary sources] and *qiyas* by jurists" (Shahristani, *Millal va Nahl*, Vol. 1, p. 180, cited in *Howzeh*, no.27, Mordad–Shahrivar 1367).

The extent to which analogical deduction deviated from "strict analogy", directly linked with the primary sources, and became instead "sound analogy", on the basis of which human reason, conditioned by "the spirit of Islam", could become the basis of law-making, is well reflected in Imam Hanifa's argument in favour of *qiyas*.

Imam Abu-Hanifa, one of the most important practitioners of analogical deduction, elevated *qiyas* to a position of great significance as a source of Islamic jurisprudence: "This knowledge of ours is an opinion, it is the best we have been able to achieve. He who is able to arrive at different conclusions is entitled to his opinion as we are entitled to our own" (Qadri, 1986, p. 94). Abu-Hanifa extended the rigid theological principle of basing rulings on the Qur'an and the *Sunna* to incorporate opinion and the exercise of free thought by jurists. "If I do not find my answers in the Book of God or in the Traditions of the Prophet, I would seek the views of the Prophet's Companions from whose opinion I would not deviate to the opinion of others. But when it comes to Ibrahim, al-Shu'aibi, ibn-Sirin, al-Hasan, Ata', and Sa'id b. Jubayr, they resorted to independent interpretation and I would do likewise" (*ibid*., p. 94). In his search for suitable responses to emerging problems, Abu-Hanifa provided greater scope for human reason and discretion. He took the final step of passing judgements not on the basis of the explicit meaning of texts in primary sources (sound analogy), but on what the jurist believed to be in the spirit of and beneficial to the general objectives of Islam. This type of ruling is usually believed to be based on public interest and the welfare of the Islamic community. Once the application of human reason in legislation was implicitly endorsed by Sunni jurists, the door was opened to greater reliance on the general spirit of Islam rather than the particular and precise primary texts. What could be loosely labelled tertiary sources of Islamic jurisprudence emerged from a twilight zone of analogy, somewhere between divine ordinance and uninhibited human reason. Imams of the different schools of Islamic jurisprudence who used this approach gave different names to the tertiary sources that they employed. Each justified the newly articulated method on the grounds that it furthered the public welfare of the Muslims and facilitated their everyday life. This new source, according to which Abu-Hanifa pronounced his Islamic rulings, is called *istihsan*, juristic equity or juristic preference. *Istihsan* is based on and "inspired by the principle of fairness and conscience" (Kamali, 1991, p. 245). According to the Hanafi jurist, al-Sarakhsi, "it involves a departure from *qiyas* in favour of a ruling which dispels hardship and brings about ease to the people" (*ibid*., p. 247).

Opponents of those juristic pronouncements which sever the direct and strict ties with the primary sources argue that such a procedure assumes that the primary sources are incapable of providing proper solutions to the emerging problems of Muslims. Such a procedure is said to open the door to rulings based on independent reasoning wrapped in religious justifications which cannot be established purely through close scrutiny of texts in the primary sources (*Howzeh*, no.27, p. 110).

It is argued that Abu-Hanifa's methodology and procedure resulted in his rejection of as many as four hundred clearly established Traditions of the Prophet (*ibid*., p. 112). The danger of such a system of legal pronouncements, according to the critics, is that Abu-Hanifa's book forbids acts which God made permissible and permits acts He forbade (*ibid.*). In other words, this type of legal procedure effectively replaces eternal divine rules with man-made rules.

Imam Malik accepted *qiyas* as a source of legislation. For him, if a parallel could be established between the effective cause of a law in the primary sources and a new case, analogical deduction could be a viable tool for a new ruling. Malik, however, goes beyond his adherence to "strict analogy" and proposes the pronouncement of rulings on the basis of what jurists consider to be the "public good" of the Islamic community (Muslehuddin, 1986, p. 156). Basing their analysis on the assumption that the objective of the *Shari'a* is the promotion of public good and the prevention of evil, legal pronouncements based on the principle of securing and engendering public interest were viewed as valid and justified by the Maliki school. The point of departure of the Maliki school in pronouncing new rulings is to analyse the "underlying or hidden meaning of the revealed text in the light of public interest" (*ibid*., p. 157). The Maliki school, however, proceeds to replace strict analogy by the wisdom of the jurist in his pursuit of the public interest. The tertiary source of law developed by Malik is called *al-masalah al-mursalah*, which means social benefit, public interest, public weal or unrestricted interest. Whereas the Hanafi school resorts to the application of *istihan* or juristic equity and juristic preference, the Maliki school relies on *al-masalah al-mursalah*, when confronted with unprecedented cases which require an Islamic ruling.

Imam Shafi'i accepted analogical deduction as one of the four valid sources of the *Shari'a*. Initially, believing that *qiyas* was a weak source, he tried to limit it to cases for which "no binding text" existed, where only strict analogy could be applied, and which dealt with matters of detail (Shafi'i, 1987, p. 292). Shafi'i criticised and rejected analogical deductions that were not firmly rooted in the primary sources of the Qur'an and the *Sunna* (*ibid*., p. 288). Whereas in their legal pronouncements, as a source of last resort, the Hanafi school depended on the discretion and preference of the jurist, and the Maliki school relied on the compliance of the ruling with the spirit of the *Shari'a*, Imam Shafi'i insisted on analogical deductions in conformity with the spirit, general rules and principles of the *Shari'a* (*ibid*., p. 39). Shafi'i rejected Abu-Hanifa's *istihsan* and Malik's *al-masalah al-mursalah* on the ground that the discretionary power of jurists based on independent reasoning and unrestrained by clear evidence in the primary sources was tantamount to man-made legislation interfering with divine law which was eternal (Mahmasani, 1358, p. 158; Qadri, 1986, p. 127). Shafi'i jurists have argued that *istihsan* and *al-masalah al-mursalah* are opposed to analogical deduction because they do not follow its rule of basing itself on primary sources (Muslehuddin, 1986, p. 148). Shafi'i discussed the adverse effect of independent human reasoning on Islamic jurisprudence and criticised the diffusion of a variety of different and, at times, contradictory rulings on the same issue. He argued that a multiplicity of rulings on one issue would ultimately result (Mahmasani, 1358, p. 159). The widespread use of such a procedure would, he argued, undermine the predictability and uniformity characteristic of a sound legal system.

Despite their official inflexible adherence to "strict analogy" based on the primary sources, the Shafi'i school realised that the extension and perpetual applicability of the *Shari'a* required mechanisms similar to those developed by the Hanafi and Maliki schools. The Shafi'i school thus adopted *istidlal* or the process of seeking guidance from the sources, which can be considered as a derivation of *istihsan*. Public interest was distinguished as the basis for the application of this Shafi'i variant of *qiyas* (Doi, 1984, p. 82). *Istidlal* allowed Shafi'i jurists to avoid "strict analogy" in cases where no precedent could be applied or direct link established in relation to the primary sources. The Shafi'i jurist, al-Amidi, has suggested that despite Shafi'i's opposition to *istihsan*, he resorted to it when necessary (Kamali, 1991, p. 259).

Among the four Sunni schools of Islamic jurisprudence, the Hanbali school is the most averse to *qiyas* and all its variants. Increasingly anxious about the destabilising effect of innovations in Islam, which could result from the application of human reason to Islamic law, Imam Hanbal was famous for his dislike of the use of personal opinion or *ra'y* in rulings and the settlement of legal disputes (Mahmasani, 1358, p. 54). Hanbal accepted the use of *qiyas* only after the search for proper guidance from the Qur'an, the *Sunna*, the rulings or *fatwas* of the Companions, the opinion of an individual Companion, and weak or discontinuous traditions of the Prophet had failed to provide a useful basis for judgement of the case under consideration (*ibid.*, p. 55). It is reported that he used to say: "Anyone who rejects any of the Traditions of the Prophet brings himself to the verge of death" (Qadri, 1986, p. 139). For Hanbal, *qiyas* was truly the last resort, limited mostly to exceptional cases of urgent necessity. According to one analysis, Hanbal rejected "human reason in any shape or form as a source of law" (Coulson, 1990, p. 71). However, even Hanbal resorted to the application of independent judgement. On issues involving transactions, where no direct evidence was found in what Hanbal considered to be primary sources, he relied on the satisfaction of public interest (Doi, 1984, p. 81). In his rulings he sought the best solution for the general public. This derivative of *qiyas* was called *istislah* or the legal process of ruling on the basis of furthering public welfare.

Members of the Hanbali school came to be known as the *Ahl-e hadith* or the proponents of reliance on the tradition of the Prophet as the most viable source of Islamic jurisprudence. They argued that the Qur'an contains difficult and complex concepts that could only be properly understood and interpreted by the Prophet. It was, therefore, necessary to rely almost entirely on *hadiths* or the tradition of the Prophet which complemented the Book and constituted its best explanation and interpretation (*Howzeh*, no.27, p. 115). The *Ahl-e hadith* were bitterly opposed to the *Ahl-e ra'y*, Abu-Hanifa's followers, who relied excessively on independent judgement as a prime source of *Shari'a*. They argued that the greater use and application of human reason would increase the scope of dissent and lead to disagreements and divisions within the Islamic community, violating the unifying purpose of Islam.

The opponents of jurists' independent judgement consider *qiyas* a Trojan horse, an infiltration leading eventually to the destabilisation of divine law. They argue that the loose, unlimited and unregulated application of human reasoning undermines the divine foundation of Islamic jurisprudence, which constitutes its most vital feature. To support their position that Qur'anic injunctions provide an adequate basis for all legal rulings, they refer to the Qur'anic verse stating that: "We have sent down to thee a Book explaining All things" [16:89]. The *Ahl-e hadith* also refer to a tradition of the Prophet, according to which he had said; "He who explains the Qur'an according to his own opinion must be prepared to occupy his seat in the Fire of Hell" (Muslehuddin, 1986, p. 138). Increasing application of human reason in Islamic legislature is believed to result in the replacement of God's *Shari'a* with that of man's, simply in order to keep the *Shari'a* in accordance with and responsive to the pressing demands of changing times. The anti-*qiyas* jurists argue that religious issues are not susceptible to human reason since reason is incapable of grasping divine injunctions and thus cannot constitute a guide to resolving legal problems (Qadri, 1986, p. 212; Motahhari, *Bist Goftar*, p. 29). Finally, they argue that Islamic law was revealed to the Prophet as complete for all times and places, to control and homogenise society on the basis if its injunctions and not to be controlled by it through adaptation to its transformations (Muslehuddin, 1986, p. 172).

### *Reason* (aql) *and independent judgement* (ijtihad)

The Shi'ites maintain that the basis for solutions to emerging legal problems should be first sought in the Qur'an and the *Sunna*, and if a relevant and appropriate reference is not found, *aql* or reason should be given free reign to deduce the proper response from the primary sources. The process whereby every possible rational effort is made by a jurist to arrive at an appropriate ruling on the basis of the *Shari'a* is called *ijtihad*. According to the Shi'ites, *ijtihad* is the proper medium through which *mujtahed* or jurists apply *aql* or reason as a source of Islamic jurisprudence. They argue that *qiyas* or analogical deduction which is used by the Sunnis as the fourth source of Islamic law is only a particular form of *ijtihad* (Doi, 1984, p. 7).

Even though the Sunni schools of jurisprudence accept *ijtihad* as a mechanism for deducing Islamic rulings, they announced an end to its practice during the thirteenth century, when the centres of Islamic knowledge, such as Baghdad,

Nishapur and Bukhara, fell into the hands of Mongols. Coulson, however, argues that the closing of the "door of *ijtihad*" occurred in the tenth century as a result of the cult of personality that shrouded the former Islamic jurists who were seen as having completed the task of "interpreting and expanding" the "material sources of the divine will" (Coulson, 1990, p. 81). For whatever reason, as far as the Sunni schools are concerned, the "door of *ijtihad*" has been closed since the tenth to thirteenth century, while for the majority of Shi'ites the "door of *ijtihad*" has always remained open. Imam Shafi'i holds that *ijtihad* and *qiyas* are one and the same (Shafi'i, 1987, p. 288). Shafi'i, who was famous for his insistence on "strict analogy", argues that ambiguous legal issues without precedent in the primary sources could be resolved through *ijtihad*, which is man's application of the "reasoning power which God has implanted in him" (Shafi'i, 1987, p. 303).

The Shi'ites argue that Islam has revealed the general principles and has outlined the fundamental contours of mankind's life in its individual and social aspects. While these general principles are fixed and eternal, particular laws dealing with time-specific and geographically specific details must be derived from the primary sources, through *ijtihad*. The adaptability of Islamic law, through its responsiveness to the emerging needs and problems of the Islamic community, allows for the dynamic sustenance and evolution of Islamic law (*Howzeh*, no.27, p. 100). Motahhari reduces the function of *ijtihad* to the adaptation of the general principles of Islam to changing circumstances and events which in turn create new problems (Motahhari, 'Adl-e Elahi, p. 33).

On the issue of *ijtihad* and the application of rational thought, the Shi'i school is itself divided into two groups. In the beginning of the seventeenth century, Mohammed-Amin Astarabadi embodied a movement against *ijtihad* and religious rulings based on reason and rational thought (*Howzeh*, no. 27, p. 116). Similar to the *Ahl-hadith*, he relied almost exclusively on the tradition of the Prophet and the infallible Shi'i Imams, whose independent judgement he accepted, although he rejected the independent judgement of ordinary jurists. Astarabadi became the founder of the Akhbari school, who were proponents of the use of *akhbar*, or *hadiths*, as the principal source of the *Shari'a*. To support their anti-*ijtihad* position, the Akhbari school invoke the *hadith* which says: "God's religion can not be measured by reason and according to human yardsticks" (*Howzeh*, no.27, p. 117). It was not until the early eighteenth century that Mullah Mohammed-Baqer-e (Vahid) Behbahani, challenged the mainstream Akhbari position and revived *ijtihad* and the application of rational thought to religious issues. Behbahani founded the Usuli school of Shi'i jurisprudence. Even though the Usuli Shi'ites believe in the application of human reason and the use of *ijtihad*, they reject the Sunni concept of *qiyas* and its derivatives of *istihsan* adopted by the Hanafi school, *al-masalah al-mursalah* adopted by the Maliki school, *istidlal* adopted by the Shafi'i school, and *istislah* adopted by the Hanbali school.

## Abrogation and the significance of the time factor

Abrogation or *naskh* means the revocation of one text in the *Shari'a* and its replacement by a different text on the grounds that the abrogating text appeared at a later date than the abrogated one (Qadri, 1986, p. 229). Abrogation is argued to be justified and valid since in the Qur'an certain texts revealed during one period were repealed by later injunctions (Mahmasani, 1358, p. 191).

According to Islamic jurisprudence the how, what and by whom of an abrogation or *naskh* falls within a highly specialised and technical field, which is by itself considered as a scientific branch of the science of Islamic jurisprudence (*usul al-fiqh*). The concept of abrogation demonstrates that Islamic jurisprudence has incorporated the important concept of time and the changing circumstances that result from its advance. The acceptance of the concept of abrogation demonstrates that Islamic jurisprudence is responsive to the objective of keeping up with changing times and conditions. The extent to which the Islamic legal and socio-economic systems are amenable to evolutionary change depends on which sources of the *Shari'a* are believed to be capable of abrogation and by which sources. Differences of opinion on the rules of abrogation constitute one of the bases for the diversity of Islamic subsystems.

There seems to be general agreement among Islamic jurists that abrogation of texts within sources of equal strength and authority is valid. A Qur'anic provision can be and has been abrogated by a later text in the Qur'an. An injunction of the Prophet narrated in one tradition has been changed into its opposite in a later tradition. The Qur'an and the Prophet's traditions are viewed by some jurists as of equal strength and authority. Therefore the abrogation of the Prophet's tradition by the Qur'an and that of the Qur'an by the tradition of the Prophet could be considered acceptable.

The majority of jurists agree that *ijma'*, which only constitutes the unanimity of opinion among jurists, cannot repeal the Qur'an and the *Sunna.* The Islamic sect of Mu'tazilah, which rejected determinism, believed that *ijma'* could repeal the primary sources, since they were convinced that God had wished man to act in perfect freedom. As for *qiyas*, it was generally agreed that a deduction on the basis of the primary sources could not result in the negation of its basis, namely the Qur'an and the *Sunna*. The majority of jurists categorically reject any contradiction of the primary sources.

It has, however, been argued that the validity of abrogating the primary sources through *ijtihad* could depend on the kind of text which is being examined (Mahmasani, 1358, p. 191). If the text is concerned with *'ibadah* or religious affairs, then it remains immutable and eternal. Divine injunctions that pertain to the laws and principles that govern the faith are not subject to change or abrogation. The element of change in time or circumstances, which could allow for the modification or abrogation of certain laws, does not apply to these eternal texts (*ibid.*, p. 191). However, in the field of public law and what relates to the worldly affairs of the faithful, it is argued that special attention should be paid to the circumstances and *raison d'être* of injunctions (*ibid.*, p. 192). In relation to this issue, it is narrated that the Prophet advised date farmers not to fecundate their palms and as a result the dates did not grow sufficiently. Once he heard about the result of his advice he is reported to have said: "I am but a human being. If I give you an order on religious matters, then you should obey. If I merely voice my opinion, you should know that I am a human being and you are more informed about your own worldly affairs" (*ibid*., p. 205). This tradition does provide some justification for the abrogation of non-'*ibadah* related texts, especially those that deal with transactions and worldly affairs.

The history of Islamic jurisprudence includes a number of cases where texts in the primary sources have been abrogated by individuals. Instead of rejecting such innovations as violations of divine law, the new rulings have been upheld by some, if not all, in the Islamic community. The second Caliph, Omar, repealed primary sources, on the basis of his own discretion, in view of changing times and circumstances. The Qur'an had explicitly announced that those whose religious convictions were not very strong had to be appeased, and therefore constituted one of the groups receiving Islamic charity (*sadaqa*), distributed by the state [9:60]. Omar refused to pay this group. He justified his decision by arguing that: "The Prophet had given you this share of public funds as a means of securing your complacence, but now that God has given Islam glory and strength and has rendered us independent of you, if you do not remain loyal to Islam the sword will judge between us, since we are not going to pay anyone for being a Muslim" (Mahmasani, 1358, p. 194). Since the reason behind the text, namely the need of a relatively weak Islamic community to appease rather than to confront the unbelievers, had disappeared, there was no further justification for state payment of charity to this group.

The Qur'an is categorical about the punishment of theft, which is the amputation of the thief's hand [5:38]. Omar abrogated the text during times of drought. Omar's abrogation was upheld by the consensus of the jurists. Shi'ite jurists supported the abrogation on the condition that an exception be made for theft of foodstuff during drought (Mahmasani, 1358, p. 196). Omar argued that his decision was based on public need and the protection of life.

While it could be argued that payment to unbelievers was a special case and that therefore its abrogation did not constitute a radical alteration of the *Shari'a*, the modification of the application of Islamic punishments ('*uqubat*), which are usually considered as fixed, opens up the issue of the degree to which Islamic laws are subject to evolution and change.

Furthermore, the Qur'an and the tradition of the Prophet allowed Muslim men to marry temporarily, for a certain agreed sum (*mut'a*) [4:3, 4:25. (al-Rafi'i, 1987, pp. 114–15). Some have argued that the text is initially abrogated by the Qur'an itself and that the Prophet forbade temporary marriage before he died [23:7] (al-Rafi'i, 1987, p. 116). Omar was, however, reported to have said: "Two forms of *mut'a* (temporary marriage) were allowed in the time of the Apostle of God but I forbid them and I will punish anyone who practices them" (*ibid*., p. 117). All Sunni schools subsequently rejected the institution of temporary marriage, while the Shi'ites consider it as permissible. What concerns us is not the legal validity of one argument or the other, but the manner in which a fallible Caliph was allowed to use his religious authority to contradict the word of God and His Prophet. Omar's action, as reported, implies that the second Caliph, an Islamic jurist and the political leader of the Islamic community, had the power to prohibit an act made permissible by God and his Prophet. Even though the fundamental sources of Islamic jurisprudence are always said to be rooted in the Qur'an and tradition, Omar's practice demonstrates that the authority of explicit primary sources did not always preclude the exercise of human judgement to the contrary. This type of precedence opened the door to the modification of the primary sources by human reason and subsequently to the emergence of different and competing Islamic subsystems.

## Conclusion

On the one hand, we have looked at arguments insisting that the texts of the primary sources have a fixed and eternal validity, since they express the will and design of God, either directly through the Qur'an or indirectly through the tradition of the Prophet. Any abrogation of the divine law by fallible human beings should be unacceptable to Muslims. On the other hand, we have seen that the secondary and tertiary sources of the *Shari'a* open the door to the application of rational human thought and legal pronouncements "verging on personal opinion" (Kamali, 1991, p. 251). The legal basis of Islamic jurisprudence, therefore, possesses both static and dynamic elements. The primary sources safeguard the continuity and permanence of certain immutable principles, while the secondary and tertiary sources can constitute an endogenous self-adjusting mechanism which enables the legal system to adapt to change. The time, place, and prevailing socio-economic conditions under which an original ruling in the primary sources appears play a crucial part in justifying the necessity of modifying and adapting the original ruling. This dynamic aspect of the *Shari'a* can be and is legitimately used by those Islamic modernists who wish to introduce change, although they feel obliged to search for an Islamic justification for it. The quest for Islamic legalisation covering scientific, social, political or economic innovations not addressed in the primary sources, and necessitated by changing times, has lead to a heated debate between Islamic modernists and the traditionalists, who question the entire adaptation process.

It could be argued that historical cases of abrogation of the divine texts by fallible human beings and the fact that they were not chastised as apostates proves that under special conditions, determined by the *fuqaha*, Islam allows for the temporary or even permanent repeal of explicit texts in the primary sources. Thus, even though the elements of the *Shari'a* are ranked in importance, beginning with the Qur'an which is the revealed word of God, it can be argued that the history of Islam, both ancient and contemporary, shows that rational thought has at times been given priority over revelations.

## Notes

1. Numbers appearing in a square bracket refer first to the *Sura* or chapter number and then the *Aya* or verse number of the Qur'an. [68:1] would therefore mean *Sura 68* or *Al Qalam* (The Pen) and Verse One: "Nun. By the Pen and by the (Record) which (men) write." All references are based on the text, translation and commentary of the Qur'an by Abdullah Yusuf'Ali.

2. Whether the immutable and eternal nature of the *Shari'a* allows the application of the term "science" to it has been the subject of debate, since science is argued to be dynamic, tending towards perfection by incorporating and reflecting change (Mahmasani, 1358, p. 17).

3. According to Tirmidhi, the Prophet permitted and even instructed certain individuals to write down the Traditions. Cited in Qadri, 1986, p. 192.

4. According to Abdolqader, the Companions and followers of Abu-Hanifa have compiled fifteen volumes of *hadiths* reported by him. Tarikh al-fiqh al-Islami, Vol. 1, p. 222. Cited in Mahmasani, 1358, p. 38.

5. For a discussion of the difference between Shi'i Akhbari and Usuli schools of jurisprudence, see Akhavi, 1980, p. 121; and Rahnema and Nomani, 1990, p. 20.

6. Mahmasani presents the following verses: 2:143, 3:103, 3:110, 4:59, 4:115, 9:119. Mahmasani, 1358, p. 143.

7. Two other important *hadiths* which convey the same message are: "What is considered good among Muslims is also considered good by God, and that which is viewed as ugly among the faithful is also viewed as ugly by God"; "God's hand is with (or over) the entire community" (cited in Mahmasani, 1358, p. 143; and Muslehuddin, 1986, p. 146).

8. This important topic will be dealt with under the section entitled *Abrogation and the significance of the time factor*, p. 17.

9. The other Qur'anic passages referred to as proof are: 59:2, 3:164, 9:122 (cited in Mahmasani, 1358, p. 149; and Qadri, 1986, p. 212).

# 2. The Economic Philosophy of Islam

Certain economic systems hold that socio-economic actors are free to act according to human nature, or as the Marxists would argue, to a historical class condition. Laws, socio-economic relations and aspirations are believed to emanate from and reflect the free, albeit economically conditioned, exercise of human nature. Human nature and the given stage of historical development supposedly set the real limits to attainable ideals. Furthermore, it is our knowledge of these factors that makes it possible for us to predict how people will react under given circumstances.

In certain other conceptions of an economic system, such as the Islamic one, notions of human nature or of a historical stage of development of the socio-economic participants do not constitute a determinant factor on the basis of which economic and social reality is constructed. Irrespective of prevalent socio-economic realities and existing human psychology, a constant attempt to mould human nature according to an ideal plays the key role. In this sense, the Islamic man's nature is prescribed.

If man constitutes the building blocks of a society and the economic system within which it operates, it could be argued that the number of tenable economic systems is directly proportional to the different conceivable concepts of human nature, at a given point in time. Economic theory, based on a given notion of human nature, tries to define and explain the causal relationships that evolve in Man's quest to secure his livelihood. Islamic economic theory is different from neo-classical or Marxian economic theory because the Islamic Man's nature is believed to be part man-made and part divinely determined. This volatile combination of real and ideal, human and divine, secular and sacred, worldly and other-worldly, presents a problem in terms of predictable behaviour.

Every economic system is shaped by a constellation of influential factors, amongst which ideology is probably the most important. A world outlook or belief system is comprised of a series of explicit or implicit assumptions and explanations about Man's relation to all that preoccupies him, such as God, state, nature and his fellow men individually and socially. Each belief system shares a common view of what constitutes the ideal life and the good society and provides its own prescription for attaining it. Subsequently each economic outlook as a subset of the belief system develops its own maximization criteria such as what and whose satisfaction is to be maximized in order to attain the Good Society through the attainment of the Ideal Life. The decisions and actions of the consumer and the producer will be a function of that which they wish to maximize. Different perceptions of what is to be maximised, such as profit, utility, social justice, equality, righteousness or a place in Heaven, and the question of whose satisfaction should be maximised, the individual's, the community's or God's, require a different set of allocative mechanisms, socio-economic institutions and social behaviours. The sum total of these essentially value-judgemental elements constitutes a particular economic philosophy. Ultimately, the way an economic system operates will be influenced by this normative constellation of values and beliefs. Whether an Islamic economic philosophy is objectively capable of reproducing a distinct Islamic economic system, easily distinguishable from other economic systems, can only be assessed through the examination of the structure and operation of particular Islamic economies.

## The Islamic concept of man

Man, according to the Qur'an, is the cause and the object of creation [2:28]. God created the sun and the moon, nature and all its fruits, time and place, colours and tastes, the plough and the sickle, only to facilitate man's life on earth [6:96–9, 17:70]. The act of creation was neither in vain nor accidental [21:16]. Against the initial recommendations of the angels, God created man as His vicegerent on earth [2:30]. Man was endowed with the capability of attaining the summits of wisdom and perfection. Yet, even though He could, God did not wish to create a homogeneous body of infallible creatures [11:118]. Nor did He banish all vice. God complicated man's life by providing him with a choice between His right path and Satan's temptations [39:18]. Man's soul possessed the potential of good as well as evil. Fulfilling his role as God's vicegerent through the adoption of good and piety thus became man's specific purpose in life [2:21].

The task of attaining righteousness was made more difficult since man was created selfish, greedy, accumulative, preoccupied with worldly pleasures and competitive. These characteristics undermined his moral and ethical convictions, distracted him from his spiritual pursuits and drove him towards the satisfaction of immediate and temporal desires. The quest for worldly objectives such as power and wealth prompted him to depend on his own powers. The belief that man's own capabilities, knowledge and power lay at the source of his material success transformed him into an egotist who substituted himself for God. Promethean man was an unbeliever and a defiant infidel.

The Qur'an refers to two specific stories in which success and wealth lead men to arrogance, conceit and subsequently the defiance of God. Polytheism or even ingratitude for God's bounties result in His show of force. To prove that true power is only vested in Him, God destroys the wealth of His ungrateful subjects so that they may realise that their possession of wealth is only subject to His will [28:71–81, 18:32–43]. God's displeasure with His ungrateful subjects should not be construed as His disapproval of material well-being. The Islamic man is not encouraged to lead a life of stoicism and asceticism. On the contrary, he is entitled to revel in material and sensual pleasures as long as such engagements remain within the bounds of the faith and do not distract him from the thought of God. The Prophet said: "There is nothing wrong in wealth for him who fears God" (Chapra, 1975, p. 5). Wealth and power are not only permitted; they are even rewarded with more favours and wealth, providing those who possess them remain grateful to God [14:7].

The individual Muslim's fate in this world and the next is the outcome of his own free choice. The Qur'an states that there can be no compulsion in religion [2:256]. The fate reserved for the unbeliever in the hereafter, however, is eternal hell. At one level, Islam gives free reign to man's hedonistic and selfish desires. Yet maximisation of pleasure and minimisation of religious duties is unacceptable from an Islamic perspective since it precipitates a rupture between man and God. Islam accepts the bifurcation of man into economic and religious spheres of interest and operation. It seeks, however, to prevent the hegemony of the economic sphere, which would ultimately result in renouncing faith in God. The utilitarian economic consumer is faced with the single constraint of a limited budget within which he may give free reign to his whims, desires and tastes to maximise his private worldly pleasures. The economic task of the Islamic man is much more complex. As both a utilitarian and a spiritual entity, he is restrained, not only by his budget, but also by the limits set on what he may or may not consume, since all worldly material pleasures are not permissible to him; how much he may or may not consume, since he is compelled to remain within the limits of moderation in consumption; what he may or may not do, since not all worldly sensual pleasures are permissible to him; how he may allocate his time between various activities, since he is not the master of all the hours in a day and all the months in a year. Islamic criteria for decision-making include maximising the infinitely long-run pleasure in the hereafter as well as satisfying short-term worldly pleasures. Incapable of attaining knowledge about the hereafter, man is obliged to entrust his fate to an omniscient God and to seek the maximisation of God's satisfaction and grace, through the righteous acts that He has prescribed in this world, as the sole path to salvation and eternal satisfaction.

The spiritual values inherent in these acts are contrary to man's selfish nature. They are intended to restrain man's perpetual drive for self-fulfilment and self-glorification, compelling him to lessen his preoccupation with his temporal self. Religious edicts act as the ultimate defence against the domination of the material and economic sphere over the religious sphere.

Whereas man is acquisitive and selfish, God instructs him to share his wealth with the poor [32:16]. Whereas man is vengeful, God instructs him to be forgiving [3:133–6]. Whereas man loves to eat well and indulge in sensual pleasures, God restrains him during the period of fasting [2:183,187]. Whereas man values his life more than anything else, God commands him to sacrifice it in Holy war — *jihad* — for His cause [9:20]. Finally, whereas man wishes to indulge in pastimes at his leisure, God instructs him to spend his spare time in communion with Him through prayers and pilgrimage [2:238–9, 2:158].

Islam accepts and to a certain degree condones the "beast" of hedonism and self-indulgence, yet it sets out to tame and domesticate it through the introduction of *'ibadah* or prayers and rites of worship. The regular and permanent practice of *'ibadah* by the individual provides God with a mechanism through which man may be directed to act according to His will and thus attain the position of His vicegerency. This control mechanism is so important that the Qur'an points out that men were created only to serve and worship God [51:56]. '*Ibadah* is an all encompassing term. On the one hand, it refers to man's submission of all aspects of his life to the code of conduct commanded by God (Afzal-ur-Rahman, 1989, Vol. 7, p. 184). On the other hand, it refers to all those acts enjoined by God which bring man closer to Him. The exercise of these practices, such as regular daily prayers, forces man to cut himself off from worldly considerations and enter an intense spiritual relation with his creator.

The object of '*ibadah* is to impose upon hedonistic man an awareness of God's power and grandeur. Through '*ibadah*, the dominant material impulses of utilitarian man are sublimated and the ideal Islamic man, the *muttaqi*, is born. The realisation that God is omniscient, omnipotent and omnipresent fills the *muttaqi* with an intense sense of awe and adoration [10:61]. The *muttaqi*'s fear and respect is based on God's unlimited power across time and His constant presence from which no event or act can be concealed. Once the *muttaqi* gains some understanding of God's attributes through '*ibadah*, he becomes compelled to follow the path paved by Him. Entering into a close relation with God opens man's eyes to God's glory and allows man to get a glimpse of his own capacities through total submission to Him. Thus man experiences himself in the process of moving closer to God (D.H.H.v.D., 1363, p. 26). '*Ibadah* also serves as the purifying catalyst that cleanses the heart from sinful temptations and shields the *muttaqi* against future evil. Total rejection of God's control is chastised, yet total rejection of material pleasures is not demanded as a necessary requirement for entrance into heaven. Islam does not prescribe a trade-off between asceticism in this world and eternal satisfaction in the next. It provides a third option, a compromise solution, which is most often emphasised as the ideal way of life for the righteous. This ideal model of life is that led by the *muttaqin* (plural of *muttaqi*).

## The ideal Islamic model of life

The Qur'an leaves no doubt that the *muttaqin* are the most honoured before God [49:13]. Their life style brings forth greater fortune both in this world and the hereafter [14:7]. The equilibrium between hedonism and spiritualism which characterises the *muttaqin*'s pattern of life is upheld as an ideal for all believers. Such an optimum balance allows man to serve God and fulfil his worldly pleasures [28:77, 24:37]. The *muttaqi* maximises the best of both worlds, given the constraints of the Islamic law (the *Shari'a*). According to a *hadith*, the Prophet said, "I like three things in this world: *thurid* (food), perfume and women, but the light of my eyes is prayer" (Afzal-ur-Rahman, Vol. 7, 1989, p. 269). Imam Ali, the fourth Caliph described the special position of the *muttaqin* in the following words: "They benefited from the joys of this transient world as they will benefit from the joys of the next world. For they shared with the people of this world in their worldly matters, while the worldly people will not share with the *muttaqin* in the matters of the next world. They lived in this world in the best manner of living and ate the best food and consequently enjoyed in this world all that the wealthy enjoyed and secured from it what the haughty and the vain secured. Then they departed from it upon taking enough provision to take them to the end of their journey and after doing a profitable transaction" (Nahjul Balagha, 1984, p. 486).

The crucial element that allows the *muttaqin* to combine the best of both worlds is their devotion to God expressed through the regular practice of *'ibadah* and the strict observance of the Divine Path, the *Shari'a*. The ideal Islamic life requires the total submission of every aspect of life, private and social, to the universally applicable law of God, the *Shari'a*. Within this framework, Islamic obligations and prohibitions are categorised in relation to four major axes:

*'Ibadah* or laws concerning religious practices, worship, religious rites, ceremonies and duties.

*Mu'amelat* or laws pertaining to transactions, commercial or otherwise.

*Munakehat* or civil and family laws.

*'Uqubat* or laws concerning punishments for transgressors of the Islamic moral order (Mahmasani, 1358. pp. 20–21; Klein, 1985, p. 120. Qadri, 1986, p. 96).

In what follows we shall try to provide a cursory outline of the manner in which a pious and righteous Muslim should conduct his life according to religious obligations. The *muttaqi* is obliged to pray five times a day (three times for Shi'ites) and is expected to participate in the Friday congregational prayer [11:114, 62:9]. In preparation for his prayers, however, he is required to follow a specific rite. This includes an elaborate process of purification and ablutions without which prayers would be invalid. The rite of purification itself involves four different forms, each specific to a particular condition and each with its own specific rites.[1] Also, it is incumbent upon all sane and adult Muslims, whose property reaches a specific value (*nisab*) to pay *zakat* or poor tax [2:177]. Fasting during the month of Ramadan is considered another duty of the righteous Muslim. This duty involves total abstinence from food, drink and cohabitation from sunrise to sunset [21:183]. If the *muttaqi* falls sick or is absent on a long journey during Ramadan, he is obliged to make up for the missed days by fasting for the same number of days during some other month. If he is incapable of fasting due to poor health, then he is obliged to pay for the meals of a poor person according to the number of days that he has missed his obligation [2:184]. Pilgrimage to *Ka'ba* or *hajj* constitutes another obligation for all Muslims who can afford the trip [22:29–30]. Finally it is incumbent on all Muslims to defend the Islamic community and nation in addition to converting the infidels to Islam. The fight against unbelievers or *jihad* is a social duty commanded by the Qur'an [9:4–5]. The principles of *'ibadah* regulate and determine man's relation with God, essentially in the private sphere. The importance of this set of obligations lies in its determining role concerning the position of man in the hereafter. It is thus the backbone of man's spirituality.

Submission to God's will or Islam applies not only to the mode of interrelation between God and man, but also to that between man and man. This aspect of divine injunctions falls under the general rubric of worldly considerations, which includes the three spheres of *mu'amelat* or transactions, *munakehat* or family laws, and *'uqubat* or punishments. The subject of *mu'amelat* covers divine injunctions on a wide range of commercial and economic topics. The *muttaqi* is informed as to the acceptable types of ownership, purchase, sale, employment, wage contract, loan, rent, profit, agricultural, commercial and manufacturing partnerships, trade practices and even consumption. Even though God is the real owner of all that exists on earth, private property is upheld as an undisputed principle of Islam — though under special circumstances limitations may be imposed upon it [3:189, 2:180] (Moussavi-Isfahani, 1360, p. 263). The *muttaqi* is, however, forbidden to dispose of his property as he wishes. He is commanded not to pay or receive interest on money borrowed or lent [2:278–9]. He is prohibited from renting his building to a producer, wholesaler or retailer of alcoholic beverages [5:90]. Islam accepts and permits the principle of freedom of trade and commerce, yet it sets restrictions on it [2:275]. First, the Qur'an warns that trade and financial gain should never impede the permanent quest of the *muttaqi* to serve his Creator. Duties to God, such as Friday prayers, have precedence over business [62:9]. Second, transactions are divided into acceptable and unacceptable ones. Transactions based on uncertainties such as speculations and forward transactions are considered as gambling and are therefore prohibited (Qadri, 1986, p. 325). Since the final objective of all economic activities is to gain the favour and blessing of God, consumption too is confined to limits set by God. On the one hand, extravagance and conspicuous consumption are deplored by the Qur'an and the *muttaqin* are encouraged to avoid them [7:31–2]. On the other hand, excessive thrift and frugality is condemned [25:67]. Other than taxes such as *zakat* and *khums* that a Muslim is obliged to pay, he is strongly encouraged to engage in charitable contributions to his family, the poor and even to wayfarers [30:38–9].[2] *Khums* is set at 20 per cent of income from natural resources, mines, petroleum, and profits from all permissible economic activities [8:41] (Doi, 1984, p. 390; Moussavi-Isfahani, 1360, p. 561). God repeatedly invites Muslims to be altruistic and charitable and promises great material recompense to those who part with their wealth in the cause of God. Moral and ethical issues based on the Islamic value system are thus a major element in all activities that could be considered as economic. A comprehensive and rigid set of normative guidelines, based on divine revelation, define the sphere of economic life for a Muslim.

*Munakehat*, or family laws is sometimes categorised under *mu'amelat* or contracts because it constitutes an agreement between the parties involved (Klein, 1985, p. 183). In the life of a Muslim, all aspects of family creation and dissolution, its rules, the rights and obligations of the parties, ground for and limitations on marriage and divorce, types and varieties, recurrence and inheritance are all elaborately determined by the *Shari'a*. Even though marriage is not an obligation, Muslims are strongly encouraged to marry. It has been reported that the Prophet said : "Young men, those of you who can support a wife should marry, for it keeps you from looking at strange women and preserves you from immorality" (Qadri, 1986, p. 359). The Qur'an provides a detailed list of all those whom a man is prohibited to marry.[3] The Muslim man is obliged to pay his wife a dower [4:24]. If perfect justice and equality can be established among wives, men are allowed to marry up to four [4:3]. Divorce is permitted by the *Shari'a* [2:229–30]. As for inheritance, Islam specifies a very detailed system of distribution [4:11, 8:75]. The exact share of each recipient is determined by the *Shari'a* according to his or her relationship to the deceased. A Muslim can only dispose of a third of his property by will and the remainder is distributed according to Islamic law.

Just as private life is regulated by the obligations of *'ibadah* and social and economic life is shaped by the obligations of *mu'amelat*, the conduct of everyday family life too is regulated by Islamic injunctions and principles of right and wrong encapsulated in *munakehat*.

*'Uqubat* or penal law in Islam, regulates the relation between criminals or non-conformists and individuals whose rights have been violated, the Islamic public whose code of conduct has been defied, and God Whose clearly delineated limits have been transgressed. *'Uqubat*, which means punishments, is divided as follows. *Hadd* (plural *Hudud*), or the limits set by God, refers to those prohibitions for which penalties are specifically fixed in the Qur'an. *Ta'zir* refers to punishments for offences not fixed by the Qur'an and left to the discretion of the Islamic judge who has to be a *faqih* or an expert on Islamic law. Finally, *Qisas* or retaliation deals with the punishment of bodily crimes committed by one against another: "Life for life, eye for eye, nose for nose, ear for ear, tooth for tooth and wounds equal for equal. But if anyone remits the retaliation by way of charity, it is an act of atonement for himself" [5:45].

Despite the multitude of obligations and prohibitions that Islam imposes on the *muttaqi*, it is adamant about the punishment of only a few offences in this world. *Hadd* is the chastisement of those who transgress the Right of God (Qadri, 1986, p. 290). The *hadd* punishments are generally believed to apply to six specific offences: adultery, slanderous allegations of licentiousness, theft, highway robbery or waging war against God, apostasy, drinking wine.[4]

Whereas the offences and punishments of *hudud* and *qisas* are clearly defined, predictable and valid for all times since they are fixed by God, *ta'zirat* (plural of *ta'zir*) introduce an element of human discretion into the Divine Order. The life of the *muttaqi* is thus shaped and regulated not only by eternal and fixed Divine laws, but by the decision of the *fuqaha* (plural of *faqih*) who have the right to impose penalties for offences or obligations whose punishments are not determined in the Qur'an.

The ideal Islamic model of life would therefore consist of closely following and minutely implementing the obligations placed on man by God while rigorously refraining from prohibitions outlined by Him in the four branches of *fiqh* (Islamic science): *'ibadah, mu'amelat, mukahaat*, and *'uqubat*. The Islamic model of life implies the unchallenged subjection of every aspect of life to a constellation of legal, political, social, economic, moral and ethical dogmas. The modalities and practical exercise of such a life style in the modern age can be best understood in contrast with the principles, objectives and practice of modern patterns of life, predominantly shaped by market-oriented economies within political democracies.

## The challenge of the economic man

Doubt has been acclaimed as the catalyst of all modern knowledge. It is also the antithesis of faith. The age of doubt and reason in the West was thus concomitant with the eclipse of the Church. Descartes' statement that "I think, therefore I am" constitutes a threshold in the development of philosophical thought. Bertrand Russell argues that Descartes introduces two fundamentally novel ideas. First, that the existence of the individual constitutes the source of knowledge. Second, that the individual's idea is as good as anyone else's ideas, therefore "the basis of knowledge is different for each person" (Russell, 1979, p. 579). The monopoly of the Catholic Church in controlling and shaping the outlook of medieval man derived its legitimacy from its claim to the possession of absolute knowledge. If man could generate knowledge, he was also capable of its proper use in the form of sound judgement which would enable him to make ethical decisions and manage his own affairs independent of the Church. By focusing on the individual's power to possess knowledge and therefore discern between vice and virtue, Descartes substituted the sovereignty of the individual not only for the Church but also indirectly for God. Man as a creature in the image of God was set loose from his obligation of strictly emulating his role-model and was given free reign to seek individually what *he* thought was right and desirable. The rupture in the relation between man and God gave birth to the individualist notion of the modern man.

Jeremy Bentham sought to explain the decision-making process of modern man, disoriented without the religious signposts that reason and doubt had dismantled. For the modern secular man, Bentham constructed a new life compass, criteria for right and wrong which were radically different from those of the Church. Bentham argued that nature had predestined man to be governed by and subjugated to "two sovereign masters, pain and pleasure" (Warnock (ed.), 1970, p. 33). The recognition of this immutable reality was called the "principle of utility". For the modern man, good was what generated happiness and bad was what generated pain. Since every decision was assumed to result in either happiness or sorrow, the rational man, capable of making the right decisions, was expected to seek greater pleasure and avoid pain. The standard of right and wrong, on the basis of pleasure generation and pain avoidance, came to dominate the ethics of modern man. The pursuit of self-interest, as modern man's purpose in life, entailed a perpetual and vigilant accounting of painful and pleasurable acts. As long as a choice generated more pleasure than pain, or less pain than pleasure, the decision was a rational or right one. Satisfaction, according to Bentham, was obtained by pleasures such as those of wealth, power, senses and piety. Displeasure, on the other hand, resulted from pains such as those of privation, awkwardness, senses and piety (*ibid.*, p. 68). Bentham criticized the "asceticism" of "moralists" and "religionists" who opposed his principle of utility (*ibid.*, p. 41). He argued that the "religionists" opposed the maximisation of happiness since they feared "future punishment at the hands of a splenetic and revengeful Deity" (*ibid.*). Bentham's "refusal to believe without rational grounds led him to reject religion, including belief in God" (Russell, 1979, p. 742). Applying his principle of utility to the function of government, Bentham argued that the principle of the greatest happiness of the greatest number should become the the guiding light of law-makers. In a modern society, therefore, laws would attain validity and legitimacy through their fulfilment of the pleasure of the greatest number.

The principle of utility challenged numerous religious canons. Unlike St Benedict, who cured himself of the "temptations of the flesh" by throwing himself naked on nettle bushes until his body was torn and gravely wounded, the modern man was to follow every pleasurable sensual instinct that augmented his total happiness (*ibid.*, p. 375). Devotion to serving God and subsequently attaining piety was replaced by serving the self through the maximisation of pleasure. Sacrifice and the practice of austerity in order to gain greater proximity to God was categorised as self-inflicted pain that the modern man would avoid or minimise. Thus utilitarianism revolted against the essence of religiosity. In the realm of economic principles too, a new calculus for rational action based on the newly articulated selfish and hedonistic nature of man was needed. The modern pleasure-maximising man could no longer be bound by the Church's concern for "just prices" and ethical business practices or by its condemnation of usury (interest) and avarice (profit) as unfair practices leading to eternal damnation. The economic dynamic had rendered spiritual and ethical issues redundant. Modern society sought to institutionalise the complete hegemony of the economic sphere over all other aspects of life.

Adam Smith, the moral philosopher and the founder of political economy, reached conclusions on human nature similar to those of Bentham. Focusing on material pleasure as life's major driving force, Smith argued that the pursuit of private interest, and not altruism, by the economic man in the market, secured a harmonious system within which social interest was maximised. Smith wrote: "It is not from the benevolence of the butcher, the brewer, or the baker, that we expect our dinner, but from their regard to their own interest. We address ourselves, not to their humanity but to their self-love, and never talk to them of our own necessities but of their advantages" (Curtis (ed.), 1962, p. 106).

Competition, acquisitiveness and selfishness did not cause anarchy; on the contrary, they secured social harmony and collective benefit. Later, Alfred Marshall, the father of modern economics, incorporated the hedonistic nature of man in what he considered to be the "scarcely changing" "kernel of man's nature" (Jensen, 1990). Marshall believed that the principle of utility was a "powerful incentive to action"(*ibid.*). Even though "he admitted that several socio-cultural forces, such as 'religious ideals', might impinge upon human nature, he was convinced that 'economic influences play' an 'incomparably more powerful [role] in the formation of ... [man's] character than any other influences'." (*ibid.*).

The whole edifice of modern economics is constructed on the fundamental assumption that human psychology in general functions on the basis of pleasure satisfaction and pain minimisation. The consumer is a satisfaction maximiser. The thirst for more consumption is insatiable since more is always considered better than less. The standard individual downward-sloping demand curve is constructed on this principle. Individuals will be enticed to purchase more if they are offered a lower price. Human wants in terms of goods, services and wealth in general are assumed to be unlimited and their satisfaction is only constrained by scarce resources and the distribution of income among individuals. It is the prospect of commanding more consumer goods and services that induces the economic man to work more. Yet work is an undesirable pain that reduces leisure. The pleasure of having more, through the income generated by more work, must be proportionately greater than the displeasure of working more hours in order for the individual to put in the extra hour of work. The ideal is to gain the most with the least possible amount of work. The rational economic man, endowed with the sacred gauge of utility or satisfaction maximisation, is expected to make all the right decisions, ultimately securing the interest of society at large.

The producer, who uses the factors of production, land, labour and capital, is a profit maximiser. He seeks to maximise his pleasure through maximising his profit. The producer's thirst for profit and wealth, like that of the consumer, is assumed to be insatiable. All economic actors are assumed to have access to perfect information which allows them to make satisfaction and profit-maximising decisions. Within this framework, the drive towards accumulation is only limited by the sanctity of private property and contract. The economic man, who is portrayed as an essentially single-purpose, hedonistic money-making machine is not constrained by ethics or morals.

The ideology and relations of production necessary to reproduce the modern pleasure-maximising socio-economic system inevitably provokes an effective rupture between man and God. Man's ever-changing and growing wants force him to abandon other time-consuming activities and fully devote himself to the lucrative task which would enable him to increase his pleasure of possession. The satisfaction of the pleasures of the senses (sex, the arts, explorations, physical exercise and all novel experiences) leaves scarcely any room for religious or spiritual activities. This does not deny that an individual may attain equal satisfaction from spiritual activities. Such behaviour, however, seems to be an exception to the rule in modern, secular societies.The guiding principles, the philosophical methodology, the assumptions and the priorities of the economic man in modern society are incompatible with those of the Islamic man — the *muttaqi* — in an Islamic society. For the pious Muslim, "not everything dictated by personal interest is permissible, and not everything that leads to a personal loss is prohibited and in bad taste" (Baqir Sadr, 1987, p. 27). The fundamental Islamic precept that *all* activities have to be performed with the objective of attaining God's pleasure and therefore His grace loses its significance in a world where man's pleasure is given precedence over that of God's. The fundamental objections of the Islamic man to the economic man and his modern society include: (i) the rejection or questioning of God as the absolute source of knowledge; (ii) the replacement of Divine revelations with human reason; (iii) prioritisation of the satisfaction of the individual's pleasure over that of God's; (iv) the belief that man's purpose in life is to maximise worldly pleasures without any consideration for the hereafter; (v) the assumption that man is *only* selfish and incapable of altruism; (vi) the assumption that man is incapable of maximising *'ibadah* and material satisfaction and is thus forced to choose the latter; (vii) the generalisation that economic pleasures rank higher than any other pleasure, even though Bentham listed piety as a source of pleasure, equal to any other; (viii) the substitution of man-made laws, representing the satisfaction of the greatest number in society, for Divine law.

## The ideal Islamic society

Historically, the ideal Islamic society has been traced back to the period between the Prophet's establishment of an Islamic community in Medina and the death of Imam Ali, the fourth Rightly Guided Caliph. Muslims consider this period as a Golden Age, during which Islam permeated every aspect of human behaviour and interaction. Much has been written on the spirit of courage, sacrifice, compassion, and fraternity, inspired by faith in God, that prevailed during the great part of this period. The Qur'an refers to these exceptional Islamic men as those with whom God is most pleased [9:100]. The Migrants (*muhajerin*) demonstrated their faith and utter selflessness before God, by sacrificing their home, property, family, status and all worldly attachments when they migrated with the Prophet to the unfamiliar land of Medina to create the ideal Islamic society. In Medina, another group of Muslims, the Helpers (*ansar*) induced by the same impregnable faith, offered and shared all their belongings with those who had chosen destitution for the sake of God. The individual's ethical system during this period was at one with the prevailing Islamic value system, upheld and pursued by those in authority. In this sense, the Islamic man's private religious practices constituted a well-integrated part of a homogeneous Islamic system, characterised by its own particular social, political and economic practices. Islam shaped and coordinated every aspect of his life: private and public; material and spiritual; political, economic and cultural. The ideal Islamic life fused each aspect of life with another in an inseparable whole.

The fragmentation and bifurcation of the Islamic man, through the disintegration of Islam's holistic system started no later than the death of the fourth Rightly Guided Caliph. The original ideal Islamic society that prevailed in Medina came under growing pressure as the community (*ummah*) expanded into a vast empire. The spiritual considerations that had motivated the original members of the community gave way to worldly preoccupations. During the rule of the Umayyids, political rivalries and the pursuit of material gain gradually ceased to even search for legitimacy in the *Shari'a* and were henceforth conducted as naked exercises in power politics and the accumulation of private fortunes.

Piety, in the sense of basing all individual and social behaviour on the cardinal principle of securing God's satisfaction before that of the self, lost its significance and social importance. Self-love and self-satisfaction, which had been muzzled, forgotten or sometimes attained as a consequence of pursuing His cause, re-emerged in a pure form. While Islam provided fuel for foreign expansion, its practical significance and influence, as an effective ideology, were gradually removed from all aspects of social life. According to Coulson, "while the Medinan Caliphs had been the servants of the religion, the Umayyads were its masters" (Coulson, 1990, p. 27). In an Islamic society where prostitution and trading in wine were legitimised by subjecting both activities to a state tax and the Guardian of the Cause (*vali-e amr*) drank wine and gambled, the Islamic man was forced to practice his religion in the quiet of his home. Under the Umayyids, Islamic society was confronted with a new age of pre-Islamic ignorance or *jahiliyya*h.[5] The Islamic man, anxious to preserve his individual faith, sacrificed the socio-political exercise of his religion, which had now come into conflict with the state, by concentrating on the practice of private Islamic rites and obligations. The primary concern of the fragmented Islamic man became to secure his place in paradise by personal obedience to divine commandments. Subsequently, Islamic social, political and economic injunctions lost their legal status and were relegated to a subsidiary position, as moral and ethical advice and exhortation.

The phenomenon of confining religion to the private domain of personal laws and separating it from socio-political, economic and cultural activities of the community, thus subverting the Ideal Islamic society of the "Golden Age of Islam", began in earnest in 661. The fact that the Islamic man "left to Caesar, what was Caesar's" and went into religious isolation has its origin not in the secularization drive of twentieth century Westernizers but the anti-Islamic practice of the seventh century Guardians of the Cause.

Western civilization's nineteenth and twentieth century offensive against Islamic lands demonstrated the practical success of a worldly ideology based on individualism, science and industry. Even though Western penetration has been viewed by Islamic scholars and jurists as a curse and an evil, in fact it was a blessing in disguise. Colonialism and imperialism compelled the Islam of quietism, introspection and acquiescence to face the challenge of the abode of unbelievers (*Dar al-kufr*) against what was left of a once complete way of life. The defence of private Islamic practices (*ibadah*) against the onslaught of Westernization necessitated the articulation of a new definition of the ideal Islamic life, based on the letter and spirit of the *Shari'a* and made relevant to the needs of the modern Islamic man. Traditional Islam was forced to question its obsession with research into minute details of religious rites and obligations and to make up for its failure to address the universal themes and concerns of the twentieth century. The Islamic counterattack focused on refuting the charges against religion in general and Islam in particular; exposing the deficiencies of the Western systems of capitalism and communism in practice; highlighting the adverse effects of colonialism and semi-colonialism on all aspects of life; and proving that Islam was a religion of liberation and emancipation, the embracing of which would break asunder all the individual, social and national shackles ushered in by the new age of ignorance (*jahiliyyah*).

Piece by piece, the pioneers of Islamic revival attempted to construct an Islamically justified blueprint of the ideal modern society, in which, in the words of Seyyed Qutb, Islam would be transformed from "a religion seeking an irrelevant, static, purely transcendental ideal" to "an operative force actively at work on modern problems" (Enayat, 1982, p. 151).

The task at hand required interpretive research in the *Shari'a*, to obtain a revised Islamic vocabulary in which familiar modern universal themes and concerns could be adressed in terms of Islam. First, the charge that an Islamic society would be averse to science, thus stunting its own economic growth, had to be forcefully confronted and rejected. Seyyed Jamal ad-din Assad-abadi (al-Afghani) asserted that: "The Islamic religion is the closest of religions to science and knowledge, and ... there is no incompatibility between science, knowledge and the foundation of Islamic faith" (Keddie, 1983, p. 107). Second, the belief that Islam did not allow for freedom of thought or action, since all was divinely predetermined, had to be challenged. Seyyed Qutb argued that, subject to a divinely created "protective 'fence' of conscience", "complete freedom of thought vis-à-vis the material world, its laws, energies and potentialities" constituted "one of the factual elements of Islam's conception of the realistic relationship between man and his Creator" (Qutb, in Afzal-ur-Rahman, 1989, p. 622). Abul-Ala Maududi argued that God had given man "freedom to choose whatever attitude in life he likes and considers proper for himself, be it Islam or *kufr* [rejection of Allah]" (Maududi, in Afzal-ur-Rahman, 1989, p. 412). Finally, it had to be proven that there was no inherent conflict between Islam and democracy, in an age of anti-despotism. The redefinition of words such as *ijma'* (consensus), *shura* (consultation) and *bay'ah* (oath of allegiance) as "public opinion", "representative democracy" and "social contract", allowed Islamic modernists to equate the Islamic system of government with that of a modern democracy.[6]

Faced with the new Islamic wave, which viewed the modern-day revival, grandeur and glory of Islam as contingent upon making Islam relevant to the needs of the present, the traditional jurists continued to defend their orthodox positions. Acting as the guardians of the authentic and unswerving Islam which did not feel compelled to adjust itself to transient political fads, they opposed the ad hoc, pragmatic and essentially expedient redefinitions of the modernists. They maintained that Islam was irreconcilable with freedom of thought, democracy and any scientific discoveries or theories which would question the Qur'anic account of creation.

The redefinition of a dynamic modern Islamic society based on compassion, social justice, freedom, democracy and equality required the formulation of certain fundamental theoretical axes which would combine the articles of the faith with contemporary socio-political and economic concepts of vital concern. *Towhid* or monotheism, *'Adl* or justice, *Amr-e be ma'ruf va nahy-e az monkar* or commanding what is good and forbidding what is evil, were taken to constitute the backbone of the new view of an ideal Islamic society in full accord with divine injunctions. To counter Islamic orthodoxy's claim that a redefinition of Islamic conduct was an act of unprecedented innovation (*ibda'*), the new

Islamic movement based its arguments on the Qur'an. It accused the old orthodoxy of abandoning the Qur'an to gather dust on library shelves, separated from everyday practical life. The reformers pledged, "To bring the Holy Qur'an from the graveyard back to the city and read it to those who are alive ! (Shariati, 1980, p. vii). Emphasising the possibility and importance of seeking applicable modern Islamic solutions in the real source of Islam, namely the Qur'an, Shariati says: "Since our enemies could not destroy the Qur'an they closed it and left it in the corner to be respected as the holy book. It is our duty to re-use it as a 'book'—a 'book to study'—as is designated by the name Qur'an" (*ibid*., p. vii).

## The fundamental theoretical axes

### *Towhid* or monotheism

The belief in *towhid* or the Oneness of God constitutes the most important principle of an Islamic society. In simple terms, it expresses the conviction that there is only one source or power that is worthy of worship and reverence. It also constitutes the basis of all other principles of the faith. According to neo-Islamic interpretations, monotheism provides the Islamic man with an ideology or world-view which directs man towards a society free of contradictions. A society based on monotheism cannot accept "legal, class, social, political, racial, national, territorial, genetic or even economic contradictions, for it implies a mode of looking upon all being as a unity" (Shariati,1979, p. 86). Thus the belief in God's singularity becomes a liberating force emancipating man from all worldly servitudes and dependencies. According to this outlook, *towhid* becomes "the sharp blade of the Islamic movement" (Shariati, *Islam-Shenasi*, p. 70). The *mu'men* or the faithful rejects any form of reverence that obscures the omnipotence of God. According to Seyyed Qutb, "there is no intermediary in the form of power or matter between the Creator and His creation" (Qutb, in Ahmad (ed.), 1988, p. 119). *Towhid* is held to arm the faithful against the worship of false gods, such as other men, nations, money or ideas. (Qutb, in Afzal-ur-Rahman, 1989, p. 590). Believing in the undisputed authority and force of these false gods, unbelievers live in constant fear and desire. In their unending search to become masters of such idols, they themselves become slaves of objects that are the creation of the Almighty. He who has no faith in *towhid* will ultimately become prey to servitude and thus complete alienation (Shariati, Collected Works, Vol. 2, pp. 88–89).

The birth of the new Islamic man is claimed to depend on the development of an Islamic consciousness, which is itself based on understanding and experiencing *towhid*. The traditional and formalistic Islamic man, concerned only with private Islamic injunctions, has to experience three different forms of liberation before he can be transformed into an unalienated social being armed with an Islamic mission that gives meaning and direction to his life (Siddiqi, in Ghazali and Omar, 1989, p. 14).[7]

First, man has to emancipate himself from all his inner instinctual sources of temptation. Self-purification or *tazkiyah*, as recommended in the Qur'an, cleanses the individual from attachment to the pleasures of wealth, power, fame and the senses. This individual and psychological aspect of *towhid* compels the new Islamic man to liberate his oppressed inner self, attaining a mystical spirit of total freedom and emancipation. Second, at the social level, *towhid* requires the new Islamic man to reject all submission and subservience to other men. This rejection of non-divine authority in socio-political relations has significant political and economic implications. In the economic realm, *towhid* has been interpreted as a call to abolish the exploitation of the weak by the strong, for the eradication of feudalism, capitalism or any other class-polarised society.[8] The more moderate Islamic modernists accept the general framework of the market system but view the elimination of *riba* or usury as the guarantor of the elimination of exploitation. In the political realm, the application of *towhid* would necessitate a relentless internal war against all despotic forms of government as well as an external war against all imperialistic forces of foreign domination (Shariati, 1980, p. 119). Third, at the cultural level, *towhid* engages the new Islamic man in a constant struggle against cultural imperialism and blind allegiance to all the fads, fashions and forms of artistic and individual expression that originate in the West. It equips the Islamic man with an endogenous source of identity, namely the Islamic value system, with which he can defend himself against cultural alienation and fetishism. The propagation of *towhid* as an ideology or world outlook represents a mission for the new Islamic man. It is incumbent upon him to speed up the process of human perfection by attaining oneness or harmony in the individual and cultural spheres of life, and equality in the social, political and economic spheres. Upon attainment of the ultimate state of human perfection, the new Islamic man will become a true representative of God, reflecting his perfection.

It would be incorrect to assume that this all-encompassing and radical concept of *towhid* is shared by all Islamic jurists or social scientists, let alone all Muslims. Traditional Islamic jurists continue to consider *towhid* as an individual and personal concern that reflects one's commitment and allegiance to God and His rules. The proper manifestation of *towhid* according to this view is neither the disappearance of alienation nor a political or social revolution. Instead, it finds its realization in the detailed practice of *'ibadah,* which is considered as the "essence" of *towhid* (Afzal-ur-Rahman, 1989, p. 16). One Islamic group views *towhid* as a private matter, another considers it to be a social issue. Each position, in turn, leads to radically different perceptions of the duty of a true Muslim.

**Justice and equity**

The Qur'an's repeated references to the establishment of a just and equitable society provides the new Islamic man with a mission. He is charged with the responsibility to fight against any source of injustice (*zulm*) be it private, political, economic or religious. Where rights are violated by despots at home or foreign imperialists, the ideal of equity and justice should provoke the Islamic man into action.

Justice or *'adl* and equity or *qist* have been used interchangeably and constitute one of the foundations of an Islamic society. After the name of Allah and the word "knowledge", "justice" and terms synonymous with it are the most frequent words in the Qur'an. It is said to occur more than a thousand times (Kahf, in Ghazali and Omar, 1989, p. 78). Shi'ite Muslims have elevated *'adl* or justice to the same sublime position as *towhid* (unity of God), *nabuwat* (prophethood), *ma'ad* (resurrection day) and *imamat* (belief in the leadership of the Twelve Imams). According to them, justice constitutes one of the five principles of the faith (*usul-e din*). Sunni sources also refer to justice and equity as one of the three principles of the religion (Afzal-ur-Rahman, 1989, p. 39).

The debate over the origin of the criteria of right and wrong, justice and injustice, has long preoccupied different Islamic schools of thought. Is theft or usury (*riba*) wrong because God prohibited it, or did God prohibit it because reason commanded against it? Should man be allowed to enquire as to why something is just and unjust? Or should he accept at face value every injunction in the *Shari'a*, on the basis of the axiom that all that God enjoins is by definition just. Different Islamic schools of thought have adopted different and even opposing positions on these issues (Motahhari, *Bist Goftar*, pp. 22–32). However, all Muslims hold that God is just and that justice (*'adl*) in all its different aspects and applications is a central concern of the ideal Islamic society.

According to Ayatollah Motahhari, the Qur'an has addressed the issue of *'adl* from four different perspectives: justice in creation, justice in religious laws, ethical justice and social justice (Motahhari, *'Adl-e Elahi*, p. 36). Justice in creation relates to the justice, balance and equilibrium that characterise the existence and operation of the universe and its components. Nature and all its constituent elements are created and set to work according to a harmonious and synchronised system. God's immaculate product is a reflection of His own balanced perfection. Motahhari invokes the Qur'an [55:7] to prove that justice and harmony constituted the criteria on which God created the world. He supports his view by referring to a statement by the Prophet that, "heaven and earth are established on the basis of justice" (Motahhari, *'Adl-e Elahi*, p. 36). Motahhari concludes that justice in creation refers to the fact that God built the universe by strictly adhering to notions of harmony, justice and balance. (Motahhari, *'Adl-e Elahi*, p. 60).

Justice in religious laws refers to the fact that the principle of justice is the guiding light illuminating all Islamic injunctions in the *Shari'a*. To implement the just Islamic society, Prophets are sent to earth. The Qur'an says that God provides His messengers with revelations in which right and wrong are differentiated. He inculcates in them a sense of balance and justice in order to understand and explain the distinction between good and evil, and arms them with iron to punish the transgressors of justice and reward those who obey, so that a just society may be established among men [57:25]. The laws of the *Shari'a* are embedded in justice and are the mirror image of it.

Ethical justice refers to God's concern with the creation of a just Man who is free of all prejudice and passes judgements on the basis of fairness and honesty [65:2, 5:95]. This is an individual duty to which God commands the faithful (*mu'men*) [16:90].

Finally, according to Motahhari, of all the different applications of the concept of justice, social justice is the one on which the Qur'an focuses the most and therefore its realization becomes of the greatest importance in an ideal Islamic society (Motahhari, *'Adl-e Elahi*, p. 38). In contrast to ethical justice which is a private concern, social justice is a social obligation. To establish social justice, the law of "giving fair share to whom it is due" has to govern society (Motahhari, *Bist Goftar*, p. 44). In his discussion of Imam Ali's justice, Motahhari argues that while ethical justice can be attained passively, social justice requires an active commitment against injustice and oppression, a commitment that may even lead to martyrdom, as it did in the case of Imam Ali (Motahhari, *Bist Goftar*, p. 8).

On the socio-economic implications of justice and equity, or Islamic social justice, opinions differ among modernist Islamic theorists. On this issue, the modernists are divided along ideological lines. The moderate Islamic modernists have interpreted a just Islamic society as one which would abolish discrimination and provide equal opportunity for all. Subsequently, however, each would be rewarded according to his ability. Radical Islamic modernists have interpreted Islamic social justice as a call for revolutionary change and the creation of a classless society based on the absolute equality of income, wealth and even consumption (Shariati, *Collected Works*, Vol.2, p. 144; Naqvi, 1981, p. 65). The different definitions and explanations of social justice can be traced back to contrasting injunctions in the Qur'an and the *Sunna*.

First, the moderate Islamic modernists believe that the Islamic concept of social justice expresses distributional equity rather than equality. Equity means fairness. Differences in human capability, effort, aptitude, dexterity, work habits and entrepreneurship should be rewarded. Motahhari argues that the system of reward on the basis of differences in capability is not discriminatory since God introduced such differences among men in the act of creation (Mottahari, *'Adl-e Elahi*, p. 115). In this interpretation, justice requires a system of reward according to varying individual contributions. Rewarding different contributions equally would actually constitute an injustice (Iqbal, 1988, p. 16; Motahhari, 1361, p. 89). "Perfect equality of money incomes would be as unjust if not more unjust than the glaring inequalities that afflict many a society in the world today" (Hasan in Iqbal (ed.), 1988, p. 40. Shafey in Iqbal (ed.), 1988, p. 68). This concept of Islamic social justice places great emphasis on equality of all before the law and equality of opportunity for members of the Islamic community. Maududi emphasises the point that equity rather than equality constitutes the basis of the Islamic economic system. He says: "Islam does not envision equal distribution of economic resources among individuals at all" (Maududi, 1984, p. 87).

The radical Islamic interpretation of social justice, on the other hand, takes a hard line against the capitalist system and the market allocation of resources. The market system is condemned, since it gives free reign to exploitation and increases injustices by rewarding those who already possess more than their share. It is ultimately viewed as the mechanism which polarizes society into the rich and poor, thus preventing the establishment of a "classless monotheistic (*towhidi*) society" (Safa and Mohsen, n.d., pp. 7–11). Based on the argument that in Islam the real ownership of all God's creations on earth belongs to Him and is only left to man in trusteeship (*amanat*), it is argued that all men should share equally in the bounties of God. This argument is further supported by reference to the Qur'an which explicitly states that the poor have a share in the wealth of the rich. The proponents of this interpretation of social justice argue that the only form of property ownership compatible with Islam is a social or collective one, since it prevents the polarization of wealth and poverty (Mustafa and Askari, in Iqbal (ed.),1988, pp. 95, 104). A certain type of class analysis is also used in their methodology. They maintain that when Islamic social justice prevails in society, the relentless war between the haves and the have-nots will come to an end in favour of the disinherited and the poor, thus realising the socio-economic aspect of *towhid* (Shariati,1362, p. 280).

Just as in the case of *towhid*, two different Islamic interpretations of the issue of social justice, each leading to different and opposed socio-economic and political policies, can be readily identified. From the radical interpretation one can derive the blueprint for the construction of a classless society, while on the basis of the more traditional interpretation one can construct a modern class-ridden market economy. Even though both positions derive their legitimacy from Islam, the rift between them as to what constitutes "true Islam" seems unbridgeable.

**Commanding good and forbidding evil**

The dissemination of Islamic thought and the shaping of correct Islamic behaviour during the initial stage of the Prophet's invitation to the faith was conducted through a campaign of *amr-e be ma'ruf* and *nahy-e az monkar* or commanding people to do what is good and forbidding them to do what is evil. God had made known what was good (*ma'ruf*) and what was evil (*monkar*) through the Qur'an [3:104, 3:110, 9:71, 31:17]. The public practice of commanding good and forbidding evil provided a grass-roots control system which assured the observance of the *Shari'a* through peer pressure. For a long time, however, the application of this principle was limited to the sphere of private affairs, having lost its social significance.

It has been argued that the proper social application of this principle would guarantee fundamental individual rights of dissent, criticism and expression, within the *Shari'a* (Bazargan, 1361, Vol.1, p. 74). In this analysis, the responsibility to struggle against injustice, inequity and corruption is placed on the shoulder of all individuals. This form of freedom of expression and thought, within the limits of the *Shari'a*, is held to prevent the Islamic society from deviation and decay. The practical and social significance of the principle is demonstrated by reference to a reported dialogue between the second Caliph, Omar, and a commoner. Omar is reported to have called on the people to remind, heed and caution him in case he deviated from the Islamic principles and objectives that he had set out to accomplish, and a commoner is reported to have said: "If you deviate from those principles I will put you on the right path not with my words, but with my sword" (Bazargan, 1361, Vol.1, p. 77).

For Islamic modernists, the social responsibility to command good and forbid evil goes beyond narrow concern for proper private Islamic behaviour. Its objective is to sensitise Muslims to the condition in which they live and to raise their socio-political consciousness. The new Islamic man has the individual responsibility of self-purification as well as the social responsibility of changing the uninitiated, his society and its political system, if need be. Social consciousness has to result in political action. It is reported that the Prophet said: "If one of you see something improper, let him change it with his hands; if he cannot, then with his tongue; if he cannot, then with his heart. That is the weakest of the faith (Ibn Taymiya,1983, p. 77). Imam Ali also argued that in the absence of the regular and permanent practice of commanding good and forbidding evil, without fear of repercussions, evil and mischief would gradually come to prevail in society (Nahjul Balagha, 1984, p. 531). In the same vein, Shariati argues that Imam Hussain's uprising against Yazid was based on the socio-political application of commanding good and forbidding evil (Shariati, *Shahadat*, p. 51). The new Islamic man had to attain an Islamic political consciousness in the colonized and semi-colonized dictatorships of the Muslim world, in order to effect change. In the principle of commanding good and forbidding evil, Islamic modernists found the justification for social criticism, civil disobedience and revolution against what they considered to be injustice and oppression.

On this issue, one finds more common ground between Muslims than on the previous two. However, the desire on the part of Islamic modernists to construct a potent political weapon out of commanding good and forbidding evil has to be contrasted with the opinion of the more traditional jurists. According to Mohaqeq-e Helli, one of the most authoritative Shi'i jurists, commanding good and forbidding evil is certainly a religious obligation. The act of enjoining good is an unconditional duty incumbent upon all Muslims. The forbidding of evil, however, is conditional upon the fulfilment of the following four requirements: the practitioner has to have full knowledge of the fact that the act which he is forbidding does constitute an evil; the practitioner has to be convinced that that his act of forbidding has a chance of being effective; the person who is committing the forbidden act has to persist in his activity; the practitioner has to be convinced that his act of forbidding would have no harmful consequences for himself or any other Muslim (Helli, 1364, Vol.1, p. 137). Helli recognises that certain theologians believe that the forbidding of evil is incumbent upon believers even if its application leads to physical injury or death, but he himself argues that no such action is allowed unless it is permitted by the Hidden Imam (Mohaqeq-e Helli, 1364, Vol.1, p. 138). Mohaqeq-e Helli effectively forbids the indiscretionary use of commanding good and forbidding evil for the purposes of violent socio-political change.

The reticence of both Shi'i and Sunni theologians to provide unconditional freedom to the practitioners of this duty has its roots in the rigid and dogmatic manner in which it was, at times, applied throughout the history of Islam. The Khawarij rebelled against Imam Ali, the fourth Caliph, invoking the primacy of commanding good and forbidding evil over pragmatism and the well-being of the community. In the application of what they believed to be their religious duty, they assassinated Imam Ali.

## Notes

1. These are: (i) *istinja*; (ii) wudu or partial ablution; (iii) *ghusl* or total ablution through immersion; (iv) *tayammum* or ablution with fine sand (Klein, pp. 123–5).

2. *Zakat* constitutes 2.5 per cent of savings which should be given to the poor (Doi, 1984, p. 388).

3. These include the ex-wife or wives of one's father or one's sons, one's first of kin, one's step-daughters, disbelievers and married women unless they have been captured as slaves in a Holy War [4:23].

4. Even though both the Shi'ites and Sunnites categorise wine drinking as a *hadd* offence, the Qur'an fixes no specific punishment for it. On the other hand, there is general agreement that the penalty for wine drinking was deduced from the penalty for slanderous allegations of unchastity by Imam Ali (Imam Malik ibn Anas,1989, p. 355).

5. With the exception of Omar ibn-Abdulaziz, unIslamic or even anti-Islamic practices were prevalent among the Ummayid Caliphs. For references, see Hassan-uz-Zaman, 1981, p. 274. Zarinkoob, 1363, p. 353.

6. For references, see Enayat, 1982, p. 135; Afzal-ur-Rahman, 1988, p. 312; Bazargan, 1361, Vol.1, p. 73; Maududi,1983, p. 26; Rahnema and Nomani, 1990, p. 109.

7. The following section is based on the ideas of Siddiqi, in Ghazali and Omar, 1989, pp. 5–7; Shariati, *Khodsazi-e Enqelabi*, pp. 97–114.

8. For references, see Maududi, "Islam: Its Meaning and Message", in Ahmad, 1988, p. 156; Shariati, *Collected Works*, Vol. 2, p. 148; Shariati, 1980, p. 129.

# 3. The Islamic Economic System

## How to recognise an economic system

An economic system, whether theoretically articulated and recorded or traditionally practised over years, is a static registration of how society organises itself to address the basic economic problems of what is to be produced, how many, how and for whom. In the process of satisfying their wants, economic agents interact individually and through organisations and institutions that they come to create. Organisations, in turn, develop their own structure, shape and mode of operation. The economic system, reflecting the interaction and participation of individuals, organisations and institutions in the process of production, consumption, exchange and distribution, is governed by a set of rules and laws specific to that system. The object of these laws is to ensure the sustained reproduction and welfare of society. These rules constitute a signalling device co-ordinating and harmonising the activity of each atomised decision-making unit (producers and consumers) in order to attain the objective of the system, which is generally held to be that of efficiently allocating scarce resources with the goal of producing the greatest combination of goods and services. The laws and the signalling device governing an economic system also play the crucial role of providing security for the participants. Risk and uncertainty in economic activities are further reduced in an economic system through the implementation of a predictable system of incentives. The incentive system provides the participants with a blueprint of what to expect as a result of their particular economic activity.

In order to distinguish one economic system from another, we need to focus on and compare their fundamental elements. Gregory and Stuart provide a systematic and very useful method of addressing the key characteristics that go to make up a particular economic system. (Gregory and Stuart, 1985, p. 12)

Their first characteristic focuses on the issue of "the organisation of decision-making arrangements" or the method and process of decision making employed by economic agents including the government. This characteristic finds its expression in two distinct domains. First, the operation of business organisations in different economic systems is governed by different socio-economic objectives. For example, the objective of firms may be to maximise profit, output, average income or even the pleasure of God (thereby securing eternal felicity by following His injunctions word by word, without undue emphasis on classical efficiency). Second, economic systems can be classified according to the different degrees of centralisation that they manifest in the process of decision-making, both within firms and between firms and consumers. For example, firms in one economic system can be characterised as decentralised at the firm level, where workers have the right to participate in and control the firm's decision-making process. In another economic system, firms managed in a centralised and hierarchical manner may respond in a decentralised manner to household preferences. Such a system would be considered as decentralised at the macro level. In a highly centralised economic system almost all decisions for the firms and households are made by a supreme planning authority. Each of these systems would obviously possess different organisational pyramids with different directions in the chain of command.

The second characteristic of an economic system is the "mechanism for the provision of information and co-ordination of decisions". This characteristic is concerned with the process through which decisions made by consumers, producers and government as to what to consume, produce and use as inputs are communicated and co-ordinated in order to guarantee the production and consumption of the "proper" basket of goods and services. Historically, three general co-ordinating mechanisms have been identified. First, the market, which operates through its price-signalling device. Second, the plan, which operates through its physical quota and target system of inputs and outputs. Third, tradition, which operates through its reliance on custom and the status quo. Each mechanism makes its own assumptions about human behaviour and establishes its own distinct economic objectives with concomitant social implications.

The third characteristic used by Gregory and Stuart to distinguish economic systems from one another is that of property rights: who is entitled to own what. Ownership in society can take one or a combination of the following forms: private, public or co-operative. Under the influence of Marxian analysis, the distribution of ownership rights was for a long time used as the sole distinguishing feature of an economic system. Even though Gregory and Stuart's multi-dimensional approach is more explanatory, one can argue that the issue of ownership still remains the most important aspect of a system. Once an economy opts for one prevalent system of ownership, the other characteristics should logically follow, if the system is to remain internally consistent. Whereas widespread public ownership would necessitate a planning mechanism along with its own hierarchical system of decision-making, an economy based on private ownership would necessitate a market system based on a horizontal system of decision-making at the macro level. The pattern of property ownership in society is also of great significance since it affects the pattern of income distribution.

Gregory and Stuart's fourth characteristic focuses on how society can employ material or moral incentives to regulate its economic activities. It is worth noting that material rewards can be further divided into private and collective incentives. Collective material incentives are meant to reward individuals materially while promoting a sense of social consciousness and solidarity, rather than competition and individualism. Private material incentives reward proper economic behaviour with a greater share of national output. Moral incentives promote man's sense of altruism and his concern for and responsibility towards the general or social good. The use of moral incentives assumes that social recognition and approbation are just as important as the provision of material goods in motivating proper economic performance.

We can now easily distinguish two very different economic systems. First, the market economic system, which is characterised by: (i) a decentralised macro decision-making structure; (ii) a co-ordinating mechanism based on the free operation of the price system; (iii) the prevalence of private property rights; and (iv) the promotion of proper economic behaviour through private material incentives. Second, the centrally planned command system, which is characterised by: (i) a centralised macro decision-making structure; (ii) a co-ordinating mechanism based on the rigorous application of the national plan, which expresses itself in terms of physical quotas and targets for firms and the absence of meaningful market prices; (iii)the prevalence of state ownership in terms of capital along with state and co-operative ownership in land; (iv) promotion of proper economic behaviour through a combination of private and collective material incentives as well as moral incentives.

Economic systems, however, do not function within a vacuum. They are significantly affected and shaped by a set of "influential factors": the level of economic development; social and cultural factors; and the environment (Bornstein, 1979, p. 7).) Religion, ideology or any strongly held set of values, ideals and mores have an impact and influence which have to be taken into serious consideration. Indeed, we shall argue that in any society claiming allegiance to Islam, the very subject of economics has to be analysed through the perspective of religious law or *Shari'a*, which expresses that which is ordained by God.

## The peculiarity of Islamic economic thought

Economic thinking in Islam does not particularly concern itself with those causal relations which Neo-classical economics treats as objective and scientific laws and tendencies. It is essentially prescriptive.

Whereas the economic and social activities of the economic man are entirely based on his own judgement as to how to achieve objectives he has defined himself, the activities of the ideal Islamic man are based on divine Islamic law, part of which is laid down and part of which has been left to human discretion. Islamic economists believe that to produce Islamic economic theory, economic hypotheses have to be based on assumptions derived from the *Shari'a*. The validity of a theory is not simply obtained by measuring it against empirical evidence; first, it has to be put to the ultimate test of compliance with Islamic axioms and criteria found in the *Shari'a*. "Any theory put forward by a human being is tested on these (Islamic) criteria and if there is a clear and undeniable contradiction, the theory is rejected straightaway without further examination" (Khan in Ghazali and Omar, 1989, p. 54). Economic objectives such as optimisation, maximisation and minimisation cannot constitute desirable criteria of assessment of and by themselves. They can only become useful if they contribute to the attainment of Islamic objectives. In this sense, value-judgements lie at the roots of the Islamic economic system and its economic theories. In this system, the Marxian notion of the economy constituting the foundation and thus determining the religious, legal, political and ethical conditions reflected in the superstructure is explicitly stood on its head.

Islam, as a system, presents itself as a well-integrated, comprehensive and universal whole which possesses the means of solving man's basic problems. As an all-embracing ideology, it does not seek to influence one or another aspect of life but its totality. It does not intervene in people's lives, since it is itself the clay of which the people in the system are made. According to Mohammad Baqir Sadr, a contemporary pioneer in the field of Islamic philosophy and economics: "It would be incorrect to analyse the Islamic economy as an independent entity, separate and distinct from other principal components of the Islamic system such as the social and political domains" (Sadr, 1350, p. 370).

The ultimate objective of Islam, as any other religion, is to mould human behaviour to the ideal laid down by the Creator. Islam is presented as a flawless way or doctrine of life, the adoption and effective use of which would enable man to experience his potential of attaining perfection. To become God's vicegerent on earth, however, man has to submit himself totally to God's will, striving to accomplish the goals He has set for him, and attaining his own pleasure only through maximising God's satisfaction. The Muslim or one who submits to God is born out of the realisation that harmony and total felicity for all mankind is possible only through the implementation of the divine order, as communicated and articulated through the Prophet, Mohammad. Total compliance with God's vision of how man should regulate his relation to Himself, other men and nature becomes the maxim and guiding torch of Islamic man in every aspect of life, including the economic. He is obliged, under contract, to behave in accordance with the precepts of Islam even if it muzzles his momentary desires or contradicts certain natural impulses [9:111]. Islamic economic relations are thus appendant to Islamic man's more comprehensive contract or "bargain" with God, according to which, "man barters his life and his possessions in exchange for the promise of Paradise in the Hereafter" (Maududi, 1986, p. 12). Islamic man's vision has to be focused on both the material world and the hereafter. This double perspective obliges him to develop a very different outlook on life compared to his secular counterpart. In the economic realm, as in any other, the objective of Islamic man is to maximise felicity across an eternally long-term horizon.

Since the objectives of the Islamic system, as outlined in Chapter 2, are incompatible with those of economic man, the practical success of Islamic economic theories hinges on the emergence and universalisation of the Islamic man's outlook. Islamic economics is, therefore, based on the internalisation and total incorporation of the Islamic value-system by all members of the Islamic community or *ummah*. This requires the development and prevalence of an Islamic individual and social psychology. This in turn is dependant upon a conducive social environment, the creation of which necessitates an Islamic state capable of promoting and upholding the Islamic value-system. Islamicisation of society and consequently the economic system therefore hinges on the establishment of an Islamic state capable of enforcing the *Shari'a*. The Islamic state established by believers is charged with the transformation of all Muslim members of society into believers with an Islamic economic outlook. Ultimately, the prevalence of such an outlook leads to the creation of an Islamic economic system. The behaviour of Islamic man, the *mu'men*, as laid down in the *Shari'a*, constitutes the basis of any theory of economic behaviour.

## Is there a single Islamic economic system?

Even though there is general consensus that Islamic economics has to be based on Islamic law, the extent to which the *Shari'a* possesses a fixed and detailed set of laws or doctrines concerning economic activities capable of resolving all present economic problems is a controversial subject of debate among Muslim social scientists and jurists. Opinions on this issue can be divided into two broad categories.

First, the traditional jurists who argue that Islamic economics, like any other aspect of life in an Islamic society, has to be and can be deducted from divine Islamic laws with the minimum of human discretion. Members in this category argue that since Islamic law has been legislated for all times and places, it is not in need of adaptation and updating and is, therefore, capable of addressing all present and future economic problems. It is argued that Islam "provides man with a definite Source, the Divine Revelation, as embodied in the Book of God and the *Sunna*. This source prescribes a standard of moral conduct that is permanent and universal and holds good in every age and under all circumstances" (Afzal-ur-Rahman, 1988, pp. 256–7). Economic issues should, therefore, be deduced from Islamic sources without involving human reasoning and discretion (Ayatollah Janati, in Va'ezzadeh Khorasani (ed.), 1369, p. 14).

Second, those who argue that in the last analysis, the primary Islamic sources do not contain sufficient information for the construction of an integrated economic system capable of resolving present economic problems. Subsequently a considerable part of Islamic economics has to be based on human reasoning. Adherents to this position argue that Islamic economics does not have a "Canon Law", leaving a great part of "the individual transactions and interrelations to the human mind" (Kahf, in Ghazali and Omar, 1989, p. 75). However, in an attempt to salvage the essential particularity of Islamic economics, namely its divine base, they immediately acknowledge the fact that human discretion has to be based on the principles laid down in the primary sources.

Recognising that economic growth over some thirteen centuries has revolutionised production and consequently the socio-economic relations, giving rise to complex economic concepts, tools, organisations, institutions and problems, not found in the socio-economic environment of seventh-century Arabia, modern Islamic economists have tried to reconcile the *Shari'a* with the requirements of a far more advanced level of capital accumulation with all its ensuing economic implications. To aid them in this task they have invoked the principle of the "spirit of the *Shari'a*", rather than its letter (Mustafa and Askari, in Iqbal (ed.), 1988, pp. 107–109). Such a theoretical approach shifts the focus from the divinely based primary sources to the application of interpretations based on independent human judgement, when the need is felt to exist.

Faced with the dilemma of solving modern economic problems by relying solely on the *Shari'a*, a prominent group of Iranian Shi'ite clerics has also tried to shift the focus away from a rigidly *Shari'a*-based economic system to one in which human discretion can be afforded greater scope. They have argued that "Islam is a religion and not a compilation of sciences necessary for man" (*Pasdar-e Eslam*, no. 110). It is, therefore, maintained that while Islamic *fiqh* (law) does possess immutable injunctions that are applicable at all times and places, it would be a mistake to assume that in particular fields such as economics, politics and military affairs, religion could provide practical and immutable policies. It is finally concluded that "there is no such thing as a well co-ordinated policy [theory] called Islamic economics that could be applied to all times and places" (*Pasdar-e Eslam*, no. 110).

As much as there is a tendency, for practical purposes, to reduce the reliance of Islamic economics on the letter of the *Shari'a*, any attempt at an exposition and explanation of Islamic economics would be meaningless without an analysis of the economic precepts of the four sources of the *Shari'a*: namely, the Qur'an or the Holy book; the *Sunna* or the Tradition of the Prophet; consensus; analogy for the Sunnis and reason for the Shi'ites.

The study of these sources with the objective of extracting relevant information for the construction of an economic system, however, does not lead to the formulation of a single, generally acceptable prototype. The difficulty of presenting a generic Islamic economic system lies in the different conceptions of what an Islamic economic system should be. Varying interpretations on the different characteristics that constitute an economic system have found their reflection in different Islamic subsystems. Even though all subsystems accept and utilise the common features of the Islamic value-system, each has searched for and provided references and proofs for its particular view of what constitutes Islam's socio-economic position.

Four apparent causes can be identified to explain the absence of a distinct, integrated and coherent theoretical construction of an Islamic economic system. First, the subjectivity of different Islamic jurists in their study and analysis of the primary sources leads to different interpretations of the same texts. Second, the existence, in the primary sources, of disparate and even contradictory positions and injunctions, on a single economically related issue such as the permissible extent of accumulating wealth, enables different subsystems to use different texts within the primary sources as proof of their particular position. This prevalent practice renders the construction of a single, universal Islamic economic model very difficult. Third, the existence of as many as forty thousand acts, injunctions and statements attributed to the Prophet and known as his Tradition or *Sunna*, provides a rich pool of information from which references to prove one economic position or another can be readily found. Islamic jurists confess that, given one's politico-economic predisposition, one would be able to seek and find a recorded proof of one's position amidst all the reports in the *hadith* and the *Sunna* (Makarem-e Shirazi, n.d., p. 149). Fourth, the prevalence of different tertiary sources allows for the pronouncement of unprecedented religious edicts by Islamic jurists, which in turn affect and influence the economic system. Pronouncements based on tertiary sources are at best linked to the spirit of Islam and are arrived at through the application of independent judgement based on different criteria and aimed at obtaining different objectives.

**The restrictive parameters of Islamic economics**

According to Muslims, everything in this world, including man's health, life and wealth belongs to God, and man is left with nothing of his own. Maududi, however, argues that the one thing that God has left for man and which fully belongs to him is his free will to follow or deviate from the path of God (Maududi, 1986, p. 13). Therefore the man who willingly renounces his freedom to deviate from the path of God and accepts His unconditional supremacy is the believer or the *mu'men.* He voluntarily sells his autonomy for the divine mode of life which would lead to "eternal bliss in Paradise" (Maududi, 1986, p. 13). The contract in which he enters into with God is faith or *Iman*.

The concept of Islamic limitations is born out of this bargain between the believer or the *mu'men* and God. Islamic economics and its system is, thus, marked by divine and man-made constraints and limitations. These limitations, which shape the Islamic economic system, may be categorised into three distinct types based on their origin (Taskhiri, in Va'ezzadeh Khorasani, 1369, p. 149).

First, those which are derived from the primary sources and are thus considered as primary ordinances (*'anavin-e avalieh*). These fixed and eternal economic ordinances include the obligation to pay two types of tax: *zakat* and *khums* for the Shi'ites and *khums* alone for the Sunnis, as well as the prohibition of usury, hoarding, excessive consumption, the private ownership of rivers and lakes.

Second, those limitations that are deduced from secondary and tertiary sources and are thus called secondary ordinances (*'anavin-e sanavieh*) (Taskhiri in Va'ezzadeh Khorasani, 1369, p. 153). These are flexible ordinances, which are only applied in exceptional conditions, subject to the requirements of changing times. Secondary ordinances, when used, replace or nullify the primary ordinances, in order to attain a higher social order of priority. It is generally accepted that since secondary ordinances are only employed under exceptional circumstances, they have to be temporary measures, abandoned in favour of the primary ordinances as soon as the abnormal circumstances requiring them are normalised. Secondary ordinances have been compared to martial law, the imposition of which temporarily suspends constitutional rights, which can be considered as primary ordinances (Makarem-e Shirazi in Va'ezzadeh Khorasani, 1369, p. 113). It is also argued that primary sources remain the main tool for solving social problems, while secondary ordinances can only be used as ad hoc solutions in the form of exceptions to the laws (*Pasdar-e Eslam*, no.39, p. 51). These secondary ordinances could, however, constitute an additional source of limitation for the Islamic economic system. For example, no stipulations for government intervention and price fixing can be deducted from the primary ordinances. It could, therefore, be argued that in the Islamic economic system prices are determined in a free market (*Pasdar-e Eslam*, no.35, p. 24). Such a primary ordinance could, however, be suspended and replaced by a secondary one that justifies the imposition of government price controls and even the introduction of administrative prices, through the invocation of exceptional conditions of overriding necessity and emergency (*zarurat va izterar*), reasons of the state or the satisfaction of the public weal (*maslahat*). Thus the Islamic economic system characterised by free market prices, according to primary ordinances could become one characterised by government-controlled or established administrative prices, through the application of secondary ordinances. State or public convenience (*maslahat*) allows Islamic jurists to suspend some of the fundamental edicts of the religion. While the application of the principle of free market prices based on primary ordinances would lead analysts to categorise the Islamic economic system as one with capitalist features, the use of state-controlled or administered prices based on secondary ordinances would lead them to categorise it as one similar to a planned economic system. Therefore in constructing an Islamic economic system, it becomes important to present the model first on the basis of primary ordinances and then on the basis of secondary ordinances as they have been developed by different Islamic subsystems within both the Sunni and Shi'i sects.

The third type of economic limitations are those imposed by the Islamic ruler, with the object of implementing social justice or those principles that are not explicit but can be considered as the spirit of the *Shari'a*. This category of limitations come under the title of *'anavin-e velayati*, *ahkame sultaniyya* or governmental ordinances (Taskhiri in Va'ezzadeh Khorasani, 1369, p. 154. Schacht, 1991, p. 114). Governmental ordinances enable the Islamic ruler to play an active role in directing society towards the objectives of an ideal Islamic society and economy. In the first place, the basic contours of this ideal society and economy are established by the *Shari'a*. However, the Islamic rulers' philosophical outlook on the socio-economic meaning of Islam and subsequently the materialisation of their independent judgements through the application of secondary and governmental ordinances constitutes a determining force in giving shape to the ideal Islamic society and economy. It could therefore be argued that the primary ordinances constitute the fixed and static factors, and the secondary and governmental ordinances the variable and dynamic factors in the Islamic economic system.[1]

## Constructing an Islamic economic system

On the basis of the four characteristics outlined at the beginning of this chapter, we will attempt to construct a pure or idealised Islamic economic system on the basis of primary and secondary sources. Wherever different ordinances on a single characteristic lead to different descriptions or specifications of the system, the various possibilities will be presented. Also, where different interpretations of a source have created a multiplicity of accounts in terms of one characteristic, all accounts along with their implications for the system will be analysed. Selective references will be made to the use of tertiary sources in relation to each characteristic and the way these have changed the original description of the economic system. The construction of an Islamic economic system on the basis of secondary and governmental ordinances can produce systems ranging from a free market to a planned Islamic economy. Our account of Islamic economic systems, however, makes no claim to being exhaustive. We acknowledge the limitations imposed on the analysis by the impracticality of making a thorough study of all the possibly relevant primary and secondary sources.The categorisations and classifications that we utilise and construct may be historically specific, yet in order to present a systematic and meaningful analysis of Islam's economic system, we have drawn on evidences and proofs that span almost fourteen centuries. We have had, therefore, to make inter-temporal comparisons and deductions. Traditional Islamic sources and texts do not refer to concepts such as centralised or decentralised decision making at the micro or macro level, market or plan co-ordinating mechanisms, or private and collective material incentives as compared to divine or spiritual ones. We are, however, trying to articulate and present the theoretical outlines of conceivable Islamic economic systems in the jargon of modern social scientists.

**The organisation of decision-making arrangements**

In an Islamic economy, the operational methodology and objectives of all economic units, the decision-making flow chart, the directions of command between various levels of the economic hierarchy, and the dispersion or concentration of decision-making power within various institutions should all be deduced from the *Shari'a*.

Various forms of economic organisation in trade, agriculture and even crafts were in practice before and during the time of the Prophet. Both Sunni and Shi'ite jurists agree that the Prophet did not set out to alter these forms radically. In this sense one can argue that Islamic economic decision-making arrangements were generally based on the organisational traditions prevalent in Arabia. Certain practices such as usury and fraud were, however, prohibited on the grounds that they violated the principles of the Islamic value-system.

In view of the predominantly pastoral economy of the Arabian peninsular at the time of the revelation of the Qur'an and the life of the Prophet, it would be unrealistic to search in primary sources for direct references to industrial decision-making structures or organisational procedures co-ordinating the relation between consumers and producers. Numerous references, however, can be found, in primary and secondary sources, to the management of society at large — who should make decisions, who constitutes the best manager, and how decisions should be co-ordinated. These references are usually concerned with leadership and decision-making organisations in the political and religious realm. We have, however, extended them, by analogy, to the economic domain.

At the national level it can be argued that the organisation of decision-making arrangements, by basic economic units, is subject to two types of centralised command. First, those injunctions emanating directly from the *Shari'a*, such as the prohibition of usury. Irrespective of the existence of an Islamic state, the pious Islamic man, the *mu'men*, is obliged to comply with this command. Second, those injunctions originating in the Islamic state, which attempts to implement the ideal Islamic economy through its own interpretation of Islamic economic objectives.

Within the constraints of the first type of centralised command, individuals have the freedom to make decisions only within the fixed and eternal set of orders coming from God. The economic directives in the *Shari'a* are legally binding and therefore compliance is compulsory. However, in contrast to the centrally planned system in which directives, targets and even economic laws are subject to change according to political decisions of the state leadership, in the Islamic economic system certain commands in the realms of production, consumption, exchange and distribution are fixed and eternal. In this sense, the Islamic economic system can be considered a permanent command economy in those aspects stipulated by primary sources.

It may be argued that outside the circle of prohibited economic activities, the Islamic economic system allows the basic economic units to make the final decisions. However, even in the realm of permissibles, the freedom of choice of the consumer and the producer is restricted and conditioned by not only the obligations but also the recommendations of Islam's elaborate value-system. For example, other than the obligatory Islamic dues or taxes of *zakat*, *khums* and *'ushr* incumbent on Islamic man, he is also strongly recommended to engage in the payment of voluntary charity known as *sadaqah* or *infaq fi sabilallah* to the poor (Doi, 1984, p. 388). Such recommendations also exist in the realms of production, consumption and exchange, further binding the free decision of producers and consumers.

Within the constraints of these commands that are imposed by Islamic governments to attain the economic objectives of the system, the degree of decentralised or centralised decision-making can ultimately be considered a function of the level of economic growth of each particular Islamic economy. In an Islamic economic system, the provision of man's basic needs is considered as a goal, compelling the Islamic state to provide for its citizens. The right to sustenance can be derived from stipulations in both the Qur'an and the *Sunna*.[2] As long as not all members of society have access to basic food, clothing and shelter, the Islamic economy will be responsible for their provision. The degree to which an Islamic government wishes to achieve this goal will determine the degree of centralisation it imposes. According to one school of thought, the decision as to what constitutes basic needs and how resources should be allocated to secure their provision should be made by economic planners. At a low level of economic development, in which the lion's share of production will have to be devoted to production geared to the satisfaction of basic needs, the majority of firms will have to produce according to targets and plans compiled by the planners. The decision-making process involving the production and consumption of goods meeting basic needs will therefore be characterised by a highly centralised arrangement, emanating from the planners and going all the way down to the basic economic units. In Islamic economies characterised by low levels of capital accumulation, decentralised decision-making aimed at maximising individual utility and profit may have to be suspended in order to maximise social utility, through centralised decision-making.

Since private ownership of factors of production is permitted by the Islamic economic system, it may be argued that once the Islamic society has provided for the basic needs of its members, decisions concerning those economic activities not prohibited by the *Shari'a* should become decentralised and diffused among the producers and consumers. At this stage of economic growth, planners' preference gives way to consumers' sovereignty and the decisions at the firm level can become decentralised. Relying on a Tradition of the Prophet, it could be argued that at this historical stage of development, the Islamic economic system can abandon a centralised national decision-making arrangement and promote a conditional decentralisation of decision-making by producers and consumers.

So far we have argued that, at the national level, two different decision-making arrangements can be discerned from the primary sources. What remains is the analysis of decision-making arrangements at the micro or unit-of-production level. This requires an analysis of the Islamic intra-firm direction of command. It has to be determined whether, according to Islam, authority and power should be dispersed or concentrated in the hands of the employers, administrators or managers.

Again, two different types of Islamic decision-making arrangements, at the micro level, can be deduced from the primary sources. First, it may be argued that the Islamic firm is based on a participatory or consultative method of decision-making. According to this position, those decisions within any economic, social or political unit which involve the worldly and not religious affairs of the people and do not transgress the limits set by the *Shari'a* should be decentralised and arrived at through the participation of all those concerned. Broad policy decisions reached at the structural base, among those directly involved, are conveyed to the management, who then apply their own technical know-how to make the most efficient decisions concerning the process of production.

This Islamic conception of decision-making is similar in form to that employed in a workers' management or workers' council system. Canonical support for it is generally found in both the Qur'an and the *Sunna*. God orders the Prophet to consult with the people in their worldly affairs [3:159]. In the famous chapter (*sura*) of the Qur'an on Consultation (*al Shura*), the Prophet is once again instructed to conduct the affairs of the people through consultation [42:38]. Those who have used these verses to support the argument that economic and political affairs in an Islamic society have to be conducted through a participatory system readily accept that divine injunctions and ordinances are clearly excluded from this rule. In support of this Islamic view of decision-making, it is argued that Islam endorses a consultative decision-making system because such a procedure provides workers with a sense of dignity and self-respect; freeing them from blind obedience and intellectual intimidation, it allows them to become innovative and creative (Taleqani, 1358, p. 397). Sunni scholars and jurists are mostly of the opinion that Islam presents consultation as a fundamental principle of management, but that it does not set any particular or specific rules concerning how it should be implemented. The form and procedure of the consultative method of administration is left to the discretion of the Muslim community, to be determined according to "the needs of time and place" (Afzal-ur-Rahman, 1988, p. 312).

A centralised Islamic interpretation of decision-making, at the firm level, can also be deduced. According to this position, the ability and wisdom of decision-making by employees or direct producers is questionable on two grounds. The decision-making structure of Islam, according to which managerial power is concentrated in the hands of God and not delegated to anyone else on the basis of a social contract, can be taken to suggest that the manager of any unit of production need not delegate his decision-making power either [12:44] (Haeri, 1364, p. 66). Decisions pertaining to the worldly affairs of the Islamic community, according to this primarily Shi'i view, therefore rest with experts on Islamic law.

Second, it can be argued that the whole issue of decentralised versus centralised decision-making, as reflected in the choice of workers' management as against "one man management", becomes a pertinent organisational issue only when the objectives and interests of labour and management differ or are contradictory. Since in Islam both labour and management are supposed to be working for the satisfaction of God's pleasure, there are no grounds for labour to doubt or take a position against that of management. It is therefore argued that the involvement and interference of workers instead of the exercise of leadership by a competent authority would lead to chaos and ruin, delaying final decisions, whereas most economic problems necessitate quick and categorical decisions (Moussavi-e Isfahani, 1368, p. 536).

Shi'i jurists have interpreted the references to consultation in the Qur'an as indicating that a correct ruling should be arrived at by consultation amongst legal experts or jurists, not by reference to a majority decision of all those directly concerned, such as the workers.[3] In abstract terms it could be argued that the primary responsibility of the managers of Islamic firms is to experts in Islamic law, not to shareholders or consumers. Practically, therefore, it is easier for the managers themselves to be experts in Islamic law or appointed by such experts. In this hierarchical system, all economic managers are ultimately responsible to the governing jurist, who is only accountable to God. Subsequently, economic decisions are not necessarily made according to any worldly criteria such as profit maximisation or efficiency, but according to what is right as specified by the interpreter of the word of God.

To provide proof from the primary sources for the position that one-man management is condoned in Islam and that centralised decisions made by Islamic managers are binding upon all employees, irrespective of their individual judgements, references can be made both to the Qur'an and *Sunna*. In Chapter 4 of the Qur'an, (*Al Nisa* or "The women") believers are ordered to obey God and his Prophet and "those charged with authority among you" [4:59]. It can be argued on the basis of this verse that the Islamic manager is fully empowered to make the appropriate economic decisions without necessarily consulting his employees. This type of argument can be considered as a derivative of the position which assumes quasi-total power for the Islamic ruler. According to this view, the Islamic ruler is justified in unilaterally imposing his decision since he is considered the best judge of the public interest (Sadr, 1350, Vol. 1, p. 362). To emphasise the importance of one-man management in Islam, reference can also be made to a report of the Prophet, according to which Muslims are ordered to choose one person as their manager or leader whenever three or more of them are involved in a group activity such as a journey.[4] Within this centralised and hierarchical conception of Islamic decision-making, the rights and responsibilities of employees in relation to their managers or employers can be deduced from a saying of the Prophet. He encourages workers to comply with the orders of managers or employers. It is reported that the Prophet said: "An employee who excels in his devotion to God and also renders to his master what is due to him of duty, sincerity and obedience, for him there is a double reward [with God]" (Chapra, 1975, p. 13).

Irrespective of the two possible positions that can be put forward in terms of Islamic decision-making arrangements at the firm level, the Islamic manager has to have two specific attributes. He is not only expected to be a technical expert in his own field, but he is also required to be have some expertise in Islamic law. According to a Tradition of the Prophet, "Anyone who appoints a person from among the Muslims to a position of responsibility with the knowledge that there is another Muslim more deserving for that job and possessing a greater knowledge of the Book of God and the Tradition of the Prophet, will betray God, the Prophet of God and the whole Muslim community" (*Pasdar-e Eslam*, no. 10). All those in positions of responsibility within a unit of production are therefore expected to prove their expertise in Islamic law.

**Mechanisms for the provision of information and co-ordination**

All durable and self-sustaining economic systems are in need of an institution and a signalling device to co-ordinate and equilibrate the availability of the factors of production with the demand for them, and further assure that the quality and quantity of goods and services produced matches the demand for them in society. Otherwise disequilibrium, either in terms of factors or goods or both, will create shortages and surpluses, wasting factors of production and leaving the consumers unsatisfied. To produce the maximum amount of goods and services with the minimum amount of inputs, thus economising on resources, constitutes an objective for all economic systems. Even though it may be argued that from an Islamic perspective resources are not considered as scarce and therefore economising does not become imperative, Islam categorically condemns and prohibits waste and thereby indirectly enjoins efficiency.

Students of Islamic economics will be understandably perplexed by the variety of opinion that exists on property rights, the system's co-ordinating mechanism, and its mechanism of distribution. The issue is not one of distinguishing between a number of variants of a single Islamic economic system, but between diametrically opposed views and interpretations of the same "mother" system. While some social scientists consider the distinguishing features of the

Islamic economic system as basically the same as those of capitalism, others categorise it as an anti-capitalist, socialistic and egalitarian system.[5] A third position can also be deduced from Islamic evidences which would demonstrate that Islam represents a sequential economic system. At first it would endorse a planned and relatively egalitarian economy, during the initial stages of economic development when unequal distribution of income combined with a market system would be incapable of meeting basic needs. During later stages of economic development, once basic needs have been met and the economy is capable of producing more, Islam would endorse a socially stratified market economy.

Each position can make a case for itself based on legal evidence in the *Shari'a*. The debate between the proponents of social solidarity, compassion and mutual obligation, who believe in coercing the rich to pay for the needy, even beyond their strict obligation to pay *zakat*, on the one hand, and the proponents of voluntary philanthropy, the sanctity of private property and the idea that the only obligatory claim on the wealth of Muslims is *zakat*, on the other, has been raging since the death of the Prophet. This debate clearly predates the modern debate over the capitalist or socialist nature of the Islamic economic system. In our opinion, since the Islamic economic system is founded on the basis of Islamic jurisprudence, divergences in opinion as to the nature of its economic system are rooted not only in the *Shari'a* but also in its interpretation. For practical economic purposes, should the emphasis be on the strict letter of the law or on the spirit of the law? Should the Islamic economic system be built on what has been explicitly prohibited, such as usury, and what has been made explicitly obligatory, such as paying *zakat* or the wealth tax, or should it be built on the numerous ethical and moral recommendations and invitations of the *Shari'a*, such as helping the needy, refraining from accumulating wealth, and providing for the basic needs of all. Focusing on the letter of the law means that the economic system would take its lead from the obligatory (*wajib*) and the prohibited (*haram*) categories and would ignore the recommended (*mustahab*), permitted (*mubah*) and reprobated (*makruh*) categories, in case their implementation brings them into conflict with the explicit commandments. Clearly, if no such conflicts arise, then such recommendations would also be observed. However, attaching an equal importance to the ethical recommendations and to the obligatory laws of the *Shari'a* could lead to an impasse in cases where the implementation of a recommended injunction would come into conflict with the operation of an obligatory law.

Respect for and defence of rightfully gained private property, for example, is assumed to be an obligation and an explicit injunction under the *Shari'a*. Provision to meet basic needs is also viewed as a first-order priority of the Islamic system, and the rich are enjoined to help the poor. Given the above suppositions, should the Islamic state be permitted to readjust the economic institutions so that everybody's basic needs are provided for, even if such a readjustment necessitates the abolition of the market and infringement on private property rights? Those who favour the letter of the law argue that where meeting basic needs would violate the obligation to respect private property emphasised in the *Shari'a*, provision for basic needs must be abandoned. Those who view the equitable spirit of the law as the true reflection of Islam argue that if subsequent to the employment of all obligatory measures the essential needs of the poor remain unmet, the market mechanism and private property rights necessarily have to be temporarily suspended. In one case the first-priority objective of the system is the defence of the market and private property, and in the other the first-priority objective is provision for basic needs.

We will argue that an economic system built on the strict letter of the law would resemble a perfectly competitive market system. This will be called the "Islamic market mechanism". An economic system rigidly built on the equitable spirit of the law would resemble an egalitarian system in which the plan would have to become the co-ordinating mechanism of the economy. This will be called the "Islamic plan mechanism". Finally, the theoretical outlines of an Islamic economic system influenced by both the letter and the equitable spirit of the *Shari'a* can be inferred. This will be called the "Islamic plan-then-market mechanism". In what follows we will present three possible co-ordinating mechanisms for the Islamic economic system, all based on the *Shari'a*.

*The Islamic market mechanism.*

Subject to restrictions on the exchange of certain goods, such as wine, pork, gambling instruments, icons, gold or silverware and musical instruments, Islam accepts the market as the basic co-ordinating mechanism of its economic system. The institution of the market, under perfect competition, allows consumers to obtain their desired basket of goods, and producers to sell what they have produced, through the establishment of a mutually acceptable price. In the absence of coercion, the market is said to gratify the profit drive of the seller and the satisfaction drive of the buyer. The market can also co-ordinate and equilibrate the national circular flow of expenditures and incomes, through the price mechanism.

The principles of freedom of exchange, private property and the security of contract which constitute the necessary and sufficient conditions for the operation of a market system can all be deduced from the primary sources of Islam.[6] There are several direct references to the significance of the freedom of exchange and trade in the Qur'an. Believers are enjoined to engage in trade based on mutual goodwill [4:29]. Rejecting the contention that trade, like usury, leads to the accumulation of wealth or capital, and is therefore prohibited, the Qur'an emphasises that exchange or trade is different from usury (*riba*) since exchange (*bey'*) is permitted and usury forbidden [2:275 and 2:279]. On the general issue of contracts, the Qur'an, on numerous occasions, commands believers to "fulfil all obligations", "faithfully observe their trusts and covenants", and refrain from breaking their oaths, once they have been confirmed [5:1, 16:91, 23:8, 17:34, 70:32]. In the longest verse in the Qur'an, the specific manner in which commercial contracts involving future and spot payments should be registered and dealt with is described in great detail [2:282].

Among the Traditions of the Prophet, many reports can be cited to provide further proof for the position that the market mechanism should be the basic co-ordinator of the Islamic economic system. Before his Prophethood, Mohammad had managed Khadija's commercial affairs and was thus familiar with the operation of the market. He had traded on her behalf between Mecca and Damascus and had proved himself an astute, honest and capable tradesman. Mohammad is reported to have said: "Welfare and blessedness is composed of ten parts, nine-tenths of which is attained through trade" (Khoshneviss, n.d., p. 97). According to another Tradition reported by Ibn Abbas, the Prophet said: "It is incumbent upon you to be kind to traders, since they are the do-gooders of the world and the trustees of God on earth" (*ibid.*, p. 99).

Even though government intervention in the market is tolerated and even encouraged under specific circumstances, it can be argued that perfect competition, operating through its own self-adjusting automatic mechanisms, should constitute the primary co-ordinating mechanism of the Islamic economic system, providing it fulfils the Islamic system's first-order priorities. Numerous general guidelines can be found in the primary sources which guarantee a free market, under normal conditions.

First, Islam prohibits price fixing by a handful of buyers or sellers who have cornered the market. It encourages exchange in a market characterised by numerous buyers and sellers, in which none possesses a controlling share. In the days of the Prophet, it was customary in the city of Medina for small groups of merchants to rush out of the city to meet the agricultural producers of the rural surroundings, once they were informed of their arrival, in order to buy their whole crop. The agricultural goods were later sold at a higher price within the city limits. A small group of merchants also undertook the transportation and sale of urban-produced goods to the rural population, again at a price set by the seller. (Afzal-ur-Rahman, 1985, Vol.2, p. 76). The fact that a small number of buyers met with producers created a quasi monopsony situation in which the few buyers could bid down the price below what it could have been in an open market, where producers could meet the multitude of consumers. Furthermore, the provision of urban-produced goods to the rural areas by a handful of suppliers created a monopoly situation where the sellers could set prices higher than those that would have prevailed had numerous producers, each possessing a small share of the market, met with the consumers. The Prophet is reported to have condemned this custom and called upon Muslims to refrain from such business practices, since they caused injury and loss to the weaker party in the transaction. His argument can be interpreted to mean that a contrived price established under conditions of imperfect competition causes injury and loss to the weaker party in the transaction, be they consumers or producers (Khoshneviss, n.d., p. 350).

Second, the above-mentioned traditions can also be put forward as evidence for the position that the Islamic market is characterised by free information. Meeting producers outside the city of Medina denies the producers access to information about the prevailing demand conditions inside the city. The fact that their source of information becomes confined to a handful of merchants, whose interest is to buy cheap and sell dear, leads producers to exchange their goods at a price lower than its free market price.

According to both the Qur'an and the *Sunna*, the ideal Islamic market is expected to be free of discrimination. This means that producers are expected to inform consumers of the quality and quantity of the good they claim to be selling, in return for the consumers' payment of the market price. In the Islamic market, therefore, cheating or short-changing consumers, committing any type of fraud or the exercise of any type of sellers' preference, as well as the payment of bribes, is prohibited. Certain schools of Islamic jurisprudence are even of the opinion that if, in a transaction, the buyer is not very experienced and is therefore swayed by the seller, the consumer may nullify the transaction, once he realises that he has been unfairly treated (Qadri, 1986, p. 322). There are numerous references in the Qur'an to the prohibition of discriminatory and dishonest means of transaction [55:9, 26:181–3, 11:84–5]. In a chapter devoted to those who deal in fraud (*Al- Mutaffifin*), the Qur'an condemns all fraudulent transactions in which one party is cheated of his due share [83:1–3].

Third, according to numerous Traditions of the Prophet, hoarding, which decreases supply and thereby causes artificial price increases, is categorically condemned in Islam. The act of hoarding has the same impact on market supply and therefore price as that of erecting barriers to the entrance of potential producers. Both measures seek to prevent market supply from increasing and the price of the good under consideration from decreasing. The Prophet is reported to have said: "Whoever hoards food for forty days to sell it at a higher price has distanced himself from God and shall be detested by Him" (Khoshneviss, n.d., p. 328). The Prophet is also reported to have stated that hoarders, murderers and thieves are of the same kind and shall all go to hell (*ibid.*, p. 327, 329). It is reported that when the Prophet saw someone bringing large quantities of a good to the market and selling it at a price lower than the prevailing one, the Prophet asked him the reason for his behaviour. The seller told him that he was doing so for the sake of God's pleasure. The Prophet is then reported to have said: "Those who increase the supply on the market are similar to those who fight for the cause of God and those who hoard in the Islamic market are similar to apostates and unbelievers" (*ibid.*, p. 331). Rejecting the monopolistic conditions that patent rights could lead to, Ayatollah Khomeini ruled against the religious legitimacy of such barriers to trade (Khomeini, *Tahrir al-Wasileh*, p. 626).

As for the profit signal,[7] Ayatollah Beheshti has argued that based on the Islamic legal principle that "intervention in the wealth of a Muslim is prohibited unless he concedes to it" and the Qur'anic verse which enjoins trading on the basis of mutual goodwill [4:29], a case could be made for unlimited profits, even though making unlimited profits would be contrary to Islam's value system (Beheshti, 1363, p. 61). Basing their argument on the *Shari'a*, some have advanced the extreme view that Islam places no limits on profits (Ahmad, 1988, p. 191). A general consensus exists among Islamic jurists and social scientists that profit-making does constitute a feature of the Islamic economic system (Mustafa and Askari, in Iqbal (ed.), 1988, pp. 101–2).

Fourth, based on the Prophet's Traditions, it can be argued that in the ideal Islamic market consumers should have access to homogenous or non-differentiated goods. In the Islamic market, as in a perfectly competitive market, consumers would be indifferent as to the source of their goods, since all the goods offered by producers would be identical in quality. The lowest price in such a market constitutes the only criterion of choice for the consumer. The Prophet is reported to have prohibited the sale of good-quality wheat mixed with bad-quality wheat at a given price (Khoshneviss, n.d., p. 335). Although this and similar injunctions are primarily aimed at discouraging fraudulent practices, they indirectly support the aim of a homogeneity of goods in a perfectly competitive market.

Finally, as long as there is mutual consent between the buyer and the seller, interference with the market mechanism to enforce a set price is discouraged in the Islamic market. Even though under exceptional circumstances, such as the protection of public interest, where the pursuit of private interest undermines social well-being, or for reasons of state, government intervention is justified and even promoted by Islam, non-interference by the government is considered as a primary ordinance which should be respected and upheld under normal conditions (Makarem-e Shirazi, in Va'ezzadeh Khorasani, 1369, p. 110). The Prophet is reported to have categorically opposed any obligatory price-setting. According to a Tradition reported by Imam Ali, the Prophet once walked through the market place and, on learning that a few traders had been hoarding, he ordered them to expose their goods so that consumers could see them. Some of his followers asked him to fix a price for the hoarded goods and he is reported to have responded angrily: "That I should set a price? Prices are set by God, He will raise and lower them when He wills" (Moussavi-e Isfahani, 1368, p. 367. Ibn Taymiya, 1983, pp. 49–50). According to another Tradition, when the price of unhoarded goods was subject to considerable fluctuations in the market and the Prophet was requested to fix prices to eliminate uncertainties, he is reported to have refused and said: "I will not set such a precedent, let the people carry on with their activities and benefit mutually; if, however, you wish to give them advice, that will not be objectionable" (Va'ezzadeh Khorasani, 1369, p. 110).

Numerous verses in the Qur'an can be cited to show that inequalities in wealth and income resulting from the operation of market forces are not considered as anomalous and reprehensible in the Islamic economic system, since they reflect God's will and His view of Islam's ideal socio-economic organisation [6:165, 16:71, 24:38, 43:32]. The Qur'an explicitly states that God has bestowed His gifts more freely on some than on others, has raised some higher in rank than others, and has allotted to each according to what they earn [4:32, 43:32]. A socio-economically stratified society, characterised by differences in rank, wealth and income, is therefore compatible with the Islamic social order. Based on the primary sources cited, any interference with the outcome of market operations — for instance, prices and legitimate incomes — may therefore be considered as meddling with God's intentions. Any attempt to place a ceiling on incomes in an Islamic economic system may therefore be considered as a violation of divine optimality, which is similar to Pareto-optimality. The price-signalling device, functioning through what in part resembles a perfectly competitive market system, is therefore held, according to one interpretation, to represent the Islamic economic system's major co-ordinating mechanism.

*The Islamic plan mechanism.*
The fact that certain primary sources explicitly designate the free market as the legitimate arbiter between producers and consumers does not prove that only an Islamic market economy can be deduced from the *Shari'a*. It would be premature and inaccurate to conclude that all the evidence indicates that the Islamic economic system is simply a morally constrained replica of the capitalist economic system. It can be convincingly argued that the spirit of the *Shari'a* is governed by a strong sense of social justice, fraternity, equality and co-operation [3:180, 4:37–9, 9:34–5, 24:61, 51:19, 70:24–5]. If the promotion of social justice is posited as a first-priority objective, then all factors, institutions and arrangements hindering the attainment of such an objective have to be replaced. Where market forces, left to their own self-regulating mechanisms, fail to attain social justice as recommended by the Qur'an, intervention, regulation and planning by the Islamic state become imperative. Particular national levels of capital accumulation, rates of growth, disparities in wealth and income distribution, and levels of absolute and relative poverty, among other factors, determine the duration (short-run or long-run) and degree (partial or complete) of state intervention in the market.

To explain the legitimacy and ease with which Islamic jurists and social scientists remain loyal to the *Shari'a*, yet switch from one first-priority objective to another, depending on their perspectives, can be better understood by citing a pertinent example often used by Islamic jurists.

Entering someone else's house, without his permission and in his absence, is categorically prohibited in Islam. Yet if someone is drowning and the only way to save that person is to go through someone's house without his permission, then the prohibited act of forced entry becomes an obligatory one. In this case a secondary ordinance (*hukm-e sanavi*) has been invoked or applied, automatically suspending the applicable primary ordinance, to solve the problem. This type of secondary ordinance falls under the rubric of *masālehe aham va mohem,* or cases of primary and secondary importance in fulfulling the public interest (Makarem-e Shirazi, in Va'ezzadeh Khorasani, 1369, p. 106). The application of the above methodology even allows for the suspension of certain pillars of the faith such as prayer, let alone the market coordinating mechanism.

The primary sources of Islam abound in the simple message that the Islamic community (*ummah*) has to provide for the basic needs of its members. The elevation of provision for basic needs to a first-priority objective can be argued on the grounds of functional necessity and the philosophical spirit of the *Shari'a*.

First, Islamic jurists agree that the objective of the *Shari'a* is to protect the Five Necessities (*Zaruriyat-e Khamese*) of life, religion, reason, progeny and property (Siddiqi, in Iqbal (ed.),1988, p. 258). Clearly the preservation of life requires provision for the basic need of sustenance. The protection of religion for and by men also depends on individual sustenance and therefore on provision for basic needs. As Ghazali argues, religion is preserved through knowledge and the offering of prayers, both of which require "bodily health, survival and availability of a minimum of clothing, housing and other supplies" (*ibid.*). One could argue that since the survival of life and religion both depend on the provision for basic needs, this objective automatically becomes a first-priority concern, transcending all other goals, including that of respect for private property. Ironically, those jurists who maintain that in Islam the right to private property is inalienable refer to the same Five Necessities to prove that the preservation of the right to private property is as sacred as that of life and religion (Saeedi, in Va'ezzadeh Khorasani, 1369, Vol.2, p. 251).

There exists a consensus among Islamic jurists and social scientists that one of Islam's distinguishing features is its concern for social justice. God's justice has to find its manifestation in the social relations established among His vicegerents [2:30]. Thus the Qur'an pronounces the establishment of a just and equitable order as a prime objective of the Islamic system [57:10]. God recommends that a fair share should be given to those who are in need, since the gifts of nature belong to all men [55:10, 57:7]. To emphasise the importance of involving all members of society in the social wealth, the Qur'an reproaches those who turn a blind eye to their social duty (*fard kifayeh*) [15:20, 59:7, 70:24–5]. It warns those who do not pray nor feed the poor that they will be led "into Hell-Fire" [74:42–44].

The Tradition of those who belong to the egalitarian school of Islamic thought, placing the provision of basic needs for all, over and above all other considerations, goes all the way back to Abu Zarr Ghifari, one of the Prophet's close companions. The Prophet is reported to have said that no one was more truthful than he (Cameron, 1982, p. 152). Abu Zarr was banished by Uthman, the third Caliph, for preaching those verses of the Qur'an which condemn hoarding by the rich, and say that they shall be branded in Hell, and for insisting on the egalitarian notion that the poor should have a share in the wealth of the rich. He taught the people that "no one should hoard up that which exceeds his needs" (*ibid.*, p. 106).

The definition of legitimate basic needs poses certain problems. According to a Tradition, the Prophet indicated what he considered to be the items of basic need in his days: "The son of man has no better right than that he would have a house wherein he may live, and a piece of cloth [with which] he may hide his nakedness, and a piece of bread and some water" (Afzal-ur-Rahman, 1980, Vol.1, p. 103). According to Ibn Hazm, an individual's basic needs comprise: (i) sufficient food to maintain the body in good health and strength; (ii) proper and suitable clothing for winter and summer; (iii) adequate shelter which protects from the weather and provides privacy (*ibid.*, p. 103). Modern Islamic social scientists have added medical care, education, fuel, electricity, and even transportation to this list (Siddiqi, in Iqbal,1988, p. 261).

Islam not only establishes the provision for basic needs for all as a most important religious and social principle, but it also indicates how this should be financed. Dues or payments for the support of the poor fall under the two categories of obligatory dues (*Sadaqeh-e Wajeb*), such as *khums* and *zakat*, and voluntary dues (*Sadaqeh-e Nafeleh*), which constitute any charitable sum over the required sum (Afzal-ur-Rahman, 1985, Vol.2, pp. 67,77; D.H.H.v.D., 1363, pp. 346–7). *Zakat*, or poor-rates, which constitutes 2.5 per cent of a Muslim's savings, income and assets, is paid to the Islamic Public Treasury (*Bait al-mal*) to provide for the poor and the needy [2:83, 2:177]. *Khums*, or the one-fifth tax, which applies to income from private ownership of natural resources and mines, has to go to the Shi'ite Islamic public treasury to be spent on relatives, orphans, the poor and the wayfarer [8:41]. *Fai'*, or the property abandoned by the enemy or taken from him without a formal war, is another source of revenue which belongs to the Islamic public treasury to be used for the poor [59:7]. Finally, there is a verse in the Qur'an which allows the needy to use the house and the food found therein of relatives and friends to satisfy their essential needs [24:61].

The division between obligatory and voluntary dues seem to be clear and free of ambiguity. The proponents of the Islamic market mechanism argue that the Muslim who has paid his obligatory dues has, in the language of jurists, cleansed his wealth and can therefore accumulate as much as he pleases, without transgressing the guidelines of the *Shari'a*. Furthermore, if God wished men to give away all their surplus income and wealth for the benefit of the poor, He would have explicitly stated so in the form of a binding obligatory injunction rather than a voluntary moral recommendation. Therefore the provision of basic needs for the poor, as desirable an objective as it is, becomes the responsibility of the Islamic government which has received the obligatory dues. The majority of both Sunni and Shi'i jurists concur with the above arguments, holding that any amount of wealth becomes legitimate once the *zakat* on it has been paid (Gerami, n.d., pp. 98–100). Some jurists consider that adjustments in the economy with the purpose of improving social justice are suggested as being ethically and morally desirable by the *Shari'a*, but deny the legal and obligatory nature of such measures (Beheshti,1363, pp. 47–8).

However, the proponents of the Islamic plan mechanism query what would happen in the eventuality that revenues from the obligatory dues prove insufficient to provide all the poor with the satisfaction of their basic needs. In a society polarised between the rich and the poor, should the property rights of some Muslims be respected at the cost of abandoning the provision for basic needs of others? Specific stipulations aimed at resolving such problems can also be found in the *Shari'a*. Those who disobey God's command to feed the poor are considered as unbelievers or those who reject the faith (*Kufar*) [36:47]. The Qur'an explicitly informs the rich that implicit in their wealth and possessions there exists a duty to provide for the needy, whether the needy ask for it or not [51:19]. Can this "duty" be interpreted as *zakat*? A saying of the Prophet can be argued to support the position that, if the needs of the poor are not met, the rich have to shoulder the responsibility. "In one's wealth there is a due (of God and His men) besides *zakat*" (Afzal-ur-Rahman, 1985, Vol.2, p. 77). A number of other Traditions can also be cited supporting the *Shari'a*'s spirit of equity and overwhelming concern for social justice. The Prophet is reported to have said: "God Almighty said: he who can sleep peacefully with a full stomach, while his

Muslim brothers go hungry is not a believer in Me" (D.H.H.v.D.,1363, p. 388). The *Shari'a* also distinguishes the means of establishing social justice. According to Abu Sa'id Khudri, the Prophet is reported to have said: "Anyone who possesses goods more than his need should give the surplus wealth to the weak (and poor); and whosoever possesses food more than his need should give the surplus food to the needy and destitute" (Afzal-ur-Rahman, 1980, Vol.1, p. 105). Imam Ali is reported to have said: "God has made it obligatory on the rich to meet the economic needs of the poor up to the extent of their absolute necessities. If they [the poor] are hungry or naked or involved in other financial difficulties, it will be merely because the rich are not performing their duty. Therefore God will question them on the day of judgement and will give them due punishment" (*ibid.*).

In the chapter on repentance (*Al Tawbah*), the Qur'an proclaims "a most grievous penalty" for those who bury their gold and silver and refuse to spend it on the poor as He has recommended [9:34]. In the next verse, the Qur'an describes the penalty: "On the Day when heat will be produced out of that (wealth) in the fire of Hell, and with it will be branded their foreheads, their flanks, and their backs — 'This is the (treasure) which ye buried for yourself: taste ye, then, the (treasure) ye buried'" [9:35].

The mere existence of hunger among the Islamic community, while some are rich, is argued to transform the recommended social obligation (*fard kifayeh*) of helping the poor into an entirely obligatory (*fard 'ain*) injunction (Islahi,1988, p. 113). Some jurists maintain that after allowing for the operation of voluntary mechanisms, if unfulfilled needs persist, then the responsibility of establishing social justice and equity becomes the responsibility of the Islamic government and the rich (Tabatabae, in Moussavi-e Isfahani, 1368, p. 434; Ibn Taymiya, in Islahi, 1988, p. 114). Ibn Taymiya goes further and argues that, "if a person possessing surplus goods refuses to lend them to one in need, and this causes the death of the latter, he will be held responsible for that death" (Islahi, 1988, p. 114). Ibn Hazm says that all the companions of the Prophet agreed that if necessary, the state could take the surplus of the rich, for the need of the poor, by force (Afzal-ur-Rahman, 1980, Vol.1, p. 106). In addition it is argued that under exceptional circumstances, such as widespread poverty, famine and malnutrition, necessity transforms all voluntary dues, which are only non-binding recommendations under normal conditions, into obligatory dues (Gerami, n.d., p. 244; Javadi, in Va'ezzadeh Khorasani, 1369, p. 310). The application of this type of secondary ordinance gives unlimited powers to the Islamic government to alleviate the economic problems of the needy. Invoking necessity, public weal, or securing what is most important at the cost of the lesser, could also legitimise the use of planning as the Islamic coordinating mechanism. It is the *Shari'a*'s ethical and moral emphasis on social justice as an objective of the system that has led many Islamic jurists and social scientists to argue that the Islamic economic system has to be egalitarian, need-driven, compassionate, cooperative and participatory.

So long as essential basic needs remain unfulfilled, while their provision is recognised as a first-priority objective of the system, production in the Islamic economy would have to be based on effective need rather than effective demand (Mannan,1984, pp. 202–4). Consumer preference would have to give way to planner preference, ideally representing the needs of the poor. The price mechanism, which allocates factors and goods, would have to be abandoned or strictly controlled if the Islamic government decides to produce and distribute what is *needed* by an assumed sub-basic needs majority, rather than what is *demanded* in a society with a highly unequal distribution of income. To direct scarce resources towards the production of basic need items and away from the production of those non-basic need items, the Islamic government needs centralised control over inputs, income and even wealth. The abandonment of the price mechanism would necessitate the introduction of a centralised system of planning to produce the socially necessary goods. The pressure for adopting the plan mechanism, to provide basic needs, becomes stronger in societies characterised by low levels of capital stock, low levels of income per capita, and highly skewed distributions of income and wealth.

Supporters of this position, having proven the necessity of suspending the market mechanism to provide the poor with basic needs, thus substituting secondary ordinances for primary ones, argue that an Islamic planned economy should be maintained indefinitely. Naqvi, an articulate representative of this position, outlines an ideal, fully fledged ethical Islamic economy in which social justice forms the cornerstone of the system. In such an economy, (i) the level and composition of production and consumption will be under direct and indirect control of the Islamic society or state; (ii) all citizens irrespective of their ability to earn will be guaranteed a reasonable level of income; (iii) feasible rates of growth will be subjected to an upper limit to "ensure a fair distribution of income and wealth *now*"; (iv) income will be absolutely equalised; (v) the distribution of wealth will be equalised; (vi)exploitation will be minimised "by making labour's share a function of the total profits of the industry"; (vii) the institution of private property will be substantially diluted; (viii) enterprises will be taken over by the state (Naqvi,1981, pp. 102–3, 96, 65, 149, 64).

The whole argument of the proponents of the Islamic plan mechanism rests on the Qur'anic verses, which (i) recommend the fulfilment of the poor's basic needs; (ii) prompt the rich to assure the realisation of this recommendation by giving away their surplus wealth for the needy; (iii) remind the rich of their financial responsibility by arguing that the poor possess a divine and social right in their wealth; and (iv) warn the rich that if they treasure their wealth, which really belongs to the poor, they will go to hell and there they shall be branded. On the basis of the evidence presented, one might argue that according to the *Shari'a* the Islamic plan mechanism is just as justifiable and legitimate as that of the Islamic market mechanism.

The proponents of the Islamic market mechanism, however, argue that even though the provision of basic needs is a Qur'anic recommendation, its fulfilment is not obligatory through the appropriation of the surplus of the rich. The rich are only obliged to pay *zakat* (according to the Sunnis) and *zakat* and *khums* (according to the Shi'ites) while all other types of recommended charity is voluntary.[8] It is argued that if the Lawmaker intended to earmark anything in addition to *zakat* and *khums* for the poor, He would have stipulated the exact amount (Gerami, n.d., p. 132).[9] Subsequently, having converted the hypothetical "right of the poor" into a clearly distinguishable sum, the Qur'an would have presented it as a binding religious law. Reports from Shi'i Imams demonstrate that the Qur'anic "right of the poor" is interpreted by them as voluntary charity, the amount of which is left entirely to the pious Muslim (*ibid.*, pp. 131–2); also that, referring to the verse in the Qur'an where God threatens those who treasure their wealth and do not help the poor, with branding in hell, the Prophet has said, "The wealth on which *zakat* has been paid does not constitute treasure ..." (*ibid.*, p. 96).

The advocates of the Islamic plan mechanism are reminded by those of the Islamic market mechanism that the suppression of the market system can be legitimately justified as long as the basic needs of a social group is not provided for, and the rich refuse to help the poor. Once essential basic needs are provided for all, and a mechanism is put into place to assure its continuation, then the market mechanism and the security of private property would have to be reinstituted; obligatory injunctions, primary ordinances and the explicit letter of the *Shari'a* cannot be suspended indefinitely in favour of ethical recommendations, secondary ordinances and the equitable spirit of the law. How can one claim that Islam is a universal and eternal religion while, in an Islamic planned economy, the majority of its economic laws would be based on extraordinary ad hoc injunctions based on tertiary sources. The indefinite suspension of the letter of the law would only prove that primary Islamic laws are incomplete and incapable of securing the felicity of man. (Makarem-e Shirazi, in Va'ezzadeh Khorasani, 1369, p. 113). It can, therefore, always be argued that an Islamic economic system devoid of its primary legal basis may no longer be considered Islamic.

*The Islamic plan-then-market mechanism*

A third Islamic coordinating mechanism can be deduced from the *Shari'a*, based on a sequential view of economic development and the imperatives of the *Shari'a* during each phase. In the initial stages of development, given low levels of capital stock and a highly unequal distribution of income, the market coordinating mechanism would allocate scarce resources towards the luxury goods demanded by the effective demand of the rich, leaving the basic needs of the majority unfulfilled. The poor, incapable of translating their effective need into effective demand, for want of sufficient income, would be left without their basic needs. The abject poverty of one section of society — leading to starvation, malnutrition, homelessness, epidemics, high child and infant mortality, and low life-expectancy — co-existing with the opulent life-styles of the rich, a situation which commonly characterises Third World countries, could be considered an aberration of the *Shari'a*'s spirit of social justice and solidarity. During this phase of development the Islamic economy would have to replace the free play of the market with some degree of state control. The Islamic government's target, which is the needy, and its responsibility, which is the provision of essential basic needs, are far more specific than the instruments that it must adopt to arrive at its objective.

Policies such as the subsidising of essential goods, direct transfer of income, or public provision of essential goods, would be able to redirect resources from luxury items demanded by the rich to necessities demanded by the poor, accompanied by a minimum of interference in the market process (Siddiqi, in Iqbal, 1988, p. 269). However, the effective implementation of such policies, to assure the provision of basic needs for all those requiring assistance (who, according to Siddiqi, could constitute as much as half of the total population of a country) without a high degree of central planning, remains unaddressed.

Baqir Sadr envisages an economy in which the state would control the entire economic life of society, through its control and ownership of raw materials and minerals; these, according to Sadr's interpretation of Islam, belong to the public and therefore to the state (Sadr, 1985, Vol.2 part 2, pp. 145–6). Yet, in Sadr's economic scheme the Islamic economy would be based on private as well as state ownership (Sadr, 1982, Vol. 1, part 2, p. 55). Sadr argues that until sufficient amounts of basic needs are produced to fulfil the needs of all in society, factors of production should not be allocated to the production of non-necessities, and that the production of luxury goods should be banned (Sadr, 1985, Vol.2 part 2, pp. 145–6). Economic planning, and its necessary corollaries of control over the mix of outputs, input allocation, prices, incomes, domestic and foreign trade, and savings, would therefore become unnecessary once basic needs are provided for. Sadr's position appears different from that of the advocates of the Islamic planning mechanism in that for the latter the plan and its attributes provide an end in themselves.

According to the plan-then-market co-ordinating mechanism, during the post-need-fulfilment phase, having established social justice, the Islamic economy can then go back to the letter of the law by adopting the Islamic market mechanism. During this stage, the market would become the medium for allocation, distribution and reward. The adoption of this mechanism would fulfil the objective of the *Shari'a*, which is to "ensure the basic needs of the absolute poor, and if they aspire for more, let them try for it" (Iqbal, 1988, p. 20).

According to Marxist development theory, consumption during socialism is characterised by "to each according to his work" and only in the later stage of communism does it become "to each according to his need". In contrast, the Islamic plan-then-market mechanism initially aims at providing for each according to their essential needs, irrespective of whether they have worked for it or not. Such a policy would result in relative equality of income and consumption. During the post-need-fulfilment stage, when society can produce enough to provide everyone with minimum basic needs, and more, the Islamic plan-then-market mechanism would distribute according to ability and factor ownership. The result of this would be a growing inequality in incomes and consumption. The Islamic plan-then-market mechanism, at least in theory, appears to be in complete contradiction to the Marxist notion of development. The early days of the Prophet in Medina in which "a portion of the private wealth of the *ansar* was given to the *muhajerin*, and except for a small portion of private fortunes, wealth was superintended by the state … and was divided among all equally, to each according to his need", can be presented as a model of the operation of the initial phase of the plan-then-market mechanism (Taleghani,1982, p. 58). Once poverty is eradicated, society can be put on a market footing. "If society in general or any portion of it is not suffering from dire misery and paralysing poverty, let there be gradation of wealth honestly earned and innocently enjoyed" (Afzal-ur-Rahman, 1980, Vol.1, p. 37).

## Property rights

At first sight, no other attribute of the Islamic economic system elicits greater unanimity among Muslim jurists and social scientists than the formal definition and extent of property rights. There are numerous categorical references in the Qur'an to the fact that God is the sole owner of all things in the heavens and on earth [2:107, 2:255, 2:284, 5:120, 48:14]. Islam's concept of property ownership is based on God's absolute, natural and divine right of possession in relation to all that is on earth. God as the ultimate and unlimited owner has, however, made man His vicegerent and entrusted him with his possessions on earth [2:30, 2:40]. *Amanat*, or the notion that God's possessions are only held in trust by man, makes man's ownership conditional, contractual and effectively usufructory. As long as he remains worthy of God's trust by following the *Shari'a*, he has the right to enjoy the use and advantages of God's property. This right is accompanied by obligations. Man is enjoined to strive with his life and wealth in the cause of God [9:16].

In a philosophical sense, man cannot become an absolute owner, since ownership of all things, including man himself, belongs to God. The original Owner, however, entrusts his property to three social categories: the Imam, as the guardian of the people and head of the Islamic government, the public and the individual. The great majority of Islamic jurists and social scientists agree that Islam recognises contractual or conditional property in terms of common or public property, Islamic state property, and individual or private property. Each category can exercise its right of use and disposition according to a set of rules. The source of disagreements among Islamic jurists and social scientists lies in varying interpretations and descriptions of what constitutes the composition and constraints of each ownership category.

### Public property

Public property in Islam refers to those natural resources created by God to which all men have an equal right. In their original property form, such items are considered as the common property of the Islamic community. Individuals may, however, use such resources according to their need. Each individual's right of use is legitimate as long as it does not undermine the equally valid right of others. Islamic common property includes forests, pastures, rivers, mountains, mines, and all that can be found in the seas (Moussavi-e Isfahani, 1368, p. 248). Uncultivated or dead land (*mawat*) is also usually categorised as public property. Those cultivated lands conquered by the Islamic army through holy war falls under the rubric of the Muslim community's common property. The common endeavour expended in its appropriation justifies its categorisation as the common property of the *ummah*. The role of the Islamic state in all the above cases is supposed to be one of supervision and guardianship, except in the latter case where it is entitled to collect rent from those who work on the conquered lands (D.H.H.v.D., 1363, p. 106; Motahhari, 1368, p. 152).

Even though in its original property form a considerable part of natural resources is designated as communal property, this proves to be highly transitory in practice. Public property is allowed to be transformed either into private or state property. According to one interpretation, a private ownership right can be established through tending, exploiting and working (*hiyazat*) communal natural resources (*mubahat-e 'ameh*), before anyone else. Water taken from a river, cultivation of unclaimed land, trees cut down, or birds and fish caught by individuals, become their private property. In other cases, control over communal property is delegated to the Islamic state, which manages it on behalf of the community.

A case in point in the debate on the acceptability of privatisation of common property is that of the ownership status of mines. Mines are divided into open or accessible mines, and underground or inaccessible mines. Two different interpretations have emerged on the basis of two sets of Traditions. According to the first set, the Prophet disagreed with the privatisation of mines. It is reported that Abyaz bin Hamal asked the Prophet to grant him a salt lake in Muarib. Once the Prophet was told that the lake possessed salt, he refused to grant him the mine (Afzal-ur-Rahman, 1980, Vol.1, p. 86). The Prophet is also reported to have prohibited the privatisation of natural resources which are of public utility and necessity, saying: "People are partners in three things; water, fire and pastures" (D.H.H.v.D., 1363, p. 165). The analogical deduction is that both natural resources and articles of public utility should remain under state control. This interpretation, shared by both Sunni and Shi'i jurists, maintains that mines should always remain common property, managed and administrated by the Islamic government, for the common welfare of the *ummah* (D.H.H.v.D., 1363, p. 153; Afzal-ur-Rahman, 1980, p. 87. Islahi, 1988, p. 117). Both the Sunni Imam Malik and the Shi'ite Baqir Sadr consider mines as common or state property. They reject the notion that such natural resources could become privatised. Malik argues that even if such mines are found on someone's private land, they would have to become the property of the Islamic state (Afzal-ur-Rahman,1980, Vol.1, p. 87; Sadr, 1357, Vol.2, p. 127).

Another set of Traditions demonstrates that the Prophet allowed the private ownership of mines. When the Prophet was informed of the private exploitation of a gold mine, he neither reprimanded the private owners nor prohibited such ownership (Afzal-ur-Rahman, 1980, Vol.1, p. 88). In another instance, the Prophet reportedly gave the mines of al-Qabaliyya to Bilal ibn Harith al-Mazini, in return for which Bilal was only obliged to pay *zakat* (Imam Malik ibn Anas, 1989, p. 95). The obligation to pay *zakat* is proof of the fact that the mine was considered as the private property of the individual. The Shi'ites place a one-fifth tax (*khums*) on mineral deposits such as gold, silver, tin and oil, which once again demonstrates that private ownership of mineral deposits is allowed in Islam (Gerami, n.d., p. 223). On the basis of these Traditions, the second interpretation, shared by both Sunnis and Shi'ites, maintains that accessible as well as inaccessible mines can be privatised so long as obligatory Islamic taxes on their produce is paid to the public treasury (Khomeini, *Resalah*, pp. 283–4; Gerami, n.d., p. 223; Mannan, 1986, p. 251; Shad,1986, p. 72). Once individuals apply their labour to public property, on a first-to-exploit, first-to-own basis, they can legitimately claim their private ownership on the same basis.

There does appear to be a general tendency among Islamic jurists to consider open or accessible mines, where the extraction of minerals does not require any application of labour, as common and non-privatisable property (D.H.H.v.D., 1363, p. 153. Zarqa, in Iqbal (ed.), 1988, pp. 168–9). Yet, as we have shown, there is no strict consensus. On the subject of inaccessible mines, however, a glaring discord exists among both Sunni and Shi'ite jurists. For example, Imam Shafi'i permits the privatisation of inaccessible or hidden mines, while Imam Malik prohibits such a practice (Zarqa, in Iqbal (ed.), 1988, p. 169).

The same kind of polarisation exists among jurists on whether or not water from a well, a spring, or diverted from a river, can be privately owned and therefore sold. Both sides support their respective positions with an array of reports from different Imams.[10]

A radical interpretation supporting nationalisation rather than privatisation of public natural resources is constructed on the basis of two verses in the Qur'an. The first states that God has left His natural resources for *all* men [1:29]. The second states that God emphasises the entitlement of *all* men equally to the necessities of life [107:7]. It is asserted that since men play no direct role in the creation of natural resources, they cannot claim a private title to them. The denial of private-property rights over natural resources is thus deduced as a Qur'anic principle (Paydar, 1357, pp. 172, 182, 205, 310; Proceedings, 1976, p. 23).

Public property is therefore a formal categorisation of natural resources in their original form, and is compelled to become either state or private property. Thus, as we have seen, whether minerals or other natural resources, originally categorised as public property, should be permitted to become private property and subsequently the source of individual gain, or state property and the source of collective gain, is the subject of lengthy and indeterminate debate among Islamic jurists.

**State property**

The Qur'an explicitly designates certain items as the property of God and the Prophet. These, in addition to certain natural resources that cannot be immediately privatised, fall under the title of state property. The Islamic state takes possession of these items and the head of the Islamic state acts as custodian, without having any private rights to them. The Qur'an places all spoils of war (*anfal*) at the disposal of God and the Prophet [8:1]. A later verse specifies that only one fifth of the booty acquired in war (*ghanimah*) belongs to God and the Prophet [8:41]. The remaining four-fifths does not constitute state property and is to be distributed among the warriors who fought in the victorious campaign. The Qur'an stipulates that the property surrendered to the Muslims without a fight (*fai*), also belongs to God and the Prophet [59:6–7].

Islamic state property can be defined as first, movables and immovables including land, either gained as spoils of war (*ghanimah* or *anfal*) or surrendered by non-believers without a fight (*fai'*) and second, miscellaneous property such as unclaimed property, uncultivated lands (*mawat*), and heirless property (Islahi, 1988, pp. 208–11; D.H.H.v.D., 1363, p. 105. Motahhari, 1368, p. 154).[11] According to the Sunnis, *anfal* and *ghanimah* are the same. The Shi'ites, however, label all the property that the *Shari'a* places at the disposal of the Islamic government through God and the Prophet as *anfal* or state property (Sadr, 1357, Vol.2, p. 124). They argue that state property is handed down by the Prophet to the Shi'i Imam's (Taskhiri,1368, pp. 250–51). For the Shi'ites, therefore, that part of the booty (*ghanimah*) distributed among those who engaged in war cannot be considered as *anfal*, due to its private form of ownership (Motahhari, 1368, p. 155).

Land constitutes the most important category of the property of the Islamic state. After the conquest of Iraq and Syria, a number of prominent Companions of the Prophet argued for the distribution of the newly acquired lands among those who had fought in the campaigns, on the basis that the Prophet had distributed the conquered lands of Khaybar, Banu Nazir and Banu Quraiza to individuals. (Afzal-ur-Rahman, 1985, Vol.2, p. 142). However, the second Caliph, Omar, accepted Ali's recommendation against land distribution among individuals. Ali argued that such a practice would concentrate the common wealth of the community in the hands of a few, thus privatising what was the common property of all present and future Muslims, the fruits of which had to be used for the general good of the community. Omar invoked the Qur'anic verses referring to the properties surrendered to Muslims by non-believers without a fight (*fai*), and ruled that land should be left in the hands of the original inhabitants in return for the payment of *kharaj* (land tax), so that this income could be utilised for the welfare of society and the payment of salaries to the warriors (Abu Yusaf, 1979, pp. 40–50). In those conquered lands where the population did embrace Islam, the original cultivators paid the Islamic Treasury a tax called *ushr* on the produce of their land. *Ushr* and *kharaj* are equivalents, yet the former is paid by Muslims and the latter by non-Muslims (Hassan-uz-Zaman, 1981, p. 172). This category of conquered land that was left to the original cultivators may only be considered state property in the sense that the government received a tax on the produce of the land. Otherwise, the original inhabitants had the right of transfer, sale and inheritance of the land (Abu Yusaf, 1979, p. 121).

All unoccupied, undeclared and uncultivated lands (*mawat*) were also considered state land. These lands were given by the Islamic ruler to individuals who could reclaim and cultivate the land, or as a reward to those who were rendering a service to the state, including warriors and the new converts to Islam

(Afzal-ur-Rahman, 1985, Vol.2, p. 159). Even though the Islamic state has been recognised as the nominal owner of uncultivated land, historically its effective function has been that of supervising and legitimising the privatisation of state lands. Individuals obtain full ownership rights, including the right of sale, transfer and inheritance, through the receipt of state grants or the rehabilitation of uncultivated or barren land.

In principle, however, the Islamic ruler is entitled to full control over state lands. He can convert such lands into state farms, cultivated by wage labourers hired by the state (*ibid.*, p. 135). To assure the implementation of social justice and avoid the excessive concentration of wealth, the head of the Islamic state can prevent individuals from reclaiming land and thus transforming it into their private property (Gerami, n.d., p. 201). Omar, the second Caliph, is said to have nullified large grants of land that had been given to individuals as their private property by the first Caliph, Abu Bakr, on the grounds that the grants were unduly large (Afzal-ur-Rahman, 1985, Vol.2, p. 157). A majority of both Shi'i and Sunni jurists maintain that the Islamic ruler can also expropriate land privatised through reclamation and subsequently left idle for a long period of time. In this case, the ownership of uncultivated land which originally belonged to the state reverts to the state if its secondary owner fails to cultivate it (D.H.H.v.D., 1363, pp. 148–9). According to a *hadith*, "A deserted plot of land will be the property of the one who brings it into use and anyone who does not make use of it for three consecutive years will have no right to it after the expiry of the said period" (Abu Yusaf, 1979, p. 116). Omar confiscated that part of a land grant given by the Prophet to Bilal bin-Harith which he could not reclaim or rehabilitate, arguing that it constituted a waste of public resources. (Afzal-ur-Rahman, 1985, Vol.2, p. 155).

State ownership can, therefore, be considered as the primitive or original property condition of uncultivated land. This state property is immediately converted into private property, even though it could revert to its primitive property condition under special circumstances. As the Prophet is reported to have said: "Old and fallow lands are for God and His Messenger, and then they are for you" (Hassan-uz-Zaman, 1981, p. 77). Ultimately, therefore, individual private ownership inherits state property.

**Private property**

There is general consensus among Sunni and Shi'i jurists and social scientists alike that Islam recognises and upholds the individual's right to private property and ownership. Respect for private property in Islam is considered an undeniable certitude. Private property ownership is considered legitimate in capital, land, cash, and other things including human beings (Ahmadi-Mianji, 1363, Vol.1, pp. 13, 135). The Qur'anic verses which deal with Islamic taxes, the legality of inheritance, the prohibition against usurping property (*gasb*), the legality of trade, the legality of ownership and emancipation of slaves, the recommendation to give away in charity, and the legality of bequeathing, are all referred to as confirmation of the fact that individuals are entitled to property in Islam. It is argued that these Qur'anic injunctions presume private property ownership [2:180, 2:188, 2:254, 4:7, 4:92,17:26]. The Qur'an guarantees the security of private property by imposing stringent punishments on those who violate its sanctity. "As to the thief, male or female, cut off his or her hand" [5:38]. The Prophet is reported to have said that a person who died defending his property was a martyr (Afzal-ur-Rahman, 1980, Vol.1, p. 74).

Islamic jurists and social scientists have argued that since man is instinctively capricious and possesses varied needs and wants, he is compelled to compete with others in society to secure his exclusive wishes. The mechanism which allows for the realisation of such a quest is that of private property, since it assures the individual the fruits of his labour (Makarem-e Shirazi, n.d., pp. 120–32. Afzal-ur-Rahman, 1980, Vol.1, p. 74). Islam recognises man's instinctual inclination to private property as beneficial both for the individual and the Islamic community (D.H.H.v.D., 1363, pp. 11–12).

Even though there is no serious doubt about the legitimacy of private property in Islam, differences of opinion and rulings emerge around three major issues. First, the permissible Islamic mechanisms of establishing private ownership. Second, the legal rights of individuals who have made a legitimate claim on land. Third, the degree, extent and limiting factors of what constitutes acceptable private property. It will be demonstrated that the different judgements of different jurists on the subject of Islamic private property could lead students of Islamic economics to construct diametrically opposed economic systems, each equally legitimate and equally well supported by the *Shari'a*.

In general, Islamic jurists and economists concur that other than property entitlements acquired through involuntary means, such as inheritance, bequests or gifts, the establishment of private property rights in Islam falls into two general categories: non-contractual and contractual mechanisms. Non-contractual mechanisms involve the collection, exploitation or hunting of those natural resources that have not been previously claimed as private property. The application of labour to communal natural resources, or *hiyazat-e mobahat*, entitles the labourer to "initial" property rights. The reclamation, cultivation or revitalisation of dead or barren land (*ihya-e mawat*), is a subset of this and therefore also attributes "initial" property rights to the cultivator. Contractual mechanisms include those economic activities that involve trade or buying and selling (*bey'*), renting land or machines and hiring labour (*ijarah*), and the Islamic business usages of profit sharing in trade, agriculture and gardening (*muzaraba, muzar'a* and *musaqat*) (Saeedi and Gorji, in Va'ezzadeh Khorasani, 1369, pp. 18 and 253). Given the above possibilities of establishing private property rights in Islam, the issue of what constitutes legitimate Islamic private property has been approached and treated in two different ways.

The first approach does not really question how "initial" property rights were established, as long as the pursuit of acquiring existing property rights did not violate any of the explicit commandments of the *Shari'a*. While Islamic jurists and economists agree that property gained has to be the fruit of one's labour, the definition of property-entitling "labour" in this approach is circular. Since ownership entitlement in Islam can only be established through legitimate labour, it is argued that labour must have been at the origin of all accumulated property. The link between individual labour and property ownership can, however, be easily broken, since Islam allows for inheritance, bequests and gifts. The proponents of this position argue that on the basis of the *Shari'a*, possession is the proof of private ownership, unless the contrary is proven (Ahmadi-Mianji, 1363, Vol.2, pp. 25–6). The fact that Islam allows factors of production to be legitimately rented, and their produce appropriated by he who rents or hires them, has given rise to arguments on the means of attaining private property identical to the capitalist approach.[12] This approach is employed by both Sunni and Shi'ite jurists.

The second approach focuses on establishing the Islamic legitimacy of property entitlements by tracing them to the direct labour that has been applied to secure "initial" ownership rights. This approach, greatly influenced by the works of Baqir Sadr, has become more common among certain contemporary Shi'ite jurists and economists. Sadr bases his economic approach on what could be referred to as a "natural resources theory of value" in contrast to the classical "labour theory of value". According to Sadr, the farmer who has established his "initial' ownership by reclaiming dead land will become the owner of its produce in the form of raw materials such as seeds or cotton. Processing the cotton into yarn through the application of labour entitles the direct producer to the legitimate ownership of yarn. Having produced the yarn, Sadr argues that the yarn owner can then legitimately hire a wage labourer to produce cloth, without the hired worker having any right to the cloth, only to his wages. Sadr calls this procedure the principle of "the permanence of ownership". Even though it seems as if he applies the labour theory of value to the mechanism of reward in the first stage of processing, he rejects its validity in the second stage. He subsequently argues that if a worker applies his labour to someone else's seed or cotton, the produce of his labour would belong to the owner of the raw material, and not to the direct labourer (Sadr, 1357, Vol.2, p. 217). The emphasis on the application of labour to natural resources as the only justifiable means of establishing "initial" ownership rights has become a pivotal concern for Islamic economists. The proponents of this method of analysis have argued that the application of direct labour to natural resources, as a prerequisite for establishing "initial" ownership, renders the Islamic notion of private property different from that of capitalism.

Sadr argues that distribution in capitalism is based on the share of factor inputs in the process of production. Income is therefore composed of factor rewards: wage, rent, profit and interest. Distribution in Islam is argued to be different, since income accrues only to the direct producer who has applied his labour to natural resources. The owners of land and capital do not receive any share of the product, but are said to be entitled to a "wage" for the role that their factors play in the final produce (*ibid.*, p. 207). Here Sadr has to assume that their title to ownership is the result of their own labour. The extent to which such an assumption in terms of modern industry could be applicable is highly suspect. Sadr maintains that labour in Islam is not considered simply one of the four factors of production, but the determining factor, which bestows ownership, and therefore a right to income, on he who applies it. He concludes that whereas in capitalism the capitalist may own numerous oil wells or wood and pulp factories on which wage labour is exploited, such a condition would be impossible in Islam, since the Islamic economic system would compel him to work on his oil fields or forests himself in order to establish his ownership title. Furthermore, Islam would not permit him to reap the product of his employees (*ibid.*, p. 209).

The problem with Sadr's grand design to distinguish the Islamic system from capitalism once and for all is rooted in his central assumption that "initial" property rights belong to the labourer who has applied his direct labour to natural resources, or more specifically to land. If it could be shown that in Islam "initial" property rights could be secured without direct application of labour, but through hiring a worker to do the work, then Sadr's whole argument falls apart. To prove his position, Sadr refers to Alameh Helli, Mohaqeq Isfahani and Sheykh Tusi to prove that in Islam it is not permitted to hire a person for the purpose of collecting wood, transporting water, reclaiming or cultivating land, and catching fish. If such a person is hired, the produce of his work would, according to the above renowned jurists, belong to himself, for the work he performed directly on nature, and not to his employer (*ibid.*, pp. 201–5). It is interesting to note that the proponents of this position have been labelled "communists" by traditional jurists (Hashemi-e Rafsanjani, ***Payam-e Inqelab***, no.82).

Opponents of this position make reference to the fact that the Prophet received five gardens through the bequest of a man called Mokhiriq, on which he did not work, but from the fruits of which he benefited (Ahmadi-Mianji, 1363, Vol.2, pp. 63–4). Furthermore, Imam Ali is said to have purchased a piece of land and then, having found water from a spring that was dug by two of his slaves, given the land to charity (*ibid.*, p. 78). The report validates the position not only that land may be owned through purchase, but that its development does not require the direct labour of its owner. A review of the pronouncements of a great number of prominent Shi'ite jurists demonstrates that a solid case can be made for the position which maintains that the hiring of labour, even for the establishment of "initial" ownership, is permissible in Islam.[13] The proponents of this position argue that the majority of jurists agree that labour could be employed to exploit and extract natural resources (*hiyazat*). By analogy, it is argued that uncultivated land, as a natural resource, can also be reclaimed by hiring labour (D.H.H.v.D., 1363, p. 209; Makarem-e Shirazi, n.d., pp. 126–7). It is further argued that Islam considers the hiring of labour (*ijarah*) permissible (Mousa Sadr, n.d., p. 89). The Islamic justification of the use of wage labour in the establishment of "initial" ownership leads to the conclusion that Islam's system of property ownership, and therefore income distribution, is similar to that of capitalism. If, however, we accept the Islamic sources used by Sadr, then we would come to a different conclusion. Once again the debate remains inconclusive.

The second subject of debate on private property in Islam concerns the legal rights of the "initial" owner of the land. Some jurists believe that cultivation merely creates a right to priority over others in the use of the land, while others believe it establishes comprehensive private property rights (D.H.H.v.D., 1363, p. 259). The real debate is whether Islamic ownership bestows the right of disposition or only of utilisation. In reference to the exploitation of natural resources (*hiyazat*), the Prophet is reported to have said, "If someone exploits an item before any other Muslim, then the exploited item becomes his possession" (Beheshti, 1363, p. 33. D.H.H.v.D., 1363, p. 117). In relation to the reclamation of dead land (*ihya mawat*), the Prophet is reported to have said, "When someone revives dead land, it belongs to him" (Imam Malik ibn Anas, 1989, p. 307). Both Traditions could be used to prove that the application of labour to natural resources gives rise to unconditional private-property rights. Uncultivated land, mineral deposits and natural water resources could, therefore, be exploited and thus privatised. In spite of the Prophet's Tradition, however, there is no unanimity among jurists on the issue of mineral deposits. Yet Sunni and Shi'i jurists concur that he who first reclaims or cultivates an uncultivated plot of land becomes its owner (Imam Malik ibn Anas, 1989, p. 307; Gerami, n.d., p. 197).

Those who believe in the right of priority and utilisation, rather than ownership, argue that as soon as the worker ceases activity on his land, the right of exploitation could be transferred to one who is ready to cultivate the land. The new cultivator acquires the title to utilisation through the application of his labour to the land, nullifying the title of the original rehabilitator who left his land unattended. According to this argument the Islamic right of ownership is one of utilisation and not possession.[14] Furthermore, the security of utilisation is argued to be guaranteed only by continuous application of labour and not the security of private property. Following the same logic, a radical argument is developed based on the grounds that since Islamic ownership simply bestows a right of utilisation, the worker's right is limited to his life period, while he works on the land. His death terminates the right of priority to utilisation that was established by him. This argument rejects the right to bequest, arguing for the return of natural resources to their original or primary owner, namely God, and subsequently the public.[15]

Other Islamic jurists, however, believe that the reclamation and cultivation (*ihya*) of uncultivated (*mawat*) land provides unconditional property rights for its owner, and that such a right cannot be abrogated even if the original owner leaves the land uncultivated for an indeterminate period of time (D.H.H.v.D., 1363, pp. 211–13).[16] It is subsequently argued that their property right allows them to sell, transfer or bequest their land according to the limits established by the *Shari'a*. There seems to be a greater consensus among jurists on this position (Hashemi-e Rafsanjani, *Payam-e Inqelab*, no.81). A variant of this position maintains that the ownership rights of a person who has bought a piece of land is absolutely eternal in Islam. It is argued that even though the rights established through reclamation and cultivation (*ihya*) are subject to debate, the general consensus of jurists gives absolute rights to the original cultivator (Ahmadi-Mianji, 1363, Vol.2. p. 6).

The third controversial issue on private ownership concerns the degree, extent and limiting factors of acceptable private ownership in Islam. Opinions among jurists and social scientists fall within three broad categories. All three support their positions with reference to the *Shari'a*. First, there are those who argue that Islam sets no limits on private property earned through permissible (*halal*) means. It is, however, incumbent upon the property owner to pay the appropriate wealth tax. Second, there are those who maintain that in a fully fledged Islamic economy property ownership should be scaled down to the minimum possible, and perhaps limited solely to consumer goods. Third, there are those who reason that even though Islam upholds the freedom to pursue private property, it also places limits on property ownership when the attainment of certain first-order objectives of the system is threatened by the process of private property accumulation.

The first position, the belief in the Islamic acceptability of unlimited property ownership, is prevalent among both Sunni and Shi'i jurists. During debates and deliberations in Iran's Assembly of Experts on the status and extent of private property in an Islamic society, Ja'far Ishraqi, a Shi'ite jurist, expressed an opinion common among Muslim jurists. He said: "Those gentlemen who are familiar with Islamic law (*fiqh*) are aware that property ownership is not limited in Islam, and it is permissible for one to earn fifteen, one thousand or one million tomans daily" (Majles-e Shouray-e Islami, 1364, p. 1539). Support for quantitatively unlimited property ownership in Islam can also be found among Sunni scholars. Al-Faruqi concurs with Ishraqi and takes his argument to its logical conclusion. Al-Faruqi maintains that, "Man's acquisition of wealth may have no limits in Islam. A person may amass boundless treasures. Indeed he can, theoretically at least, 'own' the whole world" (al-Faruqi, in Proceedings 1976, p. xiii). This position can be supported indirectly by Qur'anic verses which legitimise and condone differences in income — irrespective of size — as God's will and design. The Qur'an says: "And in nowise covet those things in which Allah hath bestowed His gifts more freely on some of you than on others ..." [4:32]. The same message is expressed in a number of different Qur'anic verses, underlining the fact that God gives to those that He wills "without measure" [16:71, 6:165, 24:38]. Mu'awiya ibn Abi Sufyan, who became Caliph after Imam Ali and is known for his love of wealth, supports the Islamic notion of unlimited private property by referring to a Tradition of the Prophet. The Prophet is quoted as saying: "O people! Nothing can keep away what Allah gives and nothing can give what Allah keeps away" (Imam Malik ibn Anas, 1989, p. 381).

The second position on the permissible extent of private property in Islam maintains that Islam is averse to and incompatible with private ownership of the means of production. Some of the most radical in this group consider Islam to be in contradiction with the institution of private ownership of land, natural resources and capital (Paydar, 1357, p. 282). Support for the Islamic anti-private-property or socialistic position is based on a number of arguments.

First, in a society based on Islamic justice, exploitation would have to be eradicated. Private ownership of the means of production is argued to be at the origin of exploitation and therefore incompatible with Islamic social justice (Shariati, *Khodsazi-e Enqelabi*, pp. 102,146). Tavanayanfard argues that in the process of production three kinds of exploitation can occur: (i) the private appropriation of rewards to natural resources, which constitute the produce of God's labour, is considered exploitation of God; (ii) the private appropriation of rewards to capital, which constitute the labour of past generations, is considered exploitation of the previous generations; (iii) the appropriation of part of rewards to current labour by someone other than the direct labourer is considered exploitation of workers. According to this position, the establishment of a classless monotheistic society requires the state to collect the share of rewards pertaining to God and previous generations and use them collectively, while guaranteeing the receipt of direct labour's whole share. Clearly, in such a society there would be no private ownership of the factors of production other than labour, and no economic categories such as profit or rent (Tavanayanfard, 1361, pp. 109–10).

Second, the institution of private property would keep wealth concentrated in the hands of a few and deepen the gap between the haves and have-nots, which is incompatible with certain Qur'anic injunctions [4:34–35, 59:7] (Naqvi, 1981, p. 77; Taleqani, pp. 108–11).

Third, the rewards to private ownership of land and capital constitute usury. It is argued that interest or *riba* constitutes an addition to the original amount of capital, or an "excess over and above the principal". Profit and rent likewise constitute an excess over the original capital of their owners, and are therefore prohibited in Islam (Tavanayanfard, in Gerami, n.d., p. 19; Abu Sulayman, Proceedings, 1976, p. 22; Paydar, 1357, pp. 283–4).

Fourth, private property is tolerated by Islam as long as all members of society profit from it, since, as God's vicegerents, all men have an equal share in His bounties (Shaltut, in Karpat, 1982, p. 114). On the basis of the arguments presented by the proponents of a socialistic view of Islam, any property-ownership system that allows for private appropriation of the fruits of land and capital, which is argued to be collective property, is incompatible with Islam.

The third position on private property in Islam accepts the inviolable right to private property under normal circumstances. Yet it recognises certain exceptional conditions under which private property could be limited or even temporarily abolished (Hashemi-e Rafsanjani, *Payam-e Inqelab*, no.81). According to this position, respect for private property constitutes a primary ordinance and its curtailment or suspension can only be justified by the prevalence of exceptional circumstances requiring secondary ordinances. If individual private property endangers public weal, welfare or interest, private interest would have to be sacrificed for the sake of social interest. According to Maliki and Hanbali jurists, dwelling units owned by landlords in excess of their immediate use could be legally expropriated, in favour of the homeless, if society swells with homeless people (Qadri, 1986, p. 311). Based on a Tradition of the Prophet, Sunni as well as Shi'i jurists agree that, if the exercise of private ownership causes injury and harm to others, Islam would rule in favour of the suspension or curtailment of such rights (Imam Malik ibn Anas, 1989, p. 307. Makarem-e Shirazi in Va'ezzadeh Khorasani, 1369, p. 106). In cases of pressing necessity, such as famine, the property and food of those who possess them is made lawful to those in need (Qadri, 1986, p. 31; Islahi, 1988, p. 180). According to the Maliki and Hanbali school of jurisprudence, if someone is driven by excessive hunger to eat someone else's food, it is not incumbent on him to pay for it (Mahmasani, 1358, p. 268). Finally, private property could be suspended for reasons of state or in cases where the survival of the Islamic government necessitates such a measure (Makarem-e Shirazi, in Va'ezzadeh Khorasani, 1369, p. 107).

If economic systems are to be distinguished by the particular property relations that govern them, the Islamic economic system would undoubtedly be a multifaceted one. Islamic economists maintain that the economy should be based upon the private, public and state-owned sectors. This they consider to be a particular feature of the Islamic economy, even though it essentially reflects the property relations of a mixed economy. On the basis of our survey, three distinct types of Islamic property relations can be discerned. Each can constitute the property base of at least one of the three co-ordinating mechanisms. First, the view that condones the pursuit and achievement of unlimited private property is perfectly compatible with the Islamic free market mechanism. Second, the interpretation which views private property in the means of production as incompatible with Islam can form the property basis of the Islamic plan mechanism. Third, the position that respects the freedom of private property, yet under particular conditions calls for limitations on it or even its temporary suspension, can be effectively used as the property foundation of the Islamic plan-then-market co-ordinating mechanism. In view of the variety of legitimate and viable Islamic positions on the issue of property relations, an attempt to put the Islamic economic system into one or another straitjacket would be simplistic and reductionist.

## Incentive mechanisms

Economic systems rely on certain incentive mechanisms to assure desirable behaviour on the part of economic agents in compliance with the system's ideology and objectives. The Islamic incentive system of rewarding Islamically approved acts and discouraging Islamically undesirable acts could employ an array of mechanisms to attain its objective.

The principle force that motivates the Islamic man to undertake any activity, economic ones included, is presented as that of securing the pleasure of God. If all activities are conducted with the intention of gaining proximity to God through serving Him according to His laws, man will be rewarded by Him, both in this world and in the hereafter. The divine incentive system, particular to Islam, requires man to substitute the love of God for the love of self. The acquisitive and greedy economic man has to be reborn as the compassionate, charitable and generous Islamic man if he is to be rewarded in the hereafter. God enjoins Muslims to be altruistic and do good to one another by helping each other financially [2:177,2:195,16:90]. Spending in the cause of God, out of what man loves most, is the price of attaining righteousness and salvation in the hereafter [2:195].

The emphasis of the divine incentive system is on benefiting and enriching others at the cost of forgoing individual gain and even reducing one's own private riches. Contrary to worldly material incentives, the divine incentive system penalises the do-gooder in the short run by decreasing his material possessions. In the long run, however, he might be compensated with an increase in his worldly wealth. Yet he would certainly attain salvation and eternal bliss in the hereafter [2:245, 57:18]. Theoretically, it is the absence of immediate private material gains as the reward for Islamically desirable acts that distinguishes the divine Islamic incentive system from other incentive mechanisms.

Islamic scholars agree that private satisfaction can only be attained through pleasing God. Acts pleasing in the eyes of God do, however, include self-satisfying activities. Numerous Traditions demonstrate that permissible work and the pursuit of livelihood is considered as performing the obligatory religious duty of worshipping (*'ibadah*) (Khoshneviss, n.d., p. 51). The Prophet is reported to have elevated the status of an honest hard worker, pursuing his own private gain, to that of a *mojahid* or a warrior for the cause of God (*ibid*., p. 49). Economic activities with the objective of attaining private material benefits could, therefore, assume the character of worshipping and thus guarantee salvation in the hereafter. On this basis, Islamically condoned acts would eventually achieve both ends, satisfying the pleasure of God first and subsequently that of man. The idea that individuals can obtain worldly material rewards as well as salvation in the hereafter for one act, without any sacrifice, undermines the charitable and altruistic basis of the Islamic divine incentive mechanism. The entanglement and interrelatedness of the pursuit of earthly and divine pleasures can become complex enough to blur the distinction between means and ends. It is argued that the crucial element that makes an act pleasing in the eyes of God, even though it results in private material gain, is that the activity is undertaken with the intention of being for His sake (Ibn Taymiya, 1983, p. 86). So once the right intention is invoked, a profitable activity could be passed off as an act in the cause of God.

The argument that God's pleasure may be secured through the fulfilment of private pleasure almost turns the divine incentive mechanism into an ethically constrained private material incentive mechanism. Chapra attempts to reconcile a worldly and private material incentive mechanism with Islam by saying: "Islam creates a harmony between the material and the moral by urging Muslims to strive for material welfare, but stressing simultaneously that they place this material effort on a moral foundation thus providing a spiritual orientation to material effort" (Chapra, 1975, p. 6). According to this formula, the pursuit of Islamically permissible private pleasures as a means to attaining divine pleasure becomes justifiable. In support of this position, a Tradition of the Prophet could be referred to. It is reported that the Companions of the Prophet saw "a young man eagerly taking away his share of the booty and remarked that the same eagerness shown in the cause of Allah would do more good to the man". Hearing of this comment, the Prophet is reported to have said that, "Even if his endeavours are for his own self, he is [endeavouring] in the cause of Allah,

Allah is Great and Glorious" (Siddiqi, 1979, p. 10). The possibility of fulfilling the pleasures of both worlds is also alluded to in the Qur'an [2:201–2]. It is therefore argued that Islam does allow for the attainment of the best of both worlds, or *fallah* (Siddiqi, 1979, pp. 3–11; Afzal-ur-Rahman, 1988, p. 285) and that the pursuit of individual worldly welfare constitutes an Islamic objective (Arif, in Ghazali and Omar (ed.), 1989, p. 87). An incentive mechanism which was originally presented as essentially spiritual and moral, according to which the love of God and selflessness constituted the motivating forces behind all acts, is ultimately transformed into an Islamic private material incentive mechanism, similar to those employed in worldly economic systems.

For those Islamic scholars who believe that the pursuit of private material rewards is compatible with the altruistic Islamic incentive system, the egotistical pursuit of material prosperity does not pose a contradiction. The private incentive mechanism is justified as Islamic, since it is looked upon as the means which would provide the Muslim with "command and control over more resources", and it is argued that "the more resources are under his command, the more he will be able to allocate according to the directions and orders of Allah" (Arif in Ghazali and Omar (ed.), 1989, p. 93). This position regards material incentives, which appeal to the Muslim's sense of material acquisitiveness, as a suitable regulating mechanism capable of fostering Islamically desirable behaviour. Private material incentives provide the most suitable mechanism for the construction of an Islamic economic system based on an Islamic free market co-ordinating mechanism, subjected to unlimited property rights.

However, again based on the *Shari'a*, it can also be argued that private material incentives encourage unIslamic behaviour, incompatible with the system's objectives. Involvement in worldly affairs and material pursuits could distract Muslims from their principle duty of gaining proximity to God through the performance of obligatory religious duties. Material incentives could therefore lead to the disorientation and alienation of the Muslim. According to this position, material incentives divert man's effort from realising his "theomorphic" nature, "dull his creative faculties" and "dry up the well-springs of his happiness" (Naqvi, 1981, p. 76). In the same spirit, Shariati rejects the use of material incentives as a possible mechanism for the motivation of Muslims. He maintains that worshipping God encourages Muslims to pursue and worship noble values, whereas material incentives, which appeal to their base material instincts, restrain them from attaining those noble ideals (Shariati, *Khodsazi-e Enqelabi*, n.d., p. 147). It is also argued that placing too much emphasis on material incentives and economic well-being would encourage Muslims to become excessively welfare and consumer oriented. It is feared that if, in an Islamic society, such materialistic tendencies overshadow the concern for religious values, piety and religious devotion, the Islamic character of society would be irreparably damaged if not completely effaced (Javadi, in Va'ezzadeh Khorasani (ed.), 1369, pp. 304–8).

There are a number of verses in the Qur'an which demonstrate that Islam disapproves of worldly preoccupations and the pursuit of material prosperity as an end, while it attaches great importance to spiritual pursuits in this world as a means of attaining salvation in the hereafter. The Qur'an informs those who desire their share of this world that they will, to some extent, be granted their wish, but that they will then have no share in the hereafter [42:20]. In much stronger words, the Qur'an elsewhere promises hellfire to those who prefer this worldly life [79:38–9]. Acquisitiveness, on the basis of which private material incentives become functional, is condemned to damnation both in its unfulfilled stage as an idea, and in its realised stage, when the individual seemingly succeeds in accumulating wealth [3:185,102:1–6]. The Prophet is also reported to have said: "Love of worldly things is the source of all evil" (Siddiqi, 1979, p. 8). These evidences have led certain Islamic jurists to conclude that the general tone and spirit of the *Shari'a* demonstrates disdain for worldly preoccupations and invites believers to lead a life of material simplicity, without falling victim to asceticism (*Pasdar-e Eslam*, no.110). The corollary of rejecting material prosperity as a life objective is the repudiation of private material incentives. The proponents of this position argue that private material incentives would have to be abandoned in favour of a divine incentive mechanism, according to which all human activities would have to be motivated by the love of God and fellow human beings. Imam Ali's behaviour and his austere lifestyle are upheld as the model to be emulated. Through the description of certain aspects of Imam Ali's way of life, the operation of the divine incentive system is explained. For example, it is said that from his private income Imam Ali fed the people with bread and meat, while he was content with eating bread and olives, (*Pasdar-e Eslam*, no.110). This divine Islamic incentive mechanism is compatible with both the plan and plan-then-market co-ordinating mechanisms.

Certain Islamic jurists have argued that under special circumstances, when social welfare is in danger, coercion can be used in respect to certain individuals in order to obtain the required behaviour. The production of certain basic necessities has to be guaranteed in an Islamic society. Those activities that provide food, clothing and shelter constitute strategic sectors, the activities of which can under no circumstances be stopped. The operation of these sectors is considered a collective obligation, since public welfare is dependant upon it. If for some reason producers refrain from the production of such goods, all four Sunni schools of jurisprudence are in agreement that coercion can be used to assure the availability of such goods (Ibn Taymiya, 1983, pp. 38–9). This Islamic coercive incentive mechanism is compatible with the Islamic plan mechanism.

## Conclusion

In the process of constructing an Islamic economic system we have demonstrated that three different types of economic systems could be deduced from and constructed on the basis of primary, secondary and tertiary sources. The market, plan and plan-then-market economic systems can make equally well-founded claims to the mantle of Islamic economics. On a single legal basis, three different and opposing economic systems can be deduced. Each particular economic system can choose its appropriate, and internally consistent, economic characteristics from the plethora of evidence available. Each Islamic economic system can be thus furnished with a suitable and justifiable set of decision-making arrangements, co-ordinating mechanisms, property rights and incentive systems. If one were to employ the categorising tool of modes of production to define an Islamic economic system, one could argue that, theoretically, Islam presents features of a slave, feudal, capitalist and socialist mode of production. As we have shown, Islamic economists differ radically on what should constitute an Islamic economic system in modern times. Since Islam constitutes a common denominator, one has to search in the different political outlooks and ideological convictions of Islamic social scientists to explain why the Islamic economic system could be designated as competitive, mixed, planned, market-socialist and so forth. The different and equally justifiable interpretations that even the primary sources can lend themselves to aggravate the problem of discerning the "genuine" Islamic economic system. The multifariousness of Islamic sources, ordinances and interpretations, based at times on the letter and at other times on the spirit of Islam, along with the inconsistencies that have evolved in the historical process of using all three types of Islamic evidences, has led to an essentially adaptive and flexible economic system; one which could be considered as an ethical and value-judgemental variant of the existing modern economic systems.

## Notes

1. For a thorough analysis of primary and secondary edicts (*ahkam-e avaliyeh va sanaviyeh*), see Makarem-e Shirazi, in Va'ezzadeh Khorasani (ed.), 1369, pp. 103–19; and Taskhiri in Va'ezzadeh Khorasani, 1369, p. 155.

2. For references, see the section on the co-ordinating mechanism of the Islamic economic system.

3. For references, see Ragheb Isfahani's *Mofradat* and Tabrasi's *Tafsir-e Majma' Al-Bayan*. Cited in *Pasdar-e Eslam*, no. 10.

4. For references, see *Kanz Al-'Aamal*, Vol. 6, p. 717, cited in Seyyed Reza Taqavi-Damghani, *Chehel Hadith*, Vol.3, Tehran: Sazeman-e Tabliqat-e Islami, 1369, p. 14; Abu Dawud, Sunan and Ahmad Ibn-Hanbal, *Musnad*. Both cited for a similar message in Ibn Taymiya, 1983, p. 22

5. Works that consider the Islamic economic system as basically market-oriented: Rodinson, 1977; Ahmadi-Mianji, 1363; Makarem-e Shirazi, n.d.; Hosseni, "Islamic Economics in Iran and other Muslim Countries: Is a New Economic Paradigm in the Making?"; Behdad, "Property Rights in Contemporary Islamic Economic Thought; A critical perspective". Works that consider the Islamic economic system as basically socialistic: Naqvi, 1981; Shariati, *Islam Shenasi*; Paydar,1357. For a variant of socialism, see Shaltut, "Socialism and Islam", in Karpat, 1982; Abu Sulayman,1968.

6. For references on the sanctity of private property in Islam, see the section on "property rights" in this chapter.

7. For references, see Makarem-e Shirazi, n.d., p. 138; Beheshti, 1363, pp. 60–1; Qureshi, 1979, pp. 33, 37; Mannan, 1986, p. 61.

8. While the Shi'ites regard *khums* as a wealth tax, and therefore a regular source of government revenue, the Sunnis consider it solely as a tax on spoils of war and therefore effectively exclude it from the government's regular source of income.

9. It should be remembered that the Qur'an does not set an exact figure for *zakat* either; this sum of 2.5 per cent of income, savings and assets is deduced from the *Sunna*. See Shad, 1986, p. 67.

10. For references, see Sadr, 1357, Vol.2, pp. 138–41; Taskhiri, 1368, p. 266; D.H.H.v.D., 1363, pp. 235–44; Makarem-e Shirazi, n.d., p. 125.

11. *Mawat* has been translated as waste, dead, barren, unrevitalised or uncultivated land. It refers to land which cannot be immediately cultivated and requires labour for it to become cultivable. Waterlogged land, land covered with stones or bushes, marshland, swamps, and unirrigated land fall under this title.

12. For references, see Afzal-ur-Rahman, 1980, Vol.1, p. 9; Beheshti, 1363, pp. 76–7; Makarem-e Shirazi, n.d., pp. 147–50; Ahmadi-Mianji, 1363, p. 8; al-Faruqi, in Contemporary Aspects of Economic Thinking in Islam, in Proceedings of the Third East Coast Regional Conference of the Muslim Students' Association of the US and Canada, 1968.

13. Allameh Helli, *Tazkerat al-Fuqaha*; Mohaqeq-e Helli, *Sharaye' al-Islam*; Mohaqeq-e Karki, *Jame' al-Maqased fi Sharh al-Qawa'ed*; Sheykh Tusi, *al-Mabsoot*; Shahid-e Dovom, *Masalek al-Afham*. All cited in D.H.H.v.D., 1363, pp. 202–8.

14. According to Allameh-e Helli, Imam Malik is of this opinion. D.H.H.v.D., 1363, p. 228. For further references on this interpretation of Islamic property rights, see Sadr,1357, Vol. 2, p. 90; Kahf, in Ghazali and Omar, 1989, p. 77; Taleqani, 1983, p. 93.

15. For references, see Sadr, 1357, Vol. 2, p. 193; Kahf in Ghazali and Omar, 1989, p. 77; Taleqani, 1982, p. 38.

16. According to Allameh-e Helli, Imams Shafi'i and Ahmad ibn-Hanbal are also of this opinion. D.H.H.v.D., 1363, p. 228.

# 4. Islamic Micro- and Macroeconomics

## The microeconomic foundation

### The economic problem

The Qur'an states that God has created everything in the precise and necessary amount to fulfil the needs of Man [7:10, 54:49, 14:34]. It is even stated that His resources are not subject to depletion (D.H.H.v.D., 1363, p. 313). The assumption of scarce resources would imply the imperfection of nature and its inadequacy in satisfying the needs of men, which would in turn insinuate a deficiency in God's creation of the world. From an Islamic perspective, "the economic problem" cannot therefore be attributed to nature, but to the predominance of the greedy, selfish and acquisitive aspect of man's nature, reflected in the syndrome of unlimited wants.[1]

Islamic economists present three different interpretations of Islam's view of the economic problem. The first group, mainly professional economists, do not draw a major distinction between the mainstream and Islamic positions on the sources of the economic problem. They either ignore the fact that the Qur'an refutes the scarcity of resources or try to reconcile the Qur'anic position with that which accepts scarcity as a point of departure. Disregarding the Qur'anic injunction which clearly states that God has provided the means for the fulfilment of man's life [7:10], Mannan argues that Islamic and modern economics share the same conception of what constitutes the economic problem, namely scarce resources and unlimited wants (Mannan, 1986, pp. 18–19). Ariff concedes that "God has created everything in the heavens and on earth to meet the needs of man", yet he seeks to reconcile the Islamic position on scarcity with that of mainstream economists. He argues that God's unlimited bounties refer to those goods that do not need the application of human labour, such as air, water and sunlight. Those that do require the application of human labour are categorised as scarce goods, because man's capacity is limited (Ariff, in Ghazali and Omar, 1989, p. 105).[2] The issue is formally resolved by claiming that scarcity of resources is a function of man's limited productive capacity and not a consequence of any inadequacy in nature.

The second group of Islamic theorists represent a more doctrinaire approach, basing their arguments on the letter of the Qur'an. They argue that there is no scarcity and that, on the contrary, everything was created in relative and absolute abundance. The scarcity of resources, therefore, does not constitute an economic constraint (Nafeli, in Va'ezzadeh Khorasani (ed.), 1369, p. 64. Al-Hassani,1988, pp. 3–4). Consequently, the primary objective of the Islamic economy is not the efficient combination of scarce resources in the production process but one of addressing the problem of "injustice" and "maldistribution" (al-Hassani, 1988, p. 4).

The third view, which is a hybrid of the first two positions, maintains that even though God has provided sufficient resources for the satisfaction of man's wants and needs, man himself is the source of the economic problem. The twin reasons presented by Baqir Sadr and based on the Qur'an are: man's "injustice" in maldistributing resources and therefore goods and services; and man's "neglect" to exploit the bounties of God (Sadr, 1982, Vol.1, part 2, p. 112).

Sadr's argument is different from Ariff's, since Sadr views man as capable of producing in abundance. He argues that man's potential to produce is constrained by "injustice in the social relations of distribution" found in the capitalist and socialist economic systems (Sadr, 1982, Vol.1, part 2, p. 112). In capitalism, man's "negligence" in exploiting resources is attributed to the system's bias in favour of inefficient resource utilisation — idle capacity and unemployment — and socially undesirable resource allocation reflected in the inadequate production of necessities (Sadr, 1984, Vol.2, part 2, p. 145). The socialist system's inability to convert God's plentiful bounties to sufficient goods and services is attributed to its stifling of individual initiative caused by its disregard for the natural relationship between work and the ownership of the fruits of labour (Sadr, 1982, Vol.1, part 2, pp. 110–16).

Sadr focuses on the structural injustice of the distribution mechanism in capitalism and socialism, as the factor that prevents the realisation of an economy of abundance. The issue of the relationship between relative scarcity and unlimited wants is not, however, directly addressed by him. It is implicitly argued that if households limit their consumption to the satisfaction of their basic necessities (food, clothing and shelter), which Islam believes to be an essential right, then resources can be viewed as sufficient (Sadr, 1984, Vol.2, part 2, p. 145). The "maldistribution" theory has to be analysed in the light of Islam's theory of consumer behaviour. In simple terms, the argument goes that that if consumers were to limit their demand to basic necessities there would be enough resources to satisfy everyone's needs. A variant of Baqir Sadr's position is that of Bani-Sadr, who maintains that sufficient natural resources would exist to provide for a society of abundance if such resources were not used for destructive purposes (Bani-Sadr, n.d., p. 220). Whereas the problem of scarcity is assumed in modern economic texts to be a function of economic man's unlimited wants, Islamic man, with a different consumer behaviour, would presumably be immune to this problem.

**Islamic consumer behaviour**

Islam acknowledges the fact that man was created acquisitive and impatient. [17:11, 70:19]. It is therefore natural to expect him to prefer more to less. Maximisation of possession in the shortest time possible, as a lifetime objective, is simply the manifestation of man's natural inclination. Based on observed human behaviour, it would be safe to assume that the maximisation of worldly possessions is motivated by the love for money, either in the form of title to assets, or converted into what money can buy in terms of consumer goods and services. Thus in the process of materialising their economic objective, men can succumb to miserliness or profligacy. The miser views the realisation of his lifetime dream in the accumulation of his current and savings accounts along with his portfolio investments, which he dreads parting with. The extravagant spendthrift views his accumulated consumer goods as witness to his success.

Islam, however, wishes to create a new man: pure and immune to intemperance. By refraining from the consumption of those commodities categorically outlawed by God, the model consumer purifies his body. Commodities such as alcoholic drinks and pork are categorised as "bads" rather than "goods', since each unit consumed will result in a punishment in the hereafter. Subsequently, the consumption of the first unit of such "bads' would cause long-run disutility or displeasure leading the rational Islamic consumer to avoid further consumption.

The Islamic consumer is also averse to excess. He neither indulges in miserliness (*iqtar*) nor in profligacy (*israf*). Muslims are commanded to base their consumption on strict adherence to the practice of moderation, or *iqtisade*, [25:67, 31:19]. Consumerism, or the satisfaction of unlimited wants, as well as meanness in expenditures, especially for the cause of God, is forbidden and subsequently repugnant to the rational Islamic man [6:141, 7:31, 30:38, 17:29, 47:38]. The Qur'an labels consumerists or transgressors of the limit of moderation as "corruptors on earth" and "brother to satan" [17: 26–7, 26:151–2]. Those who are miserly are reminded by the Qur'an that such behaviour is "at the expense of their own souls" [47:38].

The Islamic consumer has to base all his decisions on the maximisation of the pleasure of God, in the first instance. Only subsequently does he maximise his own private satisfaction, in both the here and the hereafter. Islamic man's knowledge of the transitory nature of the temporal world shields him against his instinctive drive to establish the pursuit of more material goods as his sole objective in life. The Qur'an emphasises the point that seeking satisfaction in consumption alone would be a self-inflicted disservice, since the culprit would be condemned to hellfire in the hereafter [10:7–8, 17:18]. Consumerism is argued to distract man from pursuing the cause of God, rendering him conceited, pompous and forgetful of God and life in the hereafter [17:83, 63:9, 96:6–8]. Islam forbids three different types of prodigality or excessive consumption: *israf* (extravagant consumption), *itraf* (ostentatious consumption) and *tabzir* (wasteful consumption) (Moasesehe Motale'at va Pajouheshhaye Bazargani [M.M.v.P.B.], 1368, pp. 97–102). *Israf,* or extravagant consumption, is considered a quantitative transgression of moderation. *Itraf,* or ostentatious consumption, is considered a transgression, since it is an act of vanity, conceit and narcissism, with the intention of demeaning others with one's wealth, thus in a way putting oneself in the position of God. *Tabzir,* or wasteful consumption, is forbidden since it squanders or misuses the bounties of God. This type of consumption is usually associated with the revelries and pleasure-seeking activities that make men forgetful of God (D.H.H.v.D., 1363, p. 397).

Islam does not refute the neo-classical notion that individuals have insatiable wants; it simply sets out to "rectify" this human shortcoming. Mohamed Ariff, argues that economic man is caught in an interminable vicious circle of creating wants, satisfying wants and re-creating new wants (Ariff in Ghazali and Omar,1989, p. 116). We can argue that this process starts with the object of relieving man of his pain of wanting and not having, but forces him into a situation where, like Sisyphus, every time he pushes the stone up towards the peak of the mountain of satisfaction the stone rolls back, frustrating his endeavours. Attaining the summit of wantlessness through maximising satisfaction is thus argued to be a futile and self-defeating exercise.

The desire or need for a good is a necessary but not sufficient condition for what is known as effective demand. Neo-classical economics does not question the motive or ethics of a desire or a need as long as it is backed by the ability to pay. Any effective demand, whether it is for food, a private jet, heroin or pornographic literature, will be satisfied through the market. Islamic economics, however, passes judgement on what constitutes an acceptable need, which may be fulfilled, and what constitutes an unacceptable one. It prioritises Islamic man's needs and thus assigns different ethical and value weights to different commodities. The needs of the Islamic consumer are divided into real and false or perfidious ones. Real needs are defined as basic natural needs, in addition to acquired social needs, which are compatible with Islamic injunctions and reason. Those acquired social needs that are incompatible with Islamic injunctions and reason are categorised as false needs (M.M.v.P.B., 1368, p. 10). It is argued that permissible consumption must be rooted in real needs (M.M.v.P.B., 1368, p. 67). Islamic analysts and economists have provided various classifications of real needs. Based on the works of al-Ghazali and al-Shatibi, Zarqa presents a three-tier categorisation of goods and services. He argues that all activities or things that help achieve the goals of Islam and therefore increase the social welfare of the Islamic community are considered utilities (*masalih*), and all those things and activities that undermine this effort and thus decrease social welfare are considered disutilities (*mafasid*) (Zarqa, in Ghazali and Omar, 1989, pp. 34–5). Based on this classification, three different types of commodities are identified: necessities, conveniences and refinements. Zarqa argues that each of these adds to the social welfare of the Islamic community and is therefore rooted in real needs.[3] Necessities include those commodities that are necessary for the preservation of the five foundations of a good Islamic society: religion, life, progeny, property and reason (Zarqa, in Ghazali and Omar, 1989, p. 35). Necessities include food, clothing and shelter. Conveniences refer to those commodities that are not as indispensable as basic needs, but facilitate the life of man and provide him with a minimum of comforts. Refinements or adornments go beyond the elementary comforts of life. They improve the quality of life with non-essential luxuries. Irrespective of the question of equity that the consumption of refinements would pose in a country where not all are provided with necessities, if the consumption of refinements renders its consumers arrogant and conceited, or involves morally and ethically unIslamic activities or enjoyments, such goods and services would be automatically labelled as extravagant and therefore forbidden. Despite Zarqa's approval of the consumption of refinements, one could argue that such consumptions should be subject to caution, since they border on extravagance.

Even though moderation is upheld as the Islamic guide to consumer behaviour, the limits of moderation are defined neither in qualitative nor quantitative terms. For the Islamic man who wishes to consume within the permissible limits, a set of clearly defined qualitative and quantitative norms of moderation is necessary to guide him in his everyday economic decisions. In the absence of a clearly delineated definition based on primary sources, only interpretations of what these norms ought to constitute can be presented. The fact, however, that beyond a certain quantitative point the Islamic consumer should abstain from self-indulgent consumption, even if consuming additional goods were to add to his total satisfaction, shows that the Islamic man's demand curve would be different from that of the economic man. The lower the price of a commodity, the greater the inducement for economic man to buy more of that good. His only constraint is his budget. For Islamic man, however, the moral constraint of not committing the sin of excess, as commanded by the *Shari'a*, constitutes a more important constraint. After possessing a certain quantity of a good, the Islamic consumer would not increase his consumption even were the good offered to him free of charge. A decrease in the price of a good does not, therefore, entice the Islamic consumer to demand more if the possession of the additional quantity constitutes a transgression of the permissible limit of moderation. Consequently, after a quantitative limit, the Islamic consumers' demand will become insensitive to changes in price. We shall argue that based on different interpretations of what constitutes the Islamic norm of moderation, four different types of Islamic consumer behaviour can be deduced.

The first interpretation of moderation maintains that the quantitative norm of moderation, incumbent upon Islamic consumers, should be established according to the customary level of consumption of the average citizen.[4] An average level of consumption, reflected in a typical basket of goods, can be identified and set as the national index of moderation. Any significant deviation from this index would be labelled as extravagance. This permissible average level of consumption could be readily identified as that basket of goods attainable with the per-capita gross national product of a country. As the level of average income increases over time, the permissible level of moderation increases along with it.

According to this interpretation, the norm of moderation differs among countries with different factor endowments and varying levels of productivity and is subject to change over time. The Islamic consumer is thus subjected to a quantitative-cum-qualitative constraint which, for high income consumers, will prove to be far more restrictive than their budgetary constraint, and will lead to their income remaining unexhausted. In Islam idle resources constitute waste, so that the high income consumer would be advised to give away his surplus in charity (*infaq*). It is argued that even though the possession of a marble house is not forbidden in Islam, in a society where the majority are homeless the construction of a large marble house would constitute a transgression from the permissible limit of moderation (Hashemi-e Rafsanjani, 1362, p. 34). This example demonstrates all three forbidden aspects of extravagant consumption. The large size of the house constitutes *israf*, while the luxurious quality of a marble house constitutes *tabzir*, and the ostentatious character of such a house in the midst of poverty constitutes *itraf*. The permissible act of purchasing a house becomes forbidden, even though the consumer's income was earned honestly, simply because the purchase of such a house constitutes a significant deviation from the national average. This interpretation of moderation and consumption is consistent with an Islamic plan economy and lends itself to an absolutely egalitarian view of consumption in an Islamic society (Shariati, *Khodsazi-e Inqelabi*, p. 144).

Proof of the legitimacy of this egalitarian position can be found in the Tradition of the Prophet. According to one of the Companions, Abu Sa'id Khudhri, the Prophet commanded his Companions thus: "Anyone of you who possesses cloth in excess of his needs should return it to the person who needs it, and anyone who possesses food in excess of his needs should return it to the person who needs it." Khudhri adds that on the basis of the Prophet's statement, the Companions felt that they had no right over any thing in excess (Afzal-ur-Rahman,1989, p. 532). Reference to the need-fulfilling basket of goods as the index of moderation is here understood as a socially determined measurement of need based on an average standard of living. It is possible that the Prophet himself might have entertained such an idea, if we accept the following statement attributed to him: "The children of Adam are largely entitled to three things only: a house in which to live, a piece of cloth with which to cover his private parts, and a single meal in a day" (*ibid.*, p. 534). Once this basket of goods is established as the socially determined level of moderation, the Prophetic saying reported by Abu Sa'id Khudhri becomes more meaningful. The Prophet heeded against transgressing the limits of moderation when he reportedly said: "As long as economic discrimination persists, we shall have no right over a single grain over our needs" (*ibid.*,1989, p. 533).

The second interpretation of moderation essentially defines the permissible limit in terms of individual income.[5] It maintains that the index of moderation should be based upon the customary average basket of goods that each family can command, given its budget. According to this position, the moderation norm is not based on the average standard of living of society, with any deviation registering extravagance. The norm instead is the individual household's average income, and extravagant consumption is calculated on the basis of deviation from that. In this sense, *israf* is nothing but spending beyond one's means. According to this interpretation, low-income categories may find themselves transgressing the limits of moderation, even if what they consume is a minimum subsistence, if they overspend due to their limited budget. High-income categories can, on the other hand, remain immune to extravagance, even if they consume a very large basket of goods, as long as they remain within their budget.

Moderation, according to this interpretation, is viewed as a function of each individual's income. The quantitative-cum-qualitative constraint of *israf* set by the *Shari'a* turns out to be the same as economic man's budget constraint, except in the case of ostentatious consumption (*itraf*) or wasteful consumption (*tabzir*). Yet some Islamic analysts of this opinion have argued that even if a basket of goods is within one's income, if its consumption is only for the purpose of self-glory and vanity, it becomes forbidden (Maududi, 1984, p. 79). For example, if an Islamic consumer purchases an ostentatious commodity that has a high price for the status that it imparts, while a lower price commodity could equally fulfil the same need, then the consumer would be transgressing the limits, even though the item is well within his budget. If the object of having a car is to travel between two points, then the need for a vehicle can be met equally by the purchase of an inexpensive economy car, whereas the purchase of an expensive luxury car would constitute a wasteful and ostentatious act. Secondary sources can be invoked to demonstrate that the purchase of the luxury car constitutes both *tabzir* and *itraf*.[6]

However, according to the third interpretation, the Islamic consumer can be liberated even from the constraints imposed by *tabzir* and *itraf*. It is argued that it is the intention of the consumer that constitutes the ultimate criterion of Islamic or non-Islamic consumer behaviour. "A person who feeds himself well, wears decent clothes, and supplies himself with a thousand comforts with a view to making himself more efficient and more useful in the service of the Good, is welcome to the society of Islam" (Siddiqi, 1979, p. 16). It could thus be argued that there is no limit to the basket of commodities and the quality of goods that Islamic man can possess as long as those goods and services are purchased with the intention of improving the efficiency of the consumer, who is believed to be working for the cause of God and the welfare of the Islamic community (Siddiqi, 1988, p. 16).

According to the fourth interpretation, since the Qur'anic verse on moderation refers directly to food and drink, the injunction against extravagant consumption is binding only in terms of those two items (Mannan, 1986, p. 46). It is argued that all consumer goods other than food and drink are free of the quantitative-cum-qualitative constraint set by the *Shari'a*. Mannan rejects the concept of a fixed national index of moderation, and argues that "the key to the understanding of Islamic consumption is that it is relative" (Mannan, 1990, p. 35). In essence he justifies the fact that faced with "over thirty thousand Halal items for consumption in some supermarkets in Jeddah, Saudi Arabia", the process of maximising satisfaction for an Islamic consumer would be similar to that for economic man (*ibid.*).

Too much emphasis on the notion that Islamic man is completely free to choose any quantity or quality that his budget allows him, completely blurs the distinction between the Islamic and neo-classical conceptions of human nature. Even the proponents of the last three interpretations, which we can collectively call the Islamic utilitarian position, concede that there is a quantitative limit beyond which consumption is forbidden. It is argued that extravagance and indulgence in luxuries "are *nearly* independent of the mental attitude of the person [consumer] being explicitly prohibited by the Qur'an" (Siddiqi, 1979, p. 16). However, the failure to specify the limit of moderation allows proponents of these utilitarian interpretations to turn a blind eye to the way in which the Islamic consumer comes to maximise satisfaction just like the economic man.

References are made to both primary and secondary sources to substantiate what we have called the Islamic utilitarian position. It is argued that the Qur'an provides the best answer to the dilemma of the permissible limit of moderation (Afzal-ur-Rahman, 1985, Vol.2, p. 36). The Qur'an says: "Let the man of means spend according to his means; and the man whose resources are restricted, let him spend according to what Allah has given him" [65:7]. In three other verses, the Qur'an commands the believers to consume the beautiful bounties that God has made available to them [7:32, 5:87–88]. The Prophet is also reported to have said that, "When God has bestowed his bounty upon you. He likes that the effects of His bounty should appear on you" (Afzal-ur-Rahman, 1985, Vol.2, p. 26).

Shi'ites also refer to numerous reports from different Imams to prove that God not only wishes man to consume good things in life, but that He even wishes man to display his ornaments (Moussavi-e Isfahani, 1368, pp. 475–80). It is reported that Imam Sadeq said: "God is beautiful and He admires beauty and therefore He would like to see the effect of His bounty on His servants" (D.H.H.v.D., 1363, pp. 382–3). It is reported by Imam Sadeq that, "the Prophet spent more on perfumes than on foodstuff" (Moussavi-e Isfahani,1368, p. 480). Such an attempt to demonstrate that ornaments and objects of beautification constitute a significant component of the Islamic consumer's basket of goods, undermines the repugnancy of *itraf* and *tabzir*, since it justifies the display of opulence. It further eradicates the distinction between Islamic and economic man.

So far we have concerned ourselves with the worldly options of the Islamic consumer. In our assessment of Islamic consumer behaviour, we addressed the four possible interpretations of moderation and extravagant consumption and the extent to which each would resemble or differ from that of the neo-classical consumer. The Islamic consumer differs from his neo-classical counterpart in yet another significant respect. Theoretically, based on his budget and relative prices, economic man is concerned only with maximisation of satisfaction. Islamic man, however, is confronted with two types of goods: material and spiritual (*'ibadah*). Material goods provide worldly satisfaction in the here and now, while spiritual goods provide felicity in the hereafter. Whereas economic man needs only to allocate his time between leisure and work, Islamic man must allocate his time between leisure, work and spiritual pursuits or *'ibadah*. Whereas leisure is concerned with a worldly and individualised pleasure, *'ibadah* is concerned with a spiritual and divine pleasure, and it is unjustifiable and erroneous to consider the options of the two different types of consumer in the same light.

If we accept that the Islamic consumer can reach a quantitative moderation limit, beyond which any additional unit consumed would constitute a sin and therefore add to his disutility in the hereafter, we would have to accept that material goods can become "bads". If the Islamic consumer stops consuming once he reaches that point without having exhausted his budget, neither an increase in income nor a decrease in the price of material goods could induce him to purchase more of the "bad" unless he simultaneously consumed more spiritual goods to compensate for the adverse effect of transgressing the limits.[7]

Consequently, the Islamic consumer's purchase decisions will differ from that of economic man, and the market demand curve of an Islamic society, for any given commodity, would cease to be responsive to lower prices after a certain quantitative limit.

**The Islamic theory of the firm**

The whole argument in support of the Islamic economic system is based on the assumption that Islamic man's human nature is different from that of economic man. It therefore follows that each type of man pursues the maximisation of his different objectives, and has a different rationality. An analysis of the behaviour of Islamic producers has to be based on what is considered to be the appropriate behaviour of the Islamic producer in relation to the Islamic objectives of the firm.

The Qur'an makes explicit that the primary objective of all human activities should be the satisfaction of God's will [11:52, 61:10–14]. It is further added that if man wishes to prosper both in this world and in the hereafter, he would have to seek the pleasure of God [30:38–39, 87:14]. Islamic economists have argued that "all human activity should be directed towards the achievement of *fallah*, a comprehensive term denoting all-sided welfare of this life as well as that of the Hereafter" (Siddiqi, 1979, p. 3). The Islamic producer, like the Islamic consumer, is therefore obliged to maximise his welfare in both this world and the hereafter. Islamic man is well aware that it is only in this world that he may accumulate felicity points for the hereafter. He would thus be motivated to maximise felicity points and minimise grief points through practising what is commanded and refraining from what is forbidden in this world. The Islamic producer is thus ethically bound to those productive activities satisfactory to God. Those goods that He has prohibited, the Islamic producer will not produce, even if they yield enormous profits. For the Islamic entrepreneur, the pursuit of God's pleasure, through compliance with his wishes as deduced from the *Shari'a*, replaces the profit-maximisation axiom of economic man. This axiom is at best inapplicable and inappropriate to the Islamic entrepreneur. The rational Islamic producer is not expected to maximise profits under all conditions. However, Islamic economists argue, once those conditions that maximise the pleasure of God are safely secured, the maximisation of profits under perfect market conditions is not, *a priori*, contradictory to Islamic tenets.[8]

Through reliance on the spirit of the *Shari'a*, modern Islamic economists have presented certain first-order conditions, the satisfaction of which is believed to secure the pleasure of God. The process of production in an Islamic firm should be governed by the following four golden ethical rules of the *Shari'a*: maximisation of social utility or public interest (*maslaha*); prohibition on inflicting injury on or causing grief to others (*la zarar va la zirar*) or the minimisation of social disutility (*mafsada*); primacy of social benefit over private benefit; facilitating life for others and relieving them of difficulty and hardship (*osr va haraj*) especially under conditions of dire necessity and imperative need (*zarurat va izterar*).[9]

The decision of the Islamic entrepreneur as to what, for whom, how and how much to produce should ideally be conditioned by all the above considerations. The ideal Islamic firm, according to the above constraints, does not harmonise its activities with, but becomes the ethical conscience of, the market, correcting its injustices and forcing it to abide by the rules of an ideal compassionate Islamic economic system. Each producer may be motivated by his Islamic consciousness to intervene in the market. The extent to which he corrects the market signals, according to Islamic injunctions, depends on his degree of *iman* or piety. Different degrees of piety among Islamic producers lead to different responses to market indicators. This does not allow for a consistent and predictable pattern that could be labelled rational Islamic producer behaviour. In a perfectly competitive market system, goods are produced as a function of their profitability, irrespective of other considerations. Profit-maximising producers minimise cost given their capital outlay and the prevailing factor prices. They increase or decrease the empoyment of the factors of production in response to changes in the price of the goods they produce and changes in the price of factors they employ.

We will now consider four cases in which application of ethical Islamic constraints produces behaviour and microeconomic results radically different from that expected in the market system.

*The moral duty of firms in relation to output*

Given the prevailing socio-economic conditions, the Islamic producer may not be free to produce all permissible, or *halal*, goods. Islamic firms are bound by the ethical rules of the *Shari'a* to provide sufficient quantities of basic necessities at low prices to enable all members of society to command such goods. In an Islamic economy, the provision of basic necessities must take precedence over the satisfaction of private profit. Just as Holy War (*jihad*) is considered a collective or social obligation (*fard kifayah*), so is the provision of basic necessities at a price affordable by all.[10] Let us consider an entrepreneur who decides to enter an industry and engage in the production of a good. All other factors assumed constant, he has the option of producing either a luxury or a necessity item. Assuming that the price of the luxury item is rising due to demand, and that there are abnormal or super profits to be made in the luxury industry, but normal profits in the necessity industry, the profit-maximising entrepreneur would choose to produce the luxury item. The Islamic entrepreneur, if he should realise that at the prevailing market price low-income consumers are unable to satisfy their basic needs, is obliged to forgo the production of luxury goods and the benefit of super profits, and to produce the necessity item instead. In the case of the Islamic firm, the factor that results in increased production at any price level, and is the shifting factor in the supply curve of the necessity market, is not abnormal profits, but the supposedly internalised sense of benevolence of Muslims towards one another. Furthermore, when such benevolence leads to a loss for the firms concerned, the government is expected to subsidise them.[11]

*The firm's response to changes in the market price of goods*
Faced with a decrease in the price of the good produced, one could argue that it would be unethical for an Islamic firm, which is prohibited from inflicting injury on others and obliged to prioritise social benefit, to decrease output and lay off workers. However, such lay-offs could be justified under two conditions. First, if the workers made redundant could be assured of a job in another industry. Second, if the level of output and its corollary cost is such that the total revenue of the Islamic producer falls below his wage bill, causing the infliction of a greater injury to the remaining workers. The principles of prohibiting the infliction of injury on others and giving priority to social benefit over private benefit can guarantee the operation of the Islamic firm at an output at which all factors are rewarded according to their market price and no more. Any decrease in quantity supplied or increase in quantity demanded on the market, followed by increases in price and increase in the profit of those firms that were originally breaking even, could violate the ethical rules of the *Shari'a*. Ideally, therefore, the Islamic firm is expected to operate at a level of output at which total revenue is equal to total cost.[12] In the case of an increase in the market price of the commodity, in response to an increase in demand, the Islamic firm would not be entitled to benefit from the excess of total revenue above total cost, unlike firms in a perfectly competitive market situation. Instead it would have to increase output until total cost becomes equal to total revenue. Even though this might be considered to be passing on the benefit of potential abnormal profits to the consumer through an increase in the output of the individual firm, it would in the long run adversely affect the output of the industry as a whole, which is quantitatively far more significant. At the industry level, the increase in the supply of the good and the concomitant decrease in its price would not therefore materialise. It remains for the individual Islamic firm to decide which of its available options would cause the least injury and secure the greatest social benefit.

*The firm's response to market factor prices*
The Islamic producer's notion of equity and his aversion to social disutility and injury could induce him to correct the "injustices" of the market, thus reacting in a totally unexpected way to standard market signals. As Siddiqi has argued, the Islamic producer might reject the prevailing market wage as "unfair", and adjust to a higher wage which he deems to be "just" (*ibid*., p. 143). This higher, self-determined, wage is not in response to higher productivity, but to the call of his Islamic social consciousness. Given the standard tools of microeconomics, and the fixed capital outlay of the firm, this could only be achieved through a decrease in the labour employed and its substitution with capital, the relative price of which has decreased for the producer. To avoid the inflicting of one injury (unemployment) by his concern to alleviate the disutility of an "unjustly" low wage, he might choose to retain all his workers at the "just" wage he has established. Such a decision undoubtedly generates greater social utility, yet it overlooks the fact that within the restrictions of the

Islamic producer's budget he would only be able to implement such a decision by incurring a net loss. However, since he must already be equating total cost with total revenue before his decision, the resulting increase in his total cost makes a loss inevitable. Such a decision would have to be subsidised either by the state or by the personal wealth of the individual producer, and would only be sustainable as long as the sources of subsidy last. Such a course of action rejects the inherent trade-offs involved in any economic decision-making aimed at the realistic allocation of resources. Modern economic reality and the operation of the market impose, at least in the long-run, strict limitations on such noble ideals.

*The firm's driving force: competition or compassion*

Islamic economists often argue that one of the distinguishing features of the Islamic economic system is its particular incentive system. Contrary to market economies, cooperation and mutual responsibility, rather than competition, is said to constitute the principal driving force of the production process.[13] The emphasis on securing community rather than private interest has its roots in the notion of Islamic brotherhood as the coordinating principle of production. Strict compliance by firms to these tenets has radical and important implications in terms of the operation of a market economy. Its real impact is, however, seldom analysed by Islamic economists. According to al-Ghazali (A.D. 1058–1111), Islamic brotherhood has three stages: first, *ihsan*, or benevolence, which means fulfilling the needs of fellow Muslims after the fulfilment of one's own needs; second, *movasat*, or altruism, which means fulfilling the needs of fellow Muslims at the same time as fulfilling one's own needs; and third, *isar*, or sacrifice, which means the fulfilment of the needs of fellow Muslims before one's own needs.[14] The Qur'an states that "supreme felicity" belongs to those who are benevolent and practise *ihsan* [9:100,16:91]. The Prophet is reported to have said that, "Your faith is not complete until you like the same for your brother as you like for yourself" (Siddiqi, 1979, p. 28).

In a society that is evolving along the path of Islamic brotherhood, the objective and behaviour of the Islamic firm may be classified according to three distinct levels of Islamic consciousness. The producer possessing a primitive Islamic consciousness could argue that, as long as he produces permitted goods and refrains from deceptive and fraudulent business practices, he may seek to maximise his profits, benefiting from abnormal profits in the short run. He could support his argument by referring to the absence of any explicit texts against profit maximisation or abnormal profits. The behaviour of such an Islamic producer would be similar to that of his secular counterpart, except that he would not produce forbidden goods. Here there is clearly no particular economic theory of an Islamic, as distinct from a neo-classical, firm. The producer with a social Islamic consciousness, however, would be induced to produce according to the notions of benevolence, altruism and sacrifice. The rational economic behaviour of the firm practising benevolence, or *ihsan*, would imply production at a level where total cost is equal to total revenue.

The producer who operates according to the principle of altruism, or *movasat*, would intervene to correct the injustices of the market in terms of output, the price of necessities and the price of labour. His ability to intervene, however, is limited by the extent to which his altruistic policies would threaten the survival of the firm. If, however, the producer should possess a fortune large enough to cover his annual loss, altruism obliges him to share his wealth with others, through financing a loss-making operation that generates income and necessities for society.

Finally, the producer who has attained the mystical summit of selflessness, or *isar*, intends to forgo his own reward to maximise social benefit. He who practises *isar* would, therefore, be motivated solely by the spiritual incentive of serving God, knowing that he who serves God will somehow be provided for in this life and certainly compensated in the hereafter. Even though the economic operation of a society based on altruism, let alone sacrifice, seems impractical, *movasat*, the practice of altruism, is considered, according to numerous *hadiths*, a social obligation in an Islamic society (*Howzeh*, no. 4, p. 105. D.H.H.v.D., 1363, pp. 357–61).

We have attempted to demonstrate that adherence to the principle of Islamic brotherhood, as the coordinating mechanism of production, imposes certain economic practices, the application and results of which are incompatible with the prevailing rules and conventions of a market economy. The position of those Islamic economists who wish to blend the ethical axioms of Islam with the market rules of profit maximisation and efficient production, in order to present a novel hybrid economic system of a superior nature, is at best inconsistent, and often fallacious. Any attempt to realise ethical Islamic values through the use of neo-classical economic tools and theories, based on a radically different set of values, inevitably leads to the sacrifice of one to the other. Faced with this real dichotomy, Islamic economists often use neo-classical economic tools and analyses to present technically feasible economic arguments, introduced by or concluded with a paragraph of ethical Islamic rhetoric, unassimilated into their core economic arguments. Such analysis is often based on sound modern economics, and the nature of Islamic man is implicitly assumed to be synonymous with that of economic man.

### Islamic forms of business organisation

The legal form of an Islamic enterprise sheds light on how capital is raised, how labour is employed, how factors are remunerated, who makes decisions, how such enterprises are dissolved, and who bears the risks of failure. Those types of business contracts and organisations that were in use before and during the time of the Prophet, and that he did not prohibit, are accepted as legal forms of Islamic enterprises. On the basis of the particular contracts delineating the rights and responsibilities of capital and labour, Islamic enterprises can be classified into two broad categories. First, Islamic businesses in which the investor or investors hire labour on the market, pay him a fixed wage and set him to work on machines, tools or land. Such organisations based on the payment of a fixed reward for factor services, including labour, are called *ijarah* or wage-rent enterprises. Second, Islamic business organisations in which labour joins in partnership with capital or land provided by the commercial capitalist or landowners. In this type of enterprise, rewards are distributed under a profit-sharing scheme.

*Wage-rent enterprises*

In Islamic law, a contract based on renting or hiring land, tools, machines or labour is called *ijarah*. *Ijarah* or wage-rent is derived from the word *ajr* or *ajar*, which means remuneration or reward. As we have seen, wage-rent contracts and business organisations are legal in Islam. The Qur'an refers to the hiring of the services of Moses by Jethro for a wage for a specified period of time [28:26–27]. There is a consensus among Islamic jurists that hiring labour, as well as other physical factors of production, is an acceptable Islamic practice.[15] In an Islamic wage-rent enterprise, the capitalist hires labour for a specific job, a specific period of time and at a fixed wage. The profits of such an enterprise would accrue only to the capitalist and he would be responsible for losses incurred. This type of Islamic business, in broad terms, closely resembles its classical capitalist counterpart.

The Islamic wage-rent business organisation can be established as a single proprietorship or as a partnership. The *musharaka* contract is the Islamic form of a partnership on the basis of which two or more people invest their capital in a single enterprise. Joint-stock companies or corporations have been generally accepted as legitimate Islamic entities. It has been argued that they simply constitute an advanced form of Islamic partnership (Afzal-ur-Rahman, 1980, Vol.1, p. 242; Siddiqi, 1988, p. 29). Joint-stock companies and a stock market, on which only company shares can be traded, are now allowed to function in an Islamic economy, such as in Iran. Certain Islamic jurists, however, consider the purchase and sale of stocks as a "satanic practice", permissible only under capitalism (Owhadi, in Va'ezzadeh Khorasani, 1369, Vol.1, p. 248).

*Profit-sharing enterprises*

Profit-sharing is a firmly established and broadly accepted Islamic form of contract on the basis of which Islamic businesses can be established. Traditionally, profit-sharing contracts can be concluded in agriculture, horticulture and trade. Profit-sharing contracts are called *muzar'a* in agricultural production, *musaqat* in horticultural production, and *muzaraba* or *qraz* (*qirad*) in trade.

Profit-sharing in agriculture, or *muzar'a*, can also be considered an Islamic type of share-cropping. Here, one party provides the land, while the other provides labour. Each may in addition provide other factors of production such as seed, water, implements and other farming expenses. The labourer, who becomes a partner to the landowner, does not receive a wage for his work. He shares in the profit of the enterprise, according to a mutually accepted and registered profit-distribution scheme. Profit shares cannot be based on a predetermined fixed quantity of output or sum of money. They have to be set according to an agreed proportion of total output. The percentage share of each party is entirely dependant upon the individual bargaining power of the partners.

Theoretically, therefore, the percentage share of the labourer could be equivalent to subsistence wages if there is an unlimited supply of agricultural workers. The landowner is entirely responsible for fixed costs such as land tax. If the enterprise incurs a loss, the entire financial burden of the loss is borne by the landowner. The labourer's loss will be the effort he has applied without reward. *Muzar'a*, like all Islamic profit-sharing schemes, is characterised by the fact that both parties share the risks of production. They run the risk of not receiving any reward from the factors they own and contribute to.

Two schools of thought have emerged on the legality of *muzar'a*. One prominent group of Islamic jurists, basing their arguments on reports and Traditions of the Prophet, argue that profit-sharing in agriculture is a perfectly legal Islamic form of tenancy. The supporters of the legality of *muzar'a* refer to the Prophet's ruling at the time of his victory at Khaybar, when he allowed the Jews to cultivate the land in return for one-half of the crop (Afzal-ur-Rahman, 1985, Vol.2, p. 168). A second group, basing itself on other reports and Traditions of the Prophet, argues that even though *muzar'a* was a common practice at the time of the Prophet, he ruled against its practice. According to this position, which is shared by Imam abu Hanifa, Imam Malik and Imam Shafi'i, the practice at Khaybar was of the nature of a tax or a tributary payment imposed on the Jews. Such an agreement cannot, therefore, be used as a model for agricultural contracts between individuals. According to a report by Rafey bin Khadij, when the Prophet heard that he was engaged in share-cropping and fifty–fifty profit-sharing, the Prophet forbade him to engage in such a transaction as it contained an element of *riba*, or usury (*ibid*., p. 184).[16]

*Musaqat*, a profit-sharing contract in gardening, follows exactly the same rules and procedures as that of *muzar'a*. In this type of contract, the labourer applies his labour to trees that the garden owner has cultivated but does not wish to tend. The garden owner shares the output of the garden with the labourer in return for surveillance, maintenance and irrigation of the trees, and delivery of the fruit. The respective percentage share of profits or output will again be mutually agreed upon by both parties.

The term *muzaraba*, profit-sharing in trade, explains the nature of the work that was originally involved in this type of contract. The term is derived from *zarb*, meaning walking or travelling, which applies to the function of the agent or the merchant-labourer who works for the commercial capitalist, who owns capital. The agent and the commercial capitalist may each comprise more than one person. The conditions for the establishment of a profit-sharing enterprise in trade or *muzaraba*, is similar to that in *muzar'a*. One party provides capital, which the other uses in order to make a profit, which is distributed among the partners according to mutually agreed proportions. The capital given to the agent can be in the form of merchandise or money, with which he is to trade. Some jurists argue that the legitimacy of a *muzaraba* contract is guaranteed once the agent receives money in addition to merchandise (*Howzeh*, no.37–8, p. 350). In the case of an unconditional *muzaraba* contract, the agent may take all appropriate decisions to ensure the financial success of the business. He may hire workers or rent warehouses. The agent does not receive a wage for his services and is not responsible for any losses incurred. In case of loss, the agent's efforts would be left unrewarded. His travel expenses would, however, be deducted from the original capital provided by the commercial capitalist.[17] A *muzaraba* contract is for a fixed period of time and lapses on the death of any one of the parties. If the contract is nullified by the commercial capitalist, the agent is entitled to receive a remuneration for his labour.

Even though in the reports of the Tradition of the Prophet and the classical texts of Islamic jurists, profit-sharing has been limited to agriculture, horticulture and trade, modern Islamic jurists and economists have, by analogy, applied the same concept to industrial manufacturing. The majority of modern Islamic economists, both Sunni and Shi'i, believe that profit-sharing schemes used in agriculture, horticulture and trade could just as appropriately be applied to large-scale industrial production.[18] According to these economists, profit-sharing in the manufacturing sector is also called *muzaraba*. It has been argued that if the capitalist provides a sum of money in addition to the instruments of production to the labourer, the contract would become a *muzaraba*. In the absence of this sum of money, it is argued that the capitalist cannot claim a share of the profit and would only be entitled to a fixed reward for the tools he has provided (*Howzeh*, no.37–8, p. 351). Siddiqi does not set any specific conditions for industrial *muzaraba* other than that which applies to its general conditions in trade. He argues that to the best of his knowledge, "there is nothing in the *Shari'a* or juristic injunctions that can be presented as a basis for the non-validity of this method" (Siddiqi, 1988, p. 99).

Certain Islamic jurists and economists, however, reject the simple extension and application of profit-sharing to industry and maintain that *muzaraba* is specific to trade.[19] Based on the opinion of the prominent Shi'i jurist Mohaqeq-e Helli, Baqir Sadr concludes that *muzaraba* is forbidden in the process of manufacturing, where the capitalist intends to become a partner in the profits generated by the labourer, simply through the provision of tools and implements. Sadr argues that the capitalist is entitled to a fixed reward, but not a share of the profits. He applies the same argument, based on Helli's opinion, to *muzar'a* or profit-sharing in agriculture and concludes that a person cannot become party to a *muzar'a* contract by simply providing tools and implements, or factors other than land and labour.[20] A profit-sharing contract in agriculture is therefore argued to be legitimate only if the landowner provides both land and seed. Sadr's conclusion in terms of what constitutes an acceptable type of *muzar'a*, however, contradicts Helli's own conclusion. According to Helli the contribution of any one of the factors of production can constitute the basis for a profit-sharing scheme in agriculture, which is why there may be so many different types of *muzar'a*, each based on different combinations of factors of production (Helli, 1364, p. 275).

More radical Islamic analysts go to the extreme of denying the fact that *muzaraba*, *muzar'a* and *musaqat* constitute Islamic types of contract. It is argued that productive relations or contracts which allow any factor other than labour to receive a share of the product as profit or rent violate the basic tenets of Islam (Paydar, 1357, p. 309; Abu-Sulayman, in Proceedings, 1976, p. 23).

## Islamic macroeconomics

It is difficult to construct a macroeconomic model of the Islamic economic system, because there is no unique, comprehensive or ideal system. Indeed, there are many possibilities since one can assemble a set of Qur'anic verses and practices and statements of the Prophet according to one's socio-political inclination and come up with a theoretical construct of an industrial economy that follows the Islamic faith. For this reason, it is useful to present the most important Islamic economic institutions and their role in determining the economic behaviour of participants in the economic process to obtain insight into specific features of the Islamic system. Despite differences between various schools of Islamic law, we will rely mainly on traditional interpretations conventionally used by jurists. The reason for this is that in the final analysis, as recent history has shown, the implementation of the actual Islamic order has been shaped and moulded not by the Islamic economists and intellectuals, but by the *ulama* who have to approve the compatibility of the new economic institutions and policies with their interpretation of the *Shari'a*.

### Financial assets

In the modern context, the Islamic economy can have two types of financial asset: those that cannot formally yield a return, and those that can. The former includes money, government bonds and personal loans.

Deposits in the bank, which can be invested in profit-sharing schemes, private bonds and securities that allow shares in the profits of a legitimate business or trade, and common stock sold on a stock market are financial assets that bear an explicit return (Karsten, 1982, pp. 113–6; Rahman, 1982, pp. 385–9). Deposits in the bank are different from common stock in that the former always yield a fixed proportion of the profit or loss, while the latter's dividends are discretionary; deposits invested in profit-sharing schemes cover only particular projects, while the stock's coverage need not be particular or specific, which might invalidate the Islamic legitimacy of such transactions.

### Commercial banking

The prohibition of interest affects the operation of conventional financial institutions in an Islamic economy. This means that banks are barred from paying interest on deposits and that borrowers do not pay interest on loans. However, this prohibition does not eliminate the role of banks as financial intermediaries.

In interest-free banking, banks may operate two types of deposit: current accounts and non-investment savings accounts, and investment accounts. Current accounts receive no return, but non-investment savings accounts may either receive a cash reward from the bank's profits at the end of the financial year or may be accorded some privileges by the bank. This is not the ideal Islamic banking arrangement, and such savings accounts should receive a return (positive or negative) on the basis of profit/loss-sharing schemes, either in the form of *musharaka* (equity participation) or *muzaraba* (agencies). There are differences of opinion among the five schools of Islamic law on the nature, terms and conditions of these arrangements. However, it is agreed that they should be based on sharing the profit/loss on mutually agreed terms. In the case of *musharaka* both parties contribute to the capital of the operation and divide the net profit and loss pro rata. This procedure can be used for investment projects, letters of credit, or the purchase of property or real estate. In the case of property or real estate the bank will assess an imputed rent and will share it as agreed in advance.

Under *muzaraba*, the bank contributes all the finance and the customer provides labour or management, both receiving a predetermined share of profit. However, in the case of loss the customer loses only his provision of labour, as the principal capital is provided by the bank. This financial risk, according to the *Shari'a*, justifies the bank 's claim to part of the profit (Siddiqi, 1988, pp. 9–97).

In interest-free banking, the bank acts as intermediary between financiers and users of finance. The profit of the bank is the difference between the profit it receives from the entrepreneurs, and that which it gives to the depositors.

Some Islamic economists argue that the ideal alternatives to interest in an Islamic economy are profit/loss-sharing and interest-free loans (*qarz al-hassana*). However, in view of the difficulties in applying these in a pure form, other methods that are "free" of the interest element are preferred. They include service charges, indexation of bank deposits and advances, leasing, investment auctioning, *bai mujjal*, hire-purchase and financing on the basis of normal rate of return. Interest-free loans with a service charge can also provide capital resources, in a capital-scarce economy, at low cost. Since in practice this provides no returns, there is little incentive either for the bank or for the depositor. In addition, this method in its pure form will not enable the central bank to regulate credit flow by means of changes in the cost of credit. Furthermore, in this scheme the rate of the service charge must not be proportional to the size of the loan, to avoid *riba*.

Indexation of bank deposits and advances can compensate depositors and lenders for any loss in value. However, the *Shari'a*, interpreted from an orthodox point of view, does not differentiate between currency transactions and commodity transactions. The reason is that the same quantity should be returned as was borrowed even though the price of a commodity may change over the lending period.

Leasing, under which the lessor maintains ownership of an asset and the leasee is required to pay rent for its use, is compatible with the *Shari'a* and is practised in Islamic banking. Thus, a bank can buy a product and lease it to the borrower for a given sum and a given period of time. In case of damage to the product, the risk must be shared between the bank and the borrower.

Another method of medium and long-term financing is investment auctioning. Here, commercial banks may form a consortium with long-term financing institutions; projects are awarded to the highest bidder. From the economic point of view this system reflects the potential profitability of a project, which is important for an efficient allocation of resources.

For financing current input requirements of different sectors, *bai mujjal* (*murabaha*) can be used. This is a type of sale in which a commodity is paid for on a deferred basis, either as a lump sum or in instalments. This method includes a negotiated, but fixed mark-up over the cost price which is the profit margin of the bank. However, many Islamic economists believe that such a system will sabotage interest-free banking from within, despite its conformity with the *Shari'a*.

Banks may also engage in hire-purchase contracts, both for industrial purposes and for consumer durables. Investment may also be financed on the basis of a normal rate of return. Under this method a specialised public agency would determine the normal rate of return in a given industry, and the bank would provide funds to the entrepreneur based on an agreed minimum rate of profit. If the actual rate of profit were greater than this, the difference would be paid to the bank on a voluntary basis. If the actual rate of return were lower, the bank would have the right to ask for the agreed rate of return. Thus, this device can function as an interest-bearing asset and is therefore not favoured, despite the fact that it is in accordance with the *Shari'a*.

Many firms in Muslim countries are not audited and do not keep proper accounts, so cannot be monitored by the banks. Thus, fixed-rate hire-purchase arrangements, *bai mujjal*, remain the dominant form for financing fixed investment, working capital and the purchase of consumer durables.

With respect to debenture financing, a corporate bond or security can be issued. This corporate security, which is called Participation Term Certificate in Pakistan, allows its holder to share in the profits of the issuing company. Security is guaranteed by a mortgage on the fixed assets of the company. This system is suitable for those lenders who do not want to take the risk of investment.

Personal interest-free loans (*qarz al-hassana*) by commercial banks are limited. As personal loans are not considered desirable in Islam unless they are required for the satisfaction of basic needs, it is recommended that such loans be provided from *zakat* funds (see Ahmed, Iqbal and Fahim Khan, 1983, pp. 103–43).

## Stock markets and insurance

### *Stock markets*

The reliance on equity financing favoured by the *Shari'a* clearly requires the effective operation of both primary and secondary capital markets to finance investment and provide liquidity to investors. The stock market is indispensable not only for non-institutional investors, but also for banks. However, the degree of speculation on the stock market is difficult to reconcile with the *Shari'a*. One view is that Islam prohibits the selling of things that one does not possess and transactions that have the element of chance (Rahman, n.d., pp. 115–22). Nevertheless, Islamic jurisprudence considers *bai salam* permissible. *Bai salam* (post-delivery sale) is a trading arrangement which allows advance purchase of commodities at an agreed price, and because it is so speculative it should be used only with caution (Ahmed, Iqbal and Fahim Khan, 1983, p. 252). The major problems in relation to the stock market are the advisability of having a stock market free from speculation, and a stock price that reflects only the underlying economic conditions and the future earnings of enterprises. In an ideal Islamic stock market, ownership shares could be transacted by the public, so that prices could fluctuate around the level of the original deposits. In addition, the central bank could add open market operations to the list of its policy instruments. Most existing Islamic countries have permitted the operation of stock markets on the basis of *salam* sale, as we shall see in later chapters.

### *Insurance*

Insurance, both life and general insurance, is among the most controversial issues in contemporary Islamic writings, especially among Sunnite Muslims. It is claimed that many elements forbidden in Islam, e.g. gambling (*riba*), risk (*gharar*) and uncertainty (*juhala*), are found in all kinds of insurance contracts. According to some Islamic jurists, if the elements of maturity and co-operation were present in insurance, then insurance would be admissible. However, there are those who accept only co-operative insurance as Islamic. They claim that mutual insurance does not allow capital-sharing and profits are not divided; whereas in co-operative insurance, shareholders are the clients, each member is a share-holder as well as policy-holder and profits are divided among share-holders (see Ahmad, 1981, pp. 216–18; Rahman n.d., pp. 108–242). This controversy is certainly a barrier to the development of insurance business in countries like Saudi Arabia that have sought strict observance of the *Shari'a*.

## Central banking

The central bank, as a non-profit institution, executes monetary policy by controlling flow of money and credit, acts as the government's banker, member banks' banker and supervises all financial matters dealing with foreign countries.

The regulatory power of the central bank remains largely unaffected in an Islamic economy. Its main regulatory instruments are reserve requirement ratio (RRR); overall credit ceilings on lending and investment operations; selective credit operation; and moral suasion.

The central bank requires member banks to maintain minimum cash reserves with it against their current and time deposits, and imposes daily fines on banks if this requirement is not met. In addition, the central bank may use a liquidity ratio requirement in the form of cash or non-interest-bearing assets and impose fines related to the amount of the default. The central bank can also set an overall credit ceiling on the lendings and investments of commercial banks and practise a selective credit policy. The central bank may also require maximum and minimum profit-sharing ratios for member banks in regard to finance provided by them.

The central bank's function as lender in the final instance may be replaced by a new system of assistance based on profit-sharing arrangements or other devices permissible under the *Shari'a*. However, some Islamic economists are ready to accept the provision of interest-free loans by the central bank to the government, since a profit-sharing scheme cannot be applied easily to government borrowing. This is because under the *Shari'a* revenues resulting from investment must be assigned only to the use which the borrowed funds were put to. In addition, in the case of government expenditures on public goods, it is not possible to exclude consumers who are not willing to pay for government services, and therefore direct revenues cannot be generated. Thus, it is difficult to apply the profit-sharing scheme to the financing of budget deficits and a more satisfactory way of determinating returns from government expenditures is necessary. Some economists have suggested that the government can issue interest-free bonds with a return based on the annual rate of nominal gross domestic product as a proxy for the return on capital and as an indicator of state activity (Karsten, 1982, pp. 126–7). However, there is no consensus on this and, as we shall see, Islamic governments have either paid interest on bonds or benefited from generous interest-free loans from the central banks, with inevitable inflationary consequences.

Another problem is that of currency. The currency issued by the central bank is backed by financial assets which have elements of interest, i.e. government securities and foreign exchange holdings. The *ulama* do not object to interest payments to non-Muslims; this, however, means that no single policy can accommodate the entire range of requirements and prohibitions (see Ahmed, Iqbal and Fahim Khan, 1983, pp. 27–290).

**An Islamic macroeconomic model**

Islamic economists claim that the abolition of interest (*riba*), the establishment of profit-sharing in the banking sector, the application of Islamic taxation (*zakat*), and the avoidance of wasteful consumption (*israf*) constitute the key macroeconomic features of an ideal Islamic economy. Moreover,they contend that the macroeconomic performance of an ideal Islamic economy would be far superior to that of existing systems. Many believe that business cycles are tempered in an ideal Islamic economy for the following reasons. First, interest rate would not be used to induce procyclical investment. Second, saving would be related more directly to investment, which gives rise to *ex ante* equilibrium. Third, in an Islamic economy, supply creates its own demand more than in other systems since idle savings are discouraged by the *zakat* tax on wealth. Fourth, the lower degree of financial intermediation in an Islamic economy would be less subject to liquidity shocks, which create business cycles, since the economy is an investment-centred economy. Fifth, speculation would be dampened because banks, through profit-sharing, are less induced to participate in speculative activities. Let us now turn to the main features of a formal Islamic macroeconomic model.

*Financial market*

The demand for money will be determined basically by transactions and precautionary needs based on the level of money income. Many Islamic economists categorically deny the possibility, in an ideal Islamic economy, of speculative demand for money (Choudhury, 1986, p. 176). However, in practical terms, speculation would still exist because of the availability of a variety of forms of financial assets with different returns and risks, and the fact that money demanders may hold onto money until they find a more appropriate asset to invest in, which means that there is always a demand for idle balances for speculative purposes. Furthermore, *zakat* does not significantly reduce the speculative demand for money since it is only imposed on assets lying idle for more than a year. Nevertheless, Islamic economists believe that the abolition of interest and the institution of *zakat* will weaken the speculative demand for money. They assert that the abolition of interest would reduce the options of liquid-fund holders to cash holdings with no return or investment in profit-sharing schemes with a return. The institution of *zakat* will also make cash holdings in excess of those earmarked for transactions and precautionary demands for money irrational in view of the erosive effect of *zakat* and inflation. The demand for money will become determined by the level of income and the rate of profit.

The supply of money would be under the control of the central bank, which will assume full employment, stable prices and an equitable distribution of income, and regulate the supply of money accordingly. Monetary policy is thus formulated according to the desired stock of money and not the rate of interest, although some Islamic economists insist on the influence of the rate of profit on the supply side of the market (*ibid.*, p. 172).

The mechanisms by which equilibrium is established in the money market are the system of profit-sharing and the replacement of interest by the rate of profit. The rate of profit here can be considered a weighted average rate for a random sample of firms. The rate of return is in itself the opportunity cost of holding money and is used to discount the stream of future earnings.

The market would move away from disequilibrium and towards equilibrium. For example, an excess supply of money leads to an increase in investment in capital goods. As such investments increase, the marginal efficiency of investment declines, signalling a decline in the rate of profit on invested capital. This means an increase in money demanded and, finally, an equilibrium in the money market (given a level of income and the supply of money).

Changes in the level of income and/or the supply of money by the central bank and the commercial banks would lead to a new equilibrium rate of profit, *ceteris paribus*. For example, starting at equilibrium, an increase in income with no change in the supply of money would create an excess demand for money at the former rate of profit. The excess demand can be satisfied by sales of non-monetary financial assets or equity shares, which would lead to a decline in their prices until a new equilibrium is restored at a higher profit rate, *ceteris paribus*. Likewise, an increase in the supply of money by the central bank would create an excess supply of money. This excess supply would be invested in profit-sharing schemes, driving up the price of equity shares, which is associated with a decline in the rate of profit and, finally, new equilibrium in the money market at a lower profit rate.

*Product market*
In the product market, the important analytical point according to Islamic economists is the possibility of equilibrium in the market for savings and investment. Based on the assumptions of an Islamic economy, current saving would be determined by the rate of profit and the level of income. Therefore, given a rate of profit, saving would increase with the rise in the level of income.

Investment depends on the rate of return and income. Thus, given a level of income, as new investments take place, the cost of investment will increase (or the marginal efficiency of investment will decline). This is followed by a decline in the rate of profit on invested capital.

It is argued that the change in income, *ceteris paribus*, can change the equilibrium rate of profit without creating a lasting disequilibrium, especially if it is assumed that the created disequilibrium for cash balances leads automatically to a change in the rate of return on capital. If, *ceteris paribus*, we start at equilibrium in the money and investment markets, an increase in the supply of money by the central bank would create an excess supply of cash balances, which increases investment and drives down the profit rate. The increase in investment will increase the level of income that finally leads to an increase in the rate of profit in the money market. In the investment market, the increase in income will lead to an increase in investment and saving at the former level of the rate of profit. Thus, any deviation from full-employment level of income is automatically corrected by the market forces.

So far equilibrium conditions of the macro-markets have been discussed in nominal values. It is claimed that the institutional setting of an Islamic economy would rule out the possibility of sustained increases in the price level. Therefore the real values of a macroeconomic equilibrium could not be affected by the price level, and the conversion of nominal values into real values is not relevant (see *ibid.*, p. 182). The argument for price stability in the Islamic economy is based on the power of the central bank and the institutional peculiarities of the financial, product and labour markets.

It is asserted that in an Islamic interest-free economy disequilibrium in the money market cannot easily lead to recessionary or inflationary gaps. This is because the central bank can constantly monitor the supply of money and is able to estimate the money needed for the generation of the target rate of growth in money supply and the amount of profit-sharing credit it can provide for the commercial banks. In addition, it is assumed that disequilibrium in the money market is turned into equilibrium very fast due to the absence or weakness of the speculative demand for money. Whereas in a capitalist economy an excess supply of cash balances would lead to an increase in aggregate demand and, therefore, price level. The principle of the avoidance of wasteful consumption would restrain higher expenditures on consumption goods that would increase the level of aggregate demand in such a situation. Besides, due to the co-operative nature of the Islamic labour market and the absence of monopolistic and monopsonistic practices, cost-push inflation is avoided. If, however, by any chance, an inflationary gap is created by demand-pull due to excess demand for investment, it will be only a temporary phenomenon. In such a situation "a policy of distributing increasing levels of profits in the form of cash dividends will finally satisfy the demand for investment capital, thereby restoring the monetary sector equilibrium" (*ibid.*, p. 181).

If it is possible to control inflation in an Islamic economy, would it be just as easily possible to control a recession? For example, what if prospects for making profit are not encouraging and commercial banks are not willing to expand their profit-sharing investments? In such a situation the central bank might increase the lending ability of the banks, but it cannot force the private sector to invest. In that case the government can come up with an appropriate fiscal policy that would offset the deficiency in the private sector aggregate demand by running a fiscal deficit. According to this scenario, external shocks cannot be much of a problem either. For example, an international boom can be handled by the Islamic banking sector just like the conventional banking system. If demand and prices go up in this situation, the banks are going to provide more finance and more money will be created. Under profit-sharing, however, monetary stabilisation would be different: the central bank will regulate the amount of credit so that it is in accordance with monetary stability. What if there is a disturbing capital movement in the form of "hot" speculative capital flows arising from interest rate differentials and exchange rate expectations? This need not be a problem either, because deposits are interest-free and time deposits are equity-oriented and for a longer period. Therefore this inflow can only be accepted if it is absorbed in a profit-sharing framework. In the case of money inflow due to expected exchange rate appreciation, this inflow can be discouraged by policy controls that would neutralise its monetary effect. On the other hand, price stability and Islamic behaviour would minimise current account deficits and the resulting foreign exchange rate depreciation and capital outflows (see Ahmed, Iqbal and Fahim Khan, 1983, pp. 30–32, 43–4 and 92).

With respect to macroeconomic growth, it is claimed that the abolition of interest and the institution of *zakat* can provide the stimulus for growth: the former through a profit-sharing system turns the Islamic economy into an investment-oriented economy, and the latter discourages hoarding and encourages investment, generating a high demand for investment. This investment will be financed by high-level saving. Savings will not be discouraged by the abolition of interest since savers will receive a variable return (positive or negative), rather than a fixed return, on their savings in the Islamic financial market. Besides, savings motivations are many and most of them, including the level of income, continue to operate in the Islamic system. In the case of inflation, increases in the nominal price level "are likely to be associated with increases in the nominal return on investment and this could even reduce the variability of the real yield on saving" (*ibid.*, p. 20).

Based on this system and its major institutions, greater equity, too, will be realised. This is because Islam would not allow capitalists to receive a fixed, riskless return called interest and the entrepreneur would not bear all the risks and all the losses alone. Thus, both the entrepreneurs and the suppliers of capital would share in the profit and loss in a profit-sharing system.

Of course, all the above propositions are hypothetical rather than definitive conclusions derived from observed behaviour of an Islamic economy since there is no full-fledged Islamic economy at present. This, no doubt, does not undermine the value and efforts of Islamic economists who are trying to come up with theoretical constructs that are necessary for Islamic economics and its practical application. However, the adjustment mechanisms for the stability and growth of an Islamic economy that have been discussed are easier said than done. There are many unresolved questions and "courageous" assumptions and one is not sure whether in practice different schools of Islamic law and the *ulama* find them compatible with the *Shari'a*. However, the question of why a complex industrialised economy should behave according to this model has not been effectively addressed by the proponents of Islamic economics. In the absence of realistic behavioural and institutional explanations, it would be impossible to identify and evaluate the adjustment mechanisms of an Islamic economy. In fact, the main problems of the above model, which is in permanent equilibrium, especially in the financial market, are its unclear microeconomic foundation and Islamic institutional assumptions. Many of the Muslim economists who have presented these models are aware of these problems. However, they either acknowledge the importance of these problems and postpone their incorporation into their models to future studies, or build the models based on very general institutional assumptions: e.g. the prohibition of *riba*, profit/loss-sharing contracts, the avoidance of wasteful consumption and *zakat*. Obviously this approach can create a problem considering the fact that the same institutions are interpreted differently by different schools of law in Islam. To circumvent this problem, some Muslim economists construct their models by eclectically introducing certain assumptions that are suitable for the derivation of a smooth adjustment mechanism, e.g. a variable rate of *zakat* or indexation of loans, which are problematic in Islam. To justify this, it is argued that any other approach would not be fruitful and would entangle them in the details of "indecisive Islamic scholastic views on the pricing of risk, hire-purchase, mark-up in tradeable goods, forward pricing of goods, ... the issue of residual taxation over and above *zakat* ..." (Choudhury, 1986, p. 200). Maybe they are right, but it is precisely over some of these details that Muslims have bitterly argued with each other in countries where Islam is being implemented. After all, the same economists tell us that Islam is a complete doctrine and that norms are not to be established by society's consensus, but by the *Shari'a* (*ibid.*, pp. 199–200). Besides, most Islamic economists use the tools of neo-classical economics that are not based on religious assumptions about the behaviour of the economic participants in the market. This is because many of them are of the opinion the "the encroachment of foreign elements in economic theory such as through religion ... can destroy the fabric of any self-contained and well-defined domain of economic analysis as a science" (*ibid.*, p. 198). However, this means that either it would be problematic to construct the microeconomic behaviour of Islamic man, as we have seen in the previous section, or that removing the adjective Islamic from the models "would not materially affect the analysis or the conclusions" (Khan and Mirakhor, 1987, p. xv). Thus, to come up with a new paradigm, Islamic economists must analyse the Islamic imprints for all behavioural assumptions, axioms, hypotheses and theorems (*ibid.*, pp. xv–xvii). This obviously is not an easy task. Nevertheless, given these problems, certain points can be made about the above macroeconomic model.

With respect to interest-free banking based on a profit/loss sharing system, certain factors that may affect the behaviour of savers and investors must be pointed out. Savers in such a system are ideally encouraged to participate directly in the success of the investor's business, thus sharing the risk involved. For this reason savers are not only faced with the uncertainty arising from inflation but also the uncertainty concerning the nominal yield on investment. Besides, one could agree that *zakat* further increases risk to savers, since it is a wealth tax and has to be paid whether income is earned or not. Thus the elimination of interest can discourage savings and, therefore, reduce investment unless the rate of return on financial assets increases with the rise in risk (*ibid.*, pp. 137–8). However, it is also argued that if the Islamic system coexists with the conventional interest-based banking system, savings could increase. This is because such a situation offers more conventional savings instruments and could also attract the savings of the devout Muslims, absorbing all the existing saving outlets (Karsten, 1982, p. 132).

Moreover, the availability of funds can be limited in such a system if the lenders and borrowers do not have access to the same information about the uncertainty related to a production process, the economic activities of the agent in the profit-sharing contract and the profit of the projects. As Il Haque and Mirakhor have noted, this "dishonesty" factor and the excessive monitoring cost that it requires can only be eliminated if there are extensive and advanced legal and institutional infrastructures such as a well-functioning stock market; such an institution would reduce monitoring cost and allow the trading of profit-sharing contracts for the determination of a rate of return on capital (Khan and Mirakhor, 1987, p. 159). Besides, according to the *Shari'a*, the use of funds for long-term investments should be limited to investment deposits, and current deposits should be used for short-term financing. This constraint can also reduce the availability of funds. Nevertheless, some of the Islamic economists insist that there will always be enough savings even at zero rate of profit (Choudhury, 1986, p. 171). Obviously such a position is naive in assuming that the supply of funds for investment is infinite.

There are also unresolved issues in the practical operation of the Islamic financial system. Under the profit-sharing system the calculation of profit and losses for very short periods, e.g. for loans such as working capital and consumer credits, is very difficult and it is not clear whether the variable return on such loans would accurately reflect the scarcity price of financial capital or its opportunity cost. This is because profits are earned by all factors of production and not only the money capital. Moreover, in theory the rate of return on projects of equivalent risk may be used as a discount rate for project evaluation. However, it is not known how this rate is to be determined, how the risk is to be defined and calculated, and how the difference between the rate of return and risk should be reconciled.

As we shall see in later chapters, in practice the banks in Islamic countries have implicitly guaranteed their depositors a minimum positive return, excluding possible losses, which is a questionable procedure from the Sharia's point of view. This practice indicates the fear of depositors' and the Islamic government's reaction to the abolition of interest. However, this implicit policy offsets the smooth and instantaneous adjustment to shocks resulting from banking crises that is claimed to be the proof for the superiority of Islamic banking. In other words, it is asserted that in a banking system based on profit-and-loss-sharing contracts, "the real values of assets and liabilities of banks would be equal at all points in time", and that it would thus eliminate the disequilibrium between real assets and real liabilities (Khan and Mirakhor, 1987, p. 31).

As far as business cycles are concerned, most Islamic economists would accept their possibilities and in such cases would advocate appropriate monetary and fiscal policy. However, there are problems related to the fixity of the *zakat* rate set by the *Shari'a* and non-inflationary deficit financing for counter-cyclical measures. For example, in the case of fiscal deficit the Islamic government can receive interest-free loans from the central bank, commercial banks and the public. This, obviously, can be misused and can lead to inflationary cycles. However, all the methods that might control this tendency, are either ruled out by the *ulama* for technical reasons. One possibility is the indexation of government loans to avoid interest payment; but this method is rejected by the *ulama* on the grounds that it is not in accordance with the *Shari'a* (see Mannan, 1986, p. 192). Profit-sharing is also ruled out since it is not easily applicable to the case of government projects. The public might not be ready to lend to the government by an interest-free bond either, which forces the government to finance the deficit by printing money. Moreover, if inflation occurs and the government has a deficit, the velocity of money would increase considerably because the holders of cash balances and interest-free bonds suffer a real loss and saving would be discouraged in such a situation. In that case, inflationary pressure would increase. Nevertheless, some Islamic economists dismiss these problems by simply assuming that "the stress on price stability in an Islamic economy should" minimise national and international gaps, or that the Islamic economy has a capacity "to generate real growth" and that the Islamic government is determined "not to allow its fiscal deficit to exceed the limits dictated by price stability" (Ahmed, Iqbal and Fahim Khan, 1983, pp. 43–4). If these assertions are dropped, the adjustment mechanisms for macroeconomic stability and growth of an Islamic economy would definitely be confronted with the frictions inherent in any market economy.

Finally, most Islamic economists develop their economic models based on the assumption of a "truly Islamic society", without specifying what constitutes this truly Islamic society as a system. We have already seen in Chapter 3 that there are different possibilities interpreted by different socio-economic tendencies with respect to such a system. Therefore, micro- and macroeconomic functioning of these systems can also be different. What we have discussed in this section is only one of the interpretations, even though the dominant one.

## Notes

1. The argument that man's unlimited wants are primarily responsible for the economic problem has also been made by secular economists. See Heilbroner, 1985, p. 4.

2. In a later work, Mannan acknowledges the fact that according to the Qur'an the bounties of God are unlimited and invokes Ariff's argument that scarcity is a result of man's incapacity to produce (Mannan, 1984, p. 58).

3. Other Islamic economists or jurists have provided different categorisations. Afzal-ur-Rahman, for example, presents a four-tier analysis: (i) neccesities; (ii) necessaries of efficiency; (iii) comforts; (iv) luxuries. In his analysis the first three categories are considered as utilities; luxuries are considered as disutility-bearing commodities for the Islamic community. Thus the consumption of luxuries is believed to be based on false needs (Afzal-ur-Rahman, 1985, Vol.2, pp. 18–30).

4. For references to this position, see Noori, *Pasdar-e Eslam*, no.1. Noori, *Howzeh*, no.37–8. Siddiqi, 1979, p. 21.

5. For references to this position, see Afzal-ur-Rahman, 1985, Vol.2, p. 36. Siddiqi, 1979, p. 93. D.H.H.v.D., 1363, pp. 391–4. Maududi, 1984, p. 79.

6. Imam Sadeq is reported to have considered the purchase of a horse at 10,000 dirham to constitute extravagance, when a 20 dirham horse would serve or fulfil one's needs just as well (*Tafsir al-Mizan*, Vol.8, p. 94, cited in D.H.H.v.D., 1363, p. 394).

7. In terms of standard indifference curves, if you plot Material Goods (MGs) on the x-axis and Spiritual Goods (SGs) on the y-axis, the shape of the Islamic consumers' indifference curve would reflect a negative marginal rate of substitution of material goods for spiritual goods. Every point on the indifference curve would represent an equal satisfaction or felicity level of different combinations of Material Goods and Spiritual Goods. This indifference curve should also be relatively flat, demonstrating a low marginal rate of substitution of Material Goods for Spiritual Goods, once the first few units of MGs, providing basic needs, has been obtained. Islam does not condone asceticism, therefore the possession of a minimum of material goods is obligatory. The downward sloping indifference curve would reach the saturation point measured on the x-axis and then slope positively showing the relationship between a good on the y-axis and a "bad" on the x-axis. After this respite period during which the marginal rate of substitution of Material Goods for Spiritual Goods becomes positive, demonstrating the possibility of a small deviation from moderation, the indifference curve would become vertical. The budget line used would be an hourly one, the y-axis intercept, representing the maximum hours of *'ibadah* with no hours spent on work or zero income, and the x-axis co-ordinate representing zero hours of *'ibadah* and maximum hours of work or income. The income of the consumer could also be derived from the x-axis intercept by multiplying hourly wages by the maximum number of hours of work per month. Therefore an increase in income would be shown through an outward tilt of the hourly budget line. Such a tilt could also represent a decrease in the price of the basket of goods that constitute Material Goods. Each point of tangency between the indifference curve and the budget line represents an equality between marginal utility of Material Goods over the marginal utility of Spiritual Goods and the spiritual satisfaction foregone in disobeying God over the material satisfaction foregone in disobeying the instinctual drives of the self.

8. Ariff, in Ghazali and Omar, 1989, p. 108; Siddiqi, 1979, p. 103.

9. For references to each condition, see (i) Muslehuddin, 1986, pp. 159–62; and Zarqa in Ghazali and Omar, 1989, pp. 34–5. (ii) *Sunna* of the Prophet; Malik, 1989, p. 307; and

Moussavi-e Isfahani, 1368, p. 202. (iii) Moussavi-e Isfahani, 1368, p. 202; and Siddiqi, 1979, p. 65. (iv) The Qur'an, 2:185, 5:6, 24:61 and 22:78.

10. According to Ibn Taymiya, most schools of jurisprudence subscribe to this position. Ibn Taymiya argues that the producers of basic necessities could even be forced to increase output if they do not do so according to their own free will. See Ibn Taymiya, 1983, pp. 38–9.

11. For such a position, see Siddiqi, 1979, pp. 110–12; Mannan, 1984, p. 253; Sadr, 1357, p. 314.

12. This means that Islamic firms cannot experience abnormal profits. When their average cost curve is below the market price they are obliged to produce a quantity at which price or average revenue is equal to average cost. This implies the production of a quantity of output at which marginal cost is greater than marginal revenue. For such firms equalisation at the margin (marginal revenue and marginal cost) is not a meaningful guide to production. Production at the point where average revenue and increasing average cost are equal yields an output which is greater than the profit-maximisation point of production. At this point, total revenue is equal to total cost and therefore all factors are being rewarded according to the market price, hence normal profits.

13. See Ariff, in Ghazali and Omar, 1989, p. 107; Afzal-ur-Rahman,1980, p. 8; Siddiqi, 1979, p. 33; Mannan, 1984, p. 36.

14. See al-Ghazali, *Ihya' Ulum al-Din*, Vol.3, Beirut: Dar al Nodvat al-Jadidah, 1974, pp. 171–4; Biazar-e Shirazi, *Nezam-e Iqtesade Islami*, Tehran: Daftar-e Nashr-e Farhang-e Islami, 1368, p. 117. In this Persian text the second stage of *movasat* is erroneously referred to as *mosavat* or equality. The error is certainly a typographical one.

15. For Sunni sources, see Qadri, 1986, p. 326; Doi, 1984, pp. 370–1; Mustafa and Askari, in Iqbal (ed.), 1988, p. 120 (this is probably a combined Shi'i and Sunni source). For Shi'i sources, see Helli, 1364, Vol.1, pp. 301–2; Khomeini, *Tahrir al-Wasileh*, cited in Biazar-e Shirazi, 1366, p. 202; Sadr, n.d., pp. 88–90.

16. For references to both positions, see Afzal-ur-Rahman, 1985, Vol.2, pp. 172–207; Mustafa and Askari in Iqbal (ed.), 1986, pp. 120–22. Qadi abu Yusaf, 1979, pp. 175–81; Sadr, n.d., pp. 84–7; Helli, 1364, Vol.1, pp. 272–84.

17. See Helli, 1364, Vol.1, p. 263; Afzal-ur-Rahman, 1980, Vol.1, p. 234. Ayatollah Khomeini holds that such expenses could be deducted from the original capital only if the commercial capitalist concedes to this practice. Therefore he believes that permission would be required for such deductions. Biazar-e Shirazi, 1366, p. 254.

18. For Sunni sources, see Siddiqi, 1988, pp. 99–104; Mannan, 1986, p. 178; Afzal-ur-Rahman, 1980, Vol.1, p. 230. For Shi'i sources, see Sobhani, *Howzeh*, no. 37–8, p. 351; Gerami, n.d., p. 300; Hojati-e Kermani in Va'ezzadeh Khorasani, 1369, Vol.1, p. 290; Beheshti, 1363, pp. 77–8.

19. Imam Malik, cited in Siddiqi, 1988, p. 103; Sadr, 1357, Vol.2, p. 231. Khomeini, cited in Biazar-e Shirazi, 1366, Vol.2, p. 253; Taskhiri, 1368, p. 289.

20. Seyyed Mousa Sadr is of the opinion that in a *muzar'a* contract a share of the profit cannot be allocated to factors such as seed, implements or the oxen used to plough the land. M. Sadr, n.d., p. 87.

# 5. Islamisation of Pakistan's Economy by the Bureaucracy, Military and Politicians

After more than four decades, Pakistan is still in search of the specific role of Islam in its politics and economy. Pakistan as a nation-state was created around the notion that Muslims and Hindus make up two distinct nations. This was the ideological reference of the leaders of Pakistan's independence movement, who constantly referred to Muslims, rather than to Islam; what they seemed to have in mind was a separation of religion from the established institutions of Islam (Binder, 1961, p. 63). Many of the *ulama*, including Maududi, the leading Muslim theologian in India, were opposed to this distinction. They wanted a Muslim state based on the *Shari'a*, a theocracy. This issue has constituted a matter of dispute in Pakistan ever since, and the balance of power between advocates of these two main trends has shifted back and forth throughout Pakistan's history.

## The independence movement and Islam

Pakistan's independence movement grew out of the Indian subcontinent's movement for independence, which expanded between the First and Second World Wars. Religion was an important part of the culture of the subcontinent; Hinduism and Islam inspired and provided the ideology and identity of these movements. For a long time, the Indian Nationalist Movement was led by a united front of Hindu and Muslim leaders, but this union was eventually undermined by the vast differences between the two traditional cultures.

The All India National Congress (founded in 1885) and the All India Muslim League (founded in 1906), both led by the upper and middle classes, were the two main political organisations of the subcontinent. The Congress was nationalist/secularist in outlook and claimed to represent all communities and religions in India under the leadership of high-caste Hindus. The Muslim League was led by secularists who were worried about the Muslim's political, religious and economic position in relation to Hindus. The League appealed to the Islamic sentiments of poor Muslims, who were among the poorest in India and lived in the non-industrialised regions of eastern Bengal and the north-western provinces.

In the 1930s, the Muslim League demanded political self-determination for the Muslims of India, but by 1940, when it was clear that Britain was to leave India, Muhammed Ali Jinnah, the leader of the League, raised the slogan of a separate Muslim homeland. He insisted that Islam and Hinduism were not "religions" in the strict sense of the word, but, in fact, different and distinct social orders. He could not believe that the Hindus and Muslims could evolve a common nationality. "To yoke together two such nations under a single state ... must lead to growing discontent and final destruction ..." (quoted in Esposito, 1980, p. 141). Islamic nationalism became the ideology of the mass movement of Indian Muslims, bringing all classes of Muslims together under a common platform: a Muslim country. However, Islam as a social and economic order was not clearly defined and the League's leadership, including Jinnah, was vague about it. Jinnah was, in fact, an advocate of the separation of religion and politics and as late as the early 1940s he did not even mention Islamic society as his ideal society. By 1946, the Islamic state was featured ever more prominently in the Muslim League's discussions and resolutions, referring to Pakistan as an Islamic state. However, what Jinnah had in mind in 1946 with respect to a Muslim state was a "modern democratic state with sovereignty resting in the people ... regardless of their religion" (quoted in Nayak, 1985, p. 32). It is, therefore, not surprising that a group of India's Islamic leaders, including Maududi and his Jama'at-e Islami were opposed to the concept of Pakistan as a separate secular state. For them, all citizens could not have equal rights in an Islamic state since non-Muslims did not have the right to make laws, administer them or hold public office. They were suspicious of the secular orientation of the League's leadership (Gardezi and Rashid, 1983, p. 361). For the underprivileged classes, however, the creation of Pakistan meant the prospect of economic and social liberation and this expectation was raised by the Muslim League in its call for a just economic and social order. The League had promised a guaranteed minimum wage, land reform and the elimination of usury, but had never clearly defined the Islamic social and economic order that was to be implemented (Noman, 1988, pp. 5 and 23).

In the end, the Muslim League rejected the idea of a composite Indian federation. Following a constitutional and legal path within the non-violent movement of the Congress, it steered towards the creation of Pakistan. In August 1947, the Indian subcontinent was partitioned into India and Pakistan.

Initially, it was not very clear what would be the nature of the political order of the state. In fact, it took nine years to come up with a constitution. Jinnah, the first governor general, reiterated his belief in a secular state at the inaugural session of the Constituent Assembly (Nayak, 1985, pp. 32–3). The Constituent Assembly was a small house whose members were elected indirectly by the provincial legislators. However, Jinnah died in September 1948, before any restructuring of the political system of the new state could take place.

In the meantime, the *ulama* increased their pressure on the secular rulers for an Islamic state. In early 1948, they came up with the proposal for a Ministry of Religious Affairs that would regulate religious institutions and monitor the conduct of civil servants. A religious advisory committee set up by the government in 1949 also demanded that all legislation conform with the *Shari'a*. However, when the government was forced to issue a statement of intent with respect to the future constitution, it consciously avoided the concept of a state based on the *Shari'a*, but did pay lip service to an Islamic state. Practical concerns for the survival of the new state overshadowed the issue of the state's Islamic identity.

## The dominance of the bureaucracy in Pakistan's politics: 1947–58

After independence, migrants from Muslim minority provinces in India were a majority within the leadership of the League, and senior civil servants dominated the central government. Other ethnic groups in Pakistan, Sindhis, Pathans, Baluchis and Bengalis, were not well represented at the centre. The only exception was the Punjabis, who were dominant in the military. The Muslim League was unable to develop as a national, integrative force, unlike the Congress party in India, and Jinnah had to rely on the central government to forge strong regional ties among a diversified people speaking thirty-two distinct languages and clustered in the two separate regions of West and East Pakistan. As a result, the bureaucracy filled all key posts throughout the government. Entrance into Pakistan's Civil Service (CSP), a tightly knit organisation with its own esprit de corps, sense of solidarity and contempt for politicians, was based on an elaborate and competitive system of entrance exams. In its effort to control power, the bureaucracy was backed by the army which was slowly reorganising itself along the lines of the old British Indian colonial army. At the time, this new Muslim army was not well equipped; Pakistan did not receive its full share of military equipment in Indian territory, and until 1951 the commanders-in-chief of the Pakistani Army were British officers. Jinnah had extraordinary powers as governor general and increased the power of the bureaucracy at the expense of the political leadership: bureaucratic officials were able to bypass the authority of ministers and the parliament (Gardezi and Rashid, 1983, pp. 70–79).

Jinnah died in 1948. Liaquat Ali Khan, the prime minister of the Muslim League and the only man who could have had Jinnah's authority, became prime minister. Liaquat was assassinated in October 1951 and Ghulam Muhammed, his finance minister, was elected as governor general by the Assembly and Nazimuddin became prime minister. In the same period, General Ayub Khan was appointed as the first Pakistani commander-in-chief of the army with the backing of the minister of defence, Iskander Mirza.

In March 1953, a political crisis led to the dismissal of the prime minister. The crisis was caused by the wheat crop failure, rising food prices and large-scale rioting and killing in Punjab against the Ahmadiya community, a minority Muslim sect which the *ulama* considered heretical. The prime minister was dismissed by order of the governor general, bypassing the Assembly, which approved the move a few days later. In the period 1954–58, the civil service, backed by the military, was at the height of its power. However, in 1954 its authority was challenged by East Pakistan's provincial elections, when the Muslim League was overwhelmingly unseated by the United Front of East Pakistan. The army was sent to Dacca, the United Front government was dismissed and rule by the governor general was imposed. This encouraged the members of the Constituent Assembly to take a stand against the extraordinary powers of the governor general. Ghulam Muhammed responded by declaring a state of emergency, dissolving the Assembly and assuming full power. Ayub

Khan was appointed defence minister and Iskander Mirza minister of the interior. Later, in 1955, as a result of the federal court's ruling, a new Constituent Assembly was elected which drew up the Constitution of Pakistan in March 1956. Unlike its predecessor, the new Assembly was made up of members of six political parties, of which the largest was the Muslim League (al- Mujahid, 1989, pp. 828–9). In the same year, Mirza was appointed the first president of Pakistan. However, political unrest led to the postponement of the general elections that the new constitution should have introduced. Mirza dismissed the legislature, banned the activities of political parties and introduced arbitrary measures such as price controls. He arrested a number of politicians and corrupt bureaucrats. His moves led to discontent which finally culminated in Ayub Khan's coup d'état in October 1958 (Gardezi and Rashid, 1983, pp. 70–85).

Until 1958, Pakistan had a parliamentary form of government. However, the National Assembly, which was also the Constituent Assembly, was *de facto* a legitimising facade for a dominant bureaucracy. This secular bureaucracy was backed by a rising military which was gaining legitimacy, at the expense of disorganised, unrepresentative and discredited politicians, as the guarantor of survival of the new state, a process heightened by the confrontation with India.

**Economic policy in the first decade of independence**

On the eve of independence, Pakistan, East and West, was on the periphery of the political and economic centre of the British empire in India. The areas of the Indian subcontinent with a majority Muslim population were less developed than the non-Muslim areas. East Bengal, the agricultural hinterland of the empire, was related to the commercial centre of Calcutta. It exported jute and tea, but was not able to feed its own population. In West Pakistan, only Punjab was of any significant economic value in producing foodstuffs. Agriculture, based on large and small landlordism, dominated the economy of these areas. In 1947, the output of this sector constituted more than 50 per cent of the gross domestic product (GDP). The areas lacked an industrial base and national capital. The only industrial plants of any significant size in the Muslim areas were cotton and sugar mills and cement factories, owned by Hindus who had left Pakistan after independence. Local capital was engaged in trade, shipping and finance. Most of the foreign-trade sector, which was controlled by non-Muslims, came under the control of migrating Muslim communities who settled mainly in Karachi. Thus, at the time of independence, landlords (*zamindars*, *khans* and *sandars*) and the embryonic, largely immigrant bourgeoisie from Hindu India emerged as the dominant classes and also had the upper hand in the Muslim League (*ibid.*, pp. 1 and 46–8).

In the beginning, the Jinnah administration and Liaquat's government (1947–51) were besieged by the problems of independence: creating a government out of the civil servants brought in from New Delhi and establishing a functioning government apparatus; putting together a Pakistani army; and accommodating some eight million refugees from India within a few months. In such a situation, commitment to economic development and Islamic justice did not constitute a priority (Burki and Laporte, 1986, pp. 4–6).

In September 1949, following the devaluation of the pound, India devalued its currency. Pakistan, however, refused to devalue its rupee, hoping that an overvalued rupee would protect the interests of jute exporters. The government argued that the demand for jute was price inelastic. In retaliation, India suspended trade with Pakistan. In spite of all these difficulties, tariff protection for infant industries, tax concessions and government investment in projects such as jute mills, later to be privatised, led to an expansion of import-substitution industries (Ahmed and Amjad, 1984, pp. 68–9).

The Korean war boosted raw material prices for Pakistan's raw cotton, jute and wool, leading to a sharp rise in the country's export earnings. In addition, India lifted its ban on trade with Pakistan in 1950, and the government of Pakistan kept the price of agricultural goods low. However, the economic crisis of 1953–54 led to a decline of export earnings and a trade deficit, forcing the government to impose severe controls over imports of consumer goods. With the rise of prices of imported consumer goods, the terms of trade changed in favour of industry and against the agricultural sector, making industrial production profitable. All this brought about an expansion of the accumulative capacity of merchant traders who invested part of their profit in import-substitution industries (Noman, 1988, pp. 15–16). This, however, was realised only at the expense of the agricultural sector. The prices of agricultural goods were kept at a low level to provide cheap food for urban consumers (including millions of refugees) and import-substitution industries. This policy encouraged export of raw materials, but led to a stagnant agricultural output which could not match the population growth. The balance of payments was constrained and per-capita food consumption fell. Moreover, a stagnant income in the agricultural sector could not support a growing import-substitution drive, so in 1956 the government shifted its emphasis from the industrial to the agricultural sector. Pakistan's rupee was devalued at the end of 1955, which made imports of capital goods more expensive and encouraged exports of raw materials (Ahmed and Amjad, 1984, pp. 65–75).

In 1949, the Muslim League Agrarian Reform Committee proposed the abolition of sub-tenancies and sub-letting, through a programme of compensation to landlords, reducing rents and abolishing illegal exactions by landlords. These recommendations were taken into account in the East Bengal Estate Acquisition and Tenancy Act (1950) which prohibited sub-tenancies and sub-letting, set a ceiling of thirty-three acres for self-cultivation and gave tenants full occupancy rights. Land reforms, mainly in relation to tenancy conditions, were also introduced in West Pakistan in the early 1950s in Punjab, the Sind and North West Frontier Province (NWFP). The implementation of these reforms was difficult, even though the provision of full-occupancy rights applied only to a small proportion of tenants, and illegal charges imposed by the landlords on tenants were not widespread. (*ibid.*, pp. 120–21).

In the financial sector, the State Bank (central bank) was set up in 1948 with all the conventional instruments of monetary control, such as setting a discount rate and cash reserve requirement, at its disposal. However, in this period, the State Bank was mainly reacting to changes in the balance of payments position and increases in the government's deficit financing. The central bank, like the central bank of many developing countries, could not control the government's financial operations without increasing the supply of money. Changes in the discount rate were not effective due to the vast gap between the rates offered by the State Bank and the commercial banks. The size of the credit multiplier was very low, the ratio of currency to money supply high (more than 65 per cent) and banks had excess liquidity. All these factors reduced the effectiveness of the cash reserves requirement, forcing the central bank into a passive role (*ibid.*, pp. 276–81).

Despite the creation of a Planning Board in 1953 and the drawing up of the First Five Year Plan for the period 1955–60, economic planning had little direct impact, mainly due to changes in government, inter-ministerial conflicts and rivalries and lack of political support for implementation of the plan (*ibid.*, p. 56).

In the 1950s, refugees were resettled, the administrative and military apparatus set up and the state's economic institutions established, without observance of any Islamic forms and considerations, especially with respect to interest payments and *zakat*. The government was too preoccupied with the pressing problems of the day to be directly concerned with Islamic institutions and concepts of economic justice.

In 1949–58, real GNP per capita increased moderately, but rural per-capita income and real wages of industrial workers fell. However, traders, especially migrants and industrialists and to some extent large land owners, benefited from the industrial, fiscal and agrarian policies of the government. Karachi (in Sind) and Punjab attracted most of the migrants and the government's economic attention. In fact, about 70 per cent of the workers employed in Karachi's industrial sector were refugees and by 1959 over half of Pakistan's industrial assets were controlled by migrants from India (Noman, 1988, pp. 19–21).

## The dominance of the military: 1958–71

In October 1958, General Ayub Khan, with the support of the military, proclaimed himself president of Pakistan. Martial law and military courts remained until a new political structure and constitution were set up in June 1962. Nevertheless, one month after his coup d'état, Ayub sent all the troops back to their barracks and let the civilians run the business of the government.

The twin priorities of Ayub's government were the centralisation of government power and rapid economic reform. He saw himself as a modernist Muslim and emphasised the need "to liberate the spirit of religion from the cobwebs of superstition and stagnation ..." (quoted in Esposito, 1980, p. 145). However, the continuous struggle between modernists and traditionalists limited the potential of Ayub's reforms. The net result was a compromise, ad hoc changes and a vague Islamic ideology that was reflected in the constitution of 1962 and the Family Ordinance Law.

The constitution did not recognise political parties, and the members of the National Assembly were to be elected on "personal merit", but Ayub soon allowed the formation of political parties, and in May 1963 he joined the Muslim League, which split the party in two.

The 1962 constitution formally allowed for a federal government, but it limited the autonomy of the provinces. Ayub himself had a low opinion of Bengalis who formed a numerical majority in the country; he considered them to be under Hindu cultural and linguistic influences. The central government's reliance on the bureaucracy and its emphasis on the centralisation of power led East Bengal to embark on a process of confrontation. Between 1958 and 1966, thousands of riots broke out. In fact, by 1966 the political parties of East Bengal came up with a platform which for all practical purposes represented the partition of Pakistan into two nation-states.

At the same time, Ayub denied the political parties participation in the determination of policy and brought about an enforced consensus that diverted attention away from politics and towards economics. Already, in 1959, the Martial Law Ordinance had enabled the government to close newspapers that were not in tune with the government's policies, and reform of the judicial system had expanded government control by subjecting judicial appointments to political scrutiny (Noman, 1988, pp. 27–31). However, despite economic growth, socio-economic and regional inequalities, along with rising prices and indirect taxes, broke down the consensus of the first years of the 1960s. In addition, in the mid-1960s, Ayub's personal and autocratic rule, corruption and nepotism alienated people from his government. The Indo-Pakistan War over Kashmir in 1965 had also weakened the government. Ayub had established new public institutions, but had failed to institutionalise the political process, and had excluded an important part of the population from the political process, forcing them into confrontation. A breaking point was reached in 1968–69 when spontaneous demonstrations broke out across the country. Students, religious elements and political parties became active in these demonstrations. Later, urban workers and peasants also joined in the call for Ayub to go. Ayub's concessions to political parties did not appease the opposition and forced him to hand over power to his Commander-in-Chief, General Yahya Khan. Once again, the weakness of all the political parties in Pakistan enabled the military-bureaucratic elite to take the initiative. Yahya Khan set up a nominal civilian government, while maintaining the military character of the regime. He remained president and chief martial law administrator, taking a number of largely symbolic measures against a handful of businessmen who had evaded taxes and exchange controls and dismissing a few civil servants. He also promised a return to parliamentary government by a general election in October 1970, although this was later postponed until December 1970. However, the promise of elections and the changed political atmosphere of the country led to the emergence of two major parties with mass support in West and East Pakistan: the Pakistan People's party (PPP) and the Awami League (AL). The latter won all the seats in East Pakistan, except one, and received an absolute majority in the prospective National Assembly; it won the election on the basis of an extreme form of provincial autonomy and a demand for the decentralisation of power. The PPP, the second largest party, made important gains in West Pakistan, especially in the Punjab and Sind provinces. With the victory of the AL in East Pakistan, a constitutional issue re-emerged. Normally, the largest party was legally entitled to form a government. However, the exclusively provincial character of the AL and the strong opposition of the PPP to the idea of a government by the AL led Yahya to postpone the assembly session in order to find a consensus among these two parties. In the meantime, internal upheaval in East Pakistan, followed by India's intervention in December 1971, forced the secession of East Pakistan as Bangladesh. Pakistan's military defeat discredited the military government and the military itself. Until 1971, the army was considered the ultimate arbiter. It was seen as a pillar of national survival in the long-standing conflict with India and as much less corrupt than the bureaucrats. The 1971 debacle robbed the army of the initiative. Yahya Khan fell and the PPP government led by Bhutto was installed (al- Mujahid, 1989, p. 828; Gardezi and Rashid, 1983, pp. 83–8).

**The rise and fall of the decade of development**

Ayub Khan's period of rule can be divided into three phases: a phase of controls (1958–60), a boom phase (1960–65) and a phase of economic slow-down. In the first phase, the Ayub government put the blame on previous governments and on unfair practices in the private sector, especially in industry and the retail trade, for the economic problems of the country. Price and profit controls were introduced and black marketeering, smuggling, hoarding and tax evasion were punished. The initial impact of these moves was positive and the price index showed a decline. However, such controls could not be applied to a wide range of goods, and the ensuing disruptions led to a change in economic policy and a move towards a free-market policy based on a five-year plan.

The Second Five Year Plan was launched in 1960, based on two implicit assumptions: first, that in the early stages of development rising inequalities would be necessary for savings and entrepreneurial dynamism; and, second, that foreign loans were necessary to fill the domestic savings gap. To implement this model of economic development, direct controls on prices and profit margins were lifted to ensure the free play of market forces, In addition, imports were deregulated to some extent, by easing the granting of new import licenses. Later, a number of items, mainly intermediate and capital goods, were put on the list of items that could be imported without permission. The government also freed investment in industries and projects that were listed on the government's Industrial Investment Schedule.

A pro-industry strategy was followed by maintaining an overvalued rupee. In the meantime, prices of agricultural goods were kept down in order to supply the industrial sector with cheap agricultural inputs. Protection for locally produced goods, tax concessions and low interest loans were the classic features of this industrial policy, which unsurprisingly benefited large-scale manufacturers and stimulated private industrial investment.

An export bonus scheme was introduced which provided price incentives for exporters of selected manufactured goods and some raw materials. Exporters received import permits ranging from 10 to 40 per cent of the value of their exports. The bonus vouchers could be sold at high prices, compensating the exporters for the overvalued rupee.

Export promotion policy, which gave rise to a multiplicity of bonus rates, was not effective in diversifying the country's exports. However, the import-liberalisation policy moderated importers' profit margins and led to a decrease in the price of imported goods, affecting the utilisation and expansion of industrial capacity (Ahmed and Amjad, 1984, pp. 84–6).

A limited land reform was also introduced in 1959. Its objective was to reduce the concentration of land ownership in a country in which 1.2 per cent of landlords owned 30.4 per cent of the land. Two million out of a total of 48.6 million acres were taken over by the government, and the former landlords compensated. This land distribution benefited less than 3 per cent of the peasantry (Gardezi and Rashid, 1983, p. 107).

In this phase, especially in the first few years of the 1960s, the government's priority was price stability and for this reason a conservative fiscal and monetary policy was followed. The result was positive and price stability was maintained during the Second Plan: in 1960–64, on the average, price increases did not exceed 1.5 per cent per year. At the same time increased foreign loans considerably eased the balance of payments situation.

The pattern of government expenditure in the Second Plan favoured agricultural development programmes, water resources, transport and communication, housing and industry. Private investment, however, was concentrated in manufacturing, especially on a large scale, and on transportation, communication, agriculture and private housing.

In 1965–67, Pakistan's economy started to manifest certain problems. Lagging economic growth and rising tensions between rich and poor finally ended Ayub's period in office. The combination of bad harvests in 1965–67, the increase in defence expenditure due to the India–Pakistan War of 1965, and a decrease in foreign loans, led to a slowdown in economic growth. This particularly affected the manufacturing sector, leading to a rise in prices and the reimposition of foreign-exchange controls. Finally, in 1967–68, a sugar shortage caused by a poor sugar cane crop, led to a significant increase in the price of sugar. The problems of 1965–67 also delayed the implementation of the Third Five Year Plan, which had been launched in 1965 with the objective of expanding the capacity of the intermediate and capital goods sectors. Nevertheless, the economy slowly recovered in the late 1960s, mainly because of the significant increase in agricultural production due to the introduction of high yielding varieties of wheat and rice.

The strategy of the second and third plans gave a low priority to the provision of education, health and housing. Income inequalities were implicitly supported on the grounds of stimulating savings by the rich. Industrial wages were kept low by restricting trade-union activity and a prohibition on strikes. In short, the economic strategy of the 1960s was the maximisation of output based on "strong support for the private sector and a postponement of equity and social justice for the future" (Ahmed and Amjad, 1984, p. 83). Although wages had increased in the first half of the 1960s, a sharp rise in prices in the second half of the decade wiped out the gain. In 1967–68 the level of real wages fell below that of 1954. The share of wages in the value added in industry fell from 45 per cent in 1954 to 25 per cent in 1966. While landowners were exempted from income tax and industrialists were provided with tax holidays, indirect taxes on a range of consumer goods were increased to finance the development plans. Small farmers were also hit by the low procurement prices imposed by the government; poor harvests in 1965–67 worsened their situation. Regionally, the economic development of the 1960s mainly benefited West Pakistan, which received a disproportionate share of government expenditure. Disparities in per-capita income between East and West Pakistan increased from 32 per cent in 1954–60 to 61 per cent in 1969–70 in favour of the West.

Inequalities in the distribution of wealth also grew: by 1968 twenty-two families owned 61 per cent of the industrial wealth and controlled 87 per cent of the assets of the banking and insurance sectors. Nevertheless, real per-capita income rose on the average by 3.5 and 3.7 per cent per year in the first and second half of the 1960s respectively. Growth rates of large-scale manufacturing and agricultural output, especially in 1958–67, were significant and price increases moderate (*ibid.*, pp. 57 and 77–90).

## The rule of the People's Party of Pakistan and Bhutto

In December 1971, after the military defeat of Pakistan and the secession of Bangladesh, Zulfiqar Ali Bhutto was installed as president. The National Assembly was convened and a consensus was reached among the parties for a parliamentary system of government with two houses of legislature. The prime minister was to be answerable to the lower house as the chief executive, and a constitution committee of the Assembly drafted a new constitution. However, in early 1973, opposition parties of the right, together with Islamic and regional parties formed a United Democratic Front (UDF) that pushed for amendments to the proposed constitution. The UDF favoured a more Islamic and federal structure, and were successful in moderating the socialist tone of the ruling PPP slogans. In April 1973, Pakistan's constitution was approved by the Assembly and Bhutto was elected prime minister.

Until 1971, Bhutto had been a modern secular politician with social democratic ideas. He had served as a minister in Ayub's government in the 1960s. As prime minister, out of political expediency, he increasingly appealed to Islam and advocated the Islamisation of the country. His calls for parliamentary rule and social justice appealed to the new middle classes in the urban and rural areas who were themselves a product of Ayub's decade of development. He stressed the socio-economic failure of previous government in terms of the distribution of political power and economic wealth. However, he tried to build his party on an alliance of different and opposing segments of the population — landlords, the middle classes, professionals, white-collar workers, middle peasants, farmers and radicals — while at the same time maintaining close relations with industrialists and businessmen. Such a balancing act could not be sustained for long. Bhutto also tried to accommodate those parties that claimed to represent

Islam, such as the Jama'at-e Islami. Nevertheless, these parties opposed most of his moves and finally brought about his downfall by inciting street riots and demonstrations.

Before 1971, Bhutto's socialist platform included nationalisation of industries and radical land reform. The PPP slogan "bread, clothing and shelter" reflected Bhutto's populist stance and was attractive to both the modern middle classes and the masses. The PPP also enjoyed the support of many modern large landowners in the Sind and Punjab, due to tribal and family links. However, the presence of diametrically opposed forces within the party finally led to the ousting of the radicals from the government and the party in October 1974. This in turn led to a moderation of the PPP platform and of the government's programme and its authoritarian rule. The modification of the party's populist programmes alienated the masses who had rallied behind Bhutto when the military had moved against him. At the same time, Bhutto's sweeping and flashy nationalisations, especially during the 1976 election, and the high-pitched rhetoric that accompanied each measure, turned the business community against him. The military bided its time in order to regain some of its lost credibility, and sought to promote opposition to the regime in a cautious manner.

When he came to power, Bhutto, relying on the authority of his party, made a number of changes designed to enhance his own power and that of his party in a state which, for the first time, was dominated by party rule. He purged several top generals and key commanders in the armed forces. He got rid of opponents in the army, but at the same time bestowed favour on loyal generals like Zia. He also set up a paramilitary organisation, the Federal Security Force, and a political police force, the director of which was the major prosecution witness against Bhutto following his fall. In relation to the civil bureaucracy, Bhutto purged many top officials on the grounds of corruption, replacing them with those loyal to him and the PPP. He replaced the old and elitist civil service recruitment system with a system of direct party appointment at all levels of administrative and diplomatic service.

Bhutto's policy towards trade unions was also authoritarian and self-serving. He tried to impose the PPP's hegemony over the workers' organisations in 1974, at a time of industrial recession and rising unemployment. The workers responded with strikes, factory takeovers and demonstrations. Many trade-union officers were arrested and some of their militant leaders assassinated.

The honeymoon between the political parties on the one side, and Bhutto and the PPP on the other, came to an end in 1973 when tribal fighting in Baluchistan led to the imposition of direct presidential rule and the invocation of emergency powers. Later, in 1975, when a senior minister of North-West Frontier Province was assassinated, a state of emergency was declared and the National Awami League (NAL) was banned and its leaders arrested. The National Awami League was an umbrella organisation for the Baluchi national movement and had won a majority of votes in the region. The National Assembly adopted a constitutional bill enabling the government to extend the state of emergency beyond six months, even though the bill was boycotted by the opposition parties.

In the heated general election of March 1977, the PPP acquired a very significant majority in the Assembly and the new Assembly re-elected Bhutto prime minister. The major rival of the PPP in the general election was a broadly based opposition front, the Pakistan National Alliance (PNA), consisting of nine opposition parties, including major Islamic parties such as the NAL. The campaign of the PNA emphasised the erosion of political rights and the courts' authority, the rising power of the executive organ, and the authoritarian nature of the PPP regime. After its defeat in the general election, the PNA vehemently contested the result and called for the boycott of the provincial assembly polls. It also demanded a new general election under the supervision of the judiciary, the armed forces and an election commission, and called for the lifting of the state of emergency and the restoration of fundamental rights. To back these demands, the NAL launched a movement of country-wide civil disobedience. In vain, Bhutto tried to make some concessions to the NAL. However, a number of leaders of the opposition were arrested, increasing the momentum of opposition to the government in the major urban centres, and leading to a breakdown of law and order. Political unrest disrupted the economic life of the country and on several occasions Bhutto called in the armed forces. Curfews were imposed and martial law regulations were applied in major cities. Many people were killed and injured in the demonstrations of March–June 1977 and thousands were arrested for breaking the curfew and violating martial law regulations.

The intensification of the political crisis led to some Islamic countries, notably Saudi Arabia, to mediate between the opposing sides, and after four weeks of negotiations the PNA and Bhutto came to an accord. Bhutto accepted new elections, agreed to lift the state of emergency and restore the power of the judiciary and other fundamental rights; the PNA gave up its demand for Bhutto's resignation. However, the final accord was not signed due to differences over the mechanism for free elections. Armed clashes between PPP and PNA supporters followed and, finally, on 5 July 1977, the armed forces intervened in the crisis. General Zia, chief of the army staff, became martial law administrator, and a junta, a four-member military council, was set up to rule and impose law and order. The junta arrested Bhutto, as well as the leadership of the PPP and the PNA. Later, several charges, in particular the instigation of the murder of a PPP dissident and a member of Bhutto's family, were brought against Bhutto and a member of his cabinet. Bhutto was tried and convicted of these charges. Eventually, after the Supreme Court had confirmed the verdict of the lower court, Bhutto was hanged, on 4 April 1979 (al-Mujahid, 1989, pp. 829–31; Gardezi and Rashid, 1983, pp. 13–14, 50–2, 72–6, 88–90, 97–108 and 280–88).

**Bhutto's economic reforms**

Bhutto came to power partly because he and his party advocated economic and social reform. Although before 1971 he had described his programme as socialistic, once he came to power he identified it as one based on "Islamic justice". His reforms were essentially a reaction to the socio-economic inequalities of the "decade of development".

The first major economic initiative of the Bhutto government was the nationalisation of thirty-one industrial units in January 1972 (*ibid.*, pp. 10–11). These industries included iron and steel, heavy engineering, heavy electrical goods, electricity plants and gas. Since consumer-goods industries were dominant in the economy, this policy took over less than 20 per cent of the value added of the large-scale manufacturing sector. Later, nationalisation of the vegetable oil industry and, in 1976, before the general elections, of ginning factories, rice husking and flour mills, scared off businessmen (Noman, 1988, pp. 75–6).

The nationalisation of thirty-three life insurance companies took place in March 1972 and in 1974 Pakistani banks were nationalised under the Banks Act. All these nationalisations were followed by compensation to former owners; the government announced its objective as one of breaking the link between industrial and financial capital which, it said, had led to the concentration of economic power in the hands of a few families. However, foreign companies operating in Pakistan were exempted from nationalisation (Ahmed and Amjad, 1984, p. 92).

In May 1972, on the advice of the IMF, the government devalued the rupee by 130 per cent and lifted import restrictions for over three hundred commodities. The devaluation of the rupee effectively eliminated the subsidy to industry (Gardezi and Rashid, 1983, p. 101). In addition, the government increased the procurement prices of agricultural goods by about 100 per cent, again in line with the new administration's objective of correcting the pro-industry bias of previous governments.

In March 1972, a land reform was introduced. The reform reduced the ceiling on irrigated land from 500 to 150 acres and on unirrigated land from 1,000 to 300 acres. The owners of resumed land were not compensated and the peasants received the land free. In 1977, the ceiling on land ownership was again reduced, to 100 and 200 acres for irrigated and unirrigated lands respectively. However, this time, due to religious pressure on the government, the owners of the resumed lands were compensated. Although the acreage of resumed lands was not substantial, the land reforms of the 1970s were more radical and more effective than previous ones. Besides land distribution, the government introduced measures to improve the condition of the peasantry. The ejection of tenants from their holdings by landlords was subjected to rigid controls. The share of the tenants' produce retained by landlords was also changed in favour of the peasants by making landlords responsible for the cost of inputs and taxes. However, the implementation of this measure was not effective due to the political upheavals of the mid-seventies (Ahmed and Amjad, 1984, pp. 124–8).

In the labour market, the government encouraged unionisation of the labour force, especially into PPP unions, and improved their bargaining position. Workers received benefits in the form of bonuses, cash receipts for profit participation and old-age pensions. Under a participation scheme, workers' representatives were to take part in decisions concerning hiring and firing and workers were given a share in the company's capital. Four per cent of net profits was to be set aside for this purpose. The labour code was also changed to provide greater job security and more medical insurance cover for workers.

Although quite how effective such measures were is disputable. In the period after 1973, the Bhutto government abandoned the use of a five-year plan in favour of annual plans; this was largely due to general international uncertainty and the government's suspicion of the Planning Commission's economic orientation towards Ayub's development strategy. The Commission had little control over the management of the economy except for the formulation of annual plans and the preparation of a five-year plan for 1977–82 which was revised by the Zia government (*ibid.*, pp. 57–8).

Economic management and performance in Bhutto's period can be divided into two phases: the recovery phase of 1972–73 and the stagflationary-cum-balance of payments squeeze phase of 1974–77. However, between 1970 and 1977, due mainly to the growth of services, public administration and defence sector expenditures, real GDP rose by an average of 4.2 per cent per year. Inflation remained a serious problem, but by 1977 was curbed to less than 10 per cent (Noman, 1988, pp. 84–8).

In the first phase of the 1971–77 period, devaluation of the rupee encouraged an export boom in raw material and consumer goods. The industrial sector also recovered from the shock of the secession of Bangladesh. Besides, the government's liberal commercial policies following devaluation increased the utilisation of capacity in industries. The balance of payments position improved and foreign exchange reserves increased in 1972–73. Agricultural output increased due to higher procurement prices for rice, wheat and sugar and the provision of an adequate supply of essential inputs.

However, inflation was still not under control despite the fact that the growth of monetary assets was equal to the growth of GNP. There was increased expenditure on the implementation of reforms, but the government's monetary and fiscal policy was cautious. Nevertheless, there was considerable monetary expansion after devaluation, largely as a result of the rise in export earnings.

In 1973–74, the inflation rate exceeded 30 per cent, due to the dramatic rise in the price of oil and related imported goods such as fertilisers and chemicals. The value of imports doubled while their volume did not change much, giving rise to a significant pressure on the balance of payments (Ahmed and Amjad, 1984, pp. 94–5).

The second phase (1974–77) started with the oil shock and an increase in government development expenditures on long-term projects. Political unrest, floods and the rising costs of government deficit financing adversely affected industrial and agricultural performance. Private industrial investment dropped due to the fear of nationalisation, and heavy rains led to severe flooding, destroying the cotton crops, vegetables and other crops, International recession also led to a decline in cotton exports and the cotton textile industry. The prospect of employment and higher incomes in rich Arab countries led to mass migration of Pakistanis to the Persian Gulf states. However, remittances by these workers did not cushion the balance of payments gap until 1977. Finally, mass movements against the government in spring 1977 disrupted the economic process and led to further decline in industrial output (*ibid.*, pp. 93–8).

In short, the economic performance of Pakistan in this period was greatly affected by socio-economic reforms, the oil shock and natural disasters. The reforms, some unprecedented in Pakistan's history, were always accompanied by an unnecessarily charged rhetoric against the rich, businessmen and large landlords. This combination gave rise to political tension and economic insecurity for the owners of land and capital.

Some Islamic parties and *ulama* accused Bhutto of implementing socialism in the name of Islam. In general, the reforms represented the programme of a middle class that had emerged during Ayub's rule. The reforms had a definite bias against the very rich in Pakistan and benefited modern farmers and well-to-do peasants, who gained access to more investment funds through the government's procurement price policy. Labour relations reforms raised the level of consciousness of workers and peasants about their economic rights. Workers' standards of living, measured by the index of real wages in large-scale manufacturing, improved. Increased government investment in capital goods, industries and infrastructural facilities laid the foundation for the post-1977 period of economic growth. However, the economic and social development programmes were too ambitious in relation to the available domestic and foreign resources, and the attitude of the PPP was too rigid, authoritarian and populistic to ensure their successful implementation. The reforms led to the expansion of government bureaucracy and unprofitable government firms; rising government deficit to cover the cost of the development programmes; and to the flight of capital (see Noman, 1988, pp. 74–111, Burki and La Porte, Jr., 1986, pp. 19–20 and 38)

## The rule of the military: 1978–90

### Zia's "Islamic order"

The rule of General Zia was the first truly military regime in Pakistan. Unlike the previous regimes, Zia's government depended solely on the military. However, the army had lost so much prestige and credibility during the 1971 war that if military rule was to have any legitimacy, Zia needed to present it as the ideological vanguard of an Islamic state. This process passed through three phases: in the first phase (1977–79) Zia consolidated his position and that of the military, outmanoeuvring the opposition parties by promising elections; in the second (1979–84), Zia ceased to pretend that his was an interim government, and by relying on martial law and the suppression of political opposition forces he managed to impose his Islamic Order; in the third phase (1984–88) the junta employed civilians in an administration dominated by the military and established a non-party political system.

The constitution of 1973 was not officially abrogated, but some of its clauses, including the clause prohibiting military rule, were violated. Zia declared that he was not responsible to anyone except Allah and he finally proclaimed himself president of Pakistan in September 1978 (Gardezi and Rashid, 1983, p. 95). In 1978, in order to broaden his government's base of support, he formed a council of sixteen advisers, consisting of generals, retired politicians and senior civil servants. His appointed cabinet included civilian ministers and members of the Jama'at-e Islami party. However, some conservative political parties chose not to co-operate and Zia turned towards the idea of the establishment of an Islamic economy and polity. In February 1979, when Islamic power was installed in Iran, he announced the enforcement of Islamic penal laws. *Zakat*, the Islamic tax, was introduced in July 1979, but only as a supplement to existing taxes. In January 1981, nationalised and foreign banks introduced interest-free banking. Then in 1983, another Islamic tax, *ushr*, was imposed on agricultural produce.

In May 1980, a federal *Shari'a* court replaced the *Shari'a* benches of the high courts. The Council of Islamic Ideology was expanded and reconstituted. The Council was also asked to draft an Islamic system of government and the *ulama* formulated a 21-point programme for the Islamisation process (al-Mujahid, 1989, p. 831). However, with these few measures, the government reached the limit of its commitment to Islamisation. Indeed, some members of the Council of Islamic Ideology resigned from the Council several years later because they doubted the seriousness of the government's intentions (Gardezi and Rashid, 1983, p. 92).

Zia amended several articles of the 1973 Constitution that conflicted with the arbitrary actions of martial law administrators. On 27 March 1981, he proclaimed a Provisional Constitutional Order (PCO), a step which was not accepted as constitutionally valid by the Lahore High Court. Suppression of political parties and the ruling of the Lahore court led to a new wave of political initiatives. The opposition set up a Movement for the Restoration of Democracy (MRD), which Zia promptly disbanded, but in reaction to demands for democratisation a mainly civilian cabinet was sworn in, and in December 1981 a 300-member federal council, the *majlis-e shura* was appointed. The leaders of the political parties opposed the *majlis* and demanded elections. However, these parties were weak and divided and Zia was determined to prevent the rise of a new broadly based political movement. By the end of 1983, his position was secure. In December 1984, Zia decided to hold a national referendum to legitimise his Islamic rule, asking for another five-year term as president. An eleven-party opposition alliance boycotted the poll, but two parties, the Pakistan Muslim League-Parago Group (PML-PG) and Jama'at-e Islami, supported the referendum. Zia campaigned in the name of Islam and received considerable support in rural areas, where participation was high. The government declared a 64 per cent turnout of voters and a 97.7 per cent "yes" vote for Zia. The result raised the confidence of the government; an election for national and provisional assemblies, on a non-party basis, was held. It was boycotted by the MRD. The PML-PG candidates, who participated in the election, received a majority in the national assembly (al- Mujahid, 1989, p. 832). After the election, Zia was sworn in as president and the 1973 Constitution was revised to grant extraordinary powers to the president. The newly appointed prime minister, a member of the PML-PG, pledged to work for an Islamic state, political liberalisation, the end of martial law and negotiation with the opposition. The newly elected assemblies also displayed some independence and demanded the lifting of martial law. On 30 December 1985, martial law and the state of emergency, originally imposed by Yahya Khan and continued by Bhutto and Zia, were lifted. Political parties increased their activities and Benazir Bhutto, the exiled leader of the PPP, returned to a tremendous welcome in Lahore. She demanded the ousting of Zia and called for national elections in the autumn of 1986. However, her call for mass country-wide demonstrations did not bring many people out onto the streets. As a result, she dropped the PPP's tactic of campaigning alone and agreed to co-operate with the MRD for a mid-term election. She also tried to accommodate the military by recognising their role in national life, but opposed their interference in politics. The MRD and especially the PPP held rallies in major cities. Clashes with the police ensued. In reaction to these events, in September 1987, Zia banned political parties from taking part in the local elections of November 1987. Local elections were held on a non-party basis, but all political parties took part. The government-backed PML-PG obtained a majority, benefiting from the economic recovery and the ineffective campaigning of the opposition parties. The PPP won only 20 per cent of the seats in the local elections; the party was split over Benazir Bhutto's autocratic leadership and her softening of the socialist tone of the party's rhetoric.

By May 1988, a conflict between Zia and the prime minister over the latter's opposition to Zia's foreign and national policies led to the dismissal of the national and provincial assemblies and the government. Zia claimed that he was concerned with the corruption and ineptness of the government and its inability to advance the Islamisation programme. However, he neither disbanded the Senate nor outlawed the activities of the political parties. Elections were promised and Zia, as president and acting head of the government, vowed to bring the economy, judiciary and education further in line with the *Shari'a*. However, Zia was killed in an air crash in August 1988 and the acting president and chairman of the Senate, Ghulam Ishaq Khan, declared a state of emergency. Khan announced that elections would be held as scheduled and that he would follow Zia's Islamisation policies.

One month after Zia's death, the High Court in Lahore found the dissolution of assemblies by Zia illegal and unconstitutional, and ruled that new elections should be held in November 1988. At the same time the Supreme Court ruled in favour of Benazir Bhutto's constitutional petition concerning the right of the political parties to participate in the next election. Nine Islamic and conservative parties, including different factions of the PML and the Jama'at-e Islami, came together to found the Islamic Democratic Alliance (IDA) to oppose the MRD. In November 1988, the PPP won more than 90 of the 205 seats in the National Assembly, while the IDA obtained only 54 seats. Benazir Bhutto formed a coalition government with the help of the MRD parties and in December 1988 was sworn in as prime minister, the first woman to become the head of the government in an Islamic country (al-Mujahid, 1989, pp. 833–5).

Benazir Bhutto had campaigned on a progressive platform. She had pledged to improve the lives of the rural poor and reduce corruption. Once in office, however, she avoided any controversial legislation and corruption remained as rampant as ever. Ethnic violence grew in Kashmir and in Sind, her home province, where the army was not allowed to act. The military were displeased by her intervention in their affairs. The *ulama* were against her too. She suspended certain legal procedures based on the *Shari'a*, including the severing of hands or ears for robbery and the counting of a woman's testimony in court as worth half that of a man's. She obstructed the *ulama*'s demands that women be forced to wear an opaque robe or veil and she released women who had been detained for Islamic offences. In 1989, the United Council of *Ulama* questioned her faith. The Council's spokesman stated that if 'somebody doesn't like our laws, our society, our beliefs, ... she doesn't deserve to be prime minister' (quoted in *Newsweek*, 6 August 1990). In the summer of 1990, Islamic parties sponsored a bill in the Senate, where they had a majority, to reimpose the amputation of hands as a criminal punishment. The bill also demanded the total elimination of interest rates; even under Zia, Pakistan had continued to pay interest on the national debt. In addition, the bill demanded the establishment of an Islamic commission to oversee the media. More importantly, the bill made the Assembly subservient to the *Shari'a* court. A poll by Gallup Pakistan showed that 64 per cent of voters supported the bill and only 8 per cent opposed it (*ibid.*). On 6 August 1990, Bhutto was dismissed by President Ishaq Khan on the grounds of governmental corruption and nepotism. Her political rival, Ghulam Mustafa Jatoui, a former PPP member and a recent leader of the opposition, was sworn in as caretaker prime minister. A state of emergency was declared and elections were promised for October 1990 (*International Herald Tribune*, 7 August 1990).

In the October elections, the Islamic Democratic Alliance won a majority of the votes for the National Assembly and the Assembly elected one of the country's twenty richest businessmen, Nawaz Sharif, as prime minister by a majority of 153 to 39. Sharif's electoral campaign called for "industrial revolution", Islamisation of all laws, privatisation and deregulation of the economy, cleaning up the government and respect for the role of the military in Pakistan (*Le Monde, Bilan Economique, 1991*, p. 123).

**Islamisation of the economy under Zia**

The most important economic event of the period was the introduction of Islamic economic reforms. To legitimise military rule, Zia asked the Council of Islamic Ideology (CII) to study and submit a report on an Islamic restructuring of the economy (*Nizam-e Mustafa*). He also required that this task be completed within three years, in time for the restoration of democracy. These measures were popular with the Jama'at-e Islami and other parties of the PNA who had supported the military takeover. However, the *ulama* were less enthusiastic about socio-economic reforms. They were content with uncontroversial reforms concerning the observance of prayers, Islamic punishment codes, etc. In fact, when the CII, with the help of experts in the Central Bank and the Ministry of Finance, devised an economic plan, the *ulama* made no concrete proposals and were generally muted in their praise for government measures. In the Islamisation of the economy, as in the founding of Pakistan, the *ulama* played a very minor role. (Neinhaus, 1987, p. 43).

The Islamisation programme submitted by the CII in March and November 1978 demanded the restructuring of the banking sector and taxation system. The former was designed to eliminate interest rates from all financial transactions, while the latter concerned the introduction of *zakat* and *ushr* as Islamic taxes. (Alkazaz, 1987, p. 65). Debate also took place about the possibility of financing the budget deficit without interest-bearing government borrowing. However, these discussions did not lead to any concrete change and Zia's government continued to pay interest on national and international debts.

In February 1979, Zia emphasised the necessity of the imposition of *zakat* and *ushr*, and in June 1980, after a year and a half of discussions, the *Zakat* and *Ushr* Ordinance was introduced. The nationalised banks immediately imposed a 2.5 per cent levy on all savings deposits. Shi'ites, who constitute more than 20 per cent of the population, were critical. They feared that the introduction of the *Shari'a* according to Sunni interpretation would impose a Sunni hegemony. In addition, they claimed that a Sunni government could not demand *zakat* from Shi'ites (Nayak, 1985, p. 94). There was also general resentment that no exemptions were available to the poor. Public protest led to a change of the ordinance in October 1980; the 2.5 per cent *zakat* levy became applicable to all institutional savings of 1,000 rupees and above held for at least one year and Shi'ites were exempted from the tax (Neinhaus, 1987, p. 44. Ahmed and Amjad, 1984, p. 103. Noman, 1988, p. 146).

In 1983, the government imposed *ushr* on certain agricultural incomes at the rate of 5 per cent of the crop yield. A 25 per cent deduction of the taxable yield was allowed to cover depreciation. However, the actual calculation of *ushr,* and of the *zakat* due on physical and financial assets not held in banks, was left to the individual.

The *zakat* payments were to be put into a *Zakat* Fund which was organised on a hierarchical regional basis under the direction of the Central *Zakat* Fund. Local *zakat* committees were set up, comprising eight members, seven of whom were directly elected by the people. These committees could decide on the use of funds for the poor and the needy. Saudi Arabia also provided money for the *Zakat* Fund and took part in the working committees that were to define the procedures for the Islamisation of the economy (Noman, 1988, p. 150).

In 1982, total *zakat* collection was Rs 815 million (or 0.2 per cent of the GNP), and per-capita distribution Rs 40 per month (Ahmed and Amjad, 1984, p. 103; Noman, 1988, p. 150). The sums collected and distributed have to date been small, but the institution has been favourably received by the population.

In November 1978, a panel of economists and bankers was appointed by the CII to study the question of interest rates. They submitted an interim report for a phased approach to the Islamisation of the financial sector, and the CII included its own recommendations. Finally, in June 1980, the completed report was presented to the government (Ahmed, Iqbal and Fahim Khan, 1983, p. 8). By then the government had already started to implement some of the recommendations of the interim report (*ibid.*, pp. 201–11; Neinhaus, 1987, p. 46).

In July 1979, interest was eliminated from the operations of three investment-financing institutions: the National Investment (Unit) Trust, the House

Building Finance Corporation and the Mutual Funds of the Investment Corporation of Pakistan, which functions as an equity investment company and issuing bank. Later, interest-free loans to fishermen and farmers cultivating subsistence holdings (*qarz al-hassana*) were introduced and both the Investment Corporation of Pakistan and the Small Business Corporation started to apply the interest-free loan principle.

In January 1981, special departments were set up in all five nationalised commercial banks to handle deposits on Profit and Loss Sharing (PLS) accounts (*musharaka*). In these accounts, depositors would not receive interest, but would participate in the profit or loss of the bank's transactions in interest-free assets such as export bills, inland bills, import bills and government commodity operations. Provision was made for the introduction of interest-free loans (*qarz al-hassana*) by commercial banks to students. In addition, a government ordinance was introduced to enable the establishment of *muzaraba* companies. Such companies could issue specific and general-purpose *muzaraba* certificates and invest the funds for purposes permitted by the *Shari'a*. Another scheme was introduced for issuing Participation Term Certificates (PTCs), intended to replace debentures as a means of corporate financing. The holders of the transferable and negotiable PTCs share in the profit or loss of the companies instead of receiving interest, as in the case of debentures (Third Pakistan ..., 1982, pp. 228–9). The Investment Corporation of Pakistan and the National Investment Trust offered a PTC with a five to ten year maturity to replace conventional bonds with fixed interest. This scheme reflected the Islamic principle of risk-sharing between borrowers and lenders and enabled companies to raise capital using their fixed assets as collateral. Commercial banks were also allowed to finance housing on a rent-sharing basis which operates along similar lines to the policy introduced by the House Building Finance Corporation. In this system, the Corporation finances construction of houses and apartments on a co-ownership basis and receives a share of the rent in proportion to its share of investment.

To encourage people to hold PLS accounts with the commercial banks, part of the profits were exempted from income tax. The Central Bank promulgated a list of about ten different types of financing compatible with the *Shari'a* in the areas of trade and investment finance, including the purchase and discount of trade bills, leasing and hire-purchase transactions, PLS and profit-sharing securities (*muzaraba* certificates). Where profit-sharing was not feasible, the banks would grant interest-free credit and levy charges, fixed by the Central Bank, to cover administrative costs. Such loans did not come from the bank's own funds, but from other lenders, especially the state. These credits were mainly used to finance exports.

The State Bank, i.e. the Central Bank, was enabled to provide finance against PTCs, to grant advances against promissory notes supported by PTC *Muzaraba* Certificates, and to provide funds to financial institutions on a basis other than interest. Cash reserve requirements and liquidity ratio requirements have also continued to apply to the PLS liabilities of the banks. However, for the purpose of the liquidity ratio requirement, liquid assets included funds placed by banks in a separate account with the State Bank on a profit and loss sharing basis (*ibid.*, pp. 230–38). In addition, the discount rate mechanism was replaced, empowering the Central Bank to alter the profit-sharing ratios (Ahmed, Iqbal and Fahim Khan, 1983, p. 115).

Until 1985, banks could operate either an interest-paying or the Islamic system; since April 1985, the Islamic modes of operation have become obligatory. In addition, since 1985, the Islamisation of financial and deposit operations has been applied to foreign banks in Pakistan, although transactions with foreign creditors have been exempted from the prohibition on interest payment. In view of the fact that many development projects are financed by foreign credits and that Pakistan has foreign liabilities of more than $15 billion, this exemption represents a huge breach in the Islamisation of the financial system.

In the period 1981–85, when banks could operate within either system, the share of profit-sharing deposits (PLS) grew to about 35 per cent of all deposits and the holders of such deposits received more "profits" than holders of interest-based deposits. The government granted income tax exemptions for annual earnings from these deposits up to Rs 5,000 and the banks explicitly and implicitly guaranteed their depositors a minimum rate of return, comparable to interest rates and supported by extensive government deposits. Between 1981 and 1985, the rate of profit fluctuated between 7 and 15.5 per cent for short- and long-term PLS deposits. The *ulama* find the guaranteed positive return questionable from an Islamic perspective since *a priori* it excludes any losses to the depositors.

Since 1985, the returns on PLS deposits have declined, due to a lack of investment experience on the part of banks, high transaction costs, security surcharges and market reaction to the banks' frequent surplus liquidity. A large share of national savings are still held in National Savings Centres based on interest payment. Suggestions that the calculation of "profits" on these accounts should be based on the growth rate of the economy and the rate of inflation have not been implemented (Alkazaz, 1987, pp. 77 and 81). In fact, the *ulama* and the CII have been against the indexation of loans and accounts, arguing that such allowances are not permissible under the *Shari'a*, which treats currency transactions like all other transactions in so far as lending and borrowing are concerned (Ahmed, Iqbal and Fahim Khan, 1983, p. 116).

Banks have had little success in transforming their conventional asset base into an Islamic one which favours the *musharaka* (profit and loss sharing) and direct equity investment schemes in Islamic finance. In practice, banks have adopted methods that only formally avoid using interest rates to finance domestic and foreign trade and investment. In June 1984, about 87 per cent of PLS funds were used for trade purposes, compared to 8 per cent for equity investment and only 3 per cent for *musharaka* (Alkazaz, 1987, pp. 78–82). Furthermore, many loans have been granted through buy-back agreements in which banks buy a client's assets for a fixed period and the client agrees to buy these assets back from the bank at a higher price. Mark-up, mark-down (discounting) and buy-back are all considered controversial business practices from the Sunni perspective, since they oblige the client to buy back the assets at a higher price or to accept the goods under any condition. The *Shari'a* does not even find the PTC wholly acceptable. This profit-sharing, fixed-term, tax-free bond is discountable in stock exchange dealings and allows for a portion of company profits as a percentage of the PTC.

The limited use of *musharaka*, *muzaraba* and PTCs by banks and their clients has not led to a fundamental restructuring of the banks' assets. Banks do not care for profit-sharing schemes because they are unable to predict their return in advance, while clients dislike them because they fear bank interference in the management of their businesses (*ibid.*). Consequently, a complex system has been set up to charge interest to borrowers and to pay it to lenders, using an Islamic nomenclature on which even the *ulama* and Muslim economists cannot agree.

The first economic change introduced by the Zia government was the gradual denationalisation of industries to restore the private sector's confidence. This measure was justified under the theme of Islamisation of the economy and the protection of private property according to the *Shari'a*. On 2 September 1977, the government denationalised small-scale agro-based industries such as rice-husking, flour-milling, cotton ginning and some small-scale engineering enterprises. However, denationalisation of large industries and the banking system met with the opposition of the unions and the middle classes. Therefore, most large industries and the nationalised commercial banks remained under government ownership. For this reason, the business community kept its distance from the government and major business houses turned to traditional mercantile activities where profits were high and there was no fear of nationalisation (Nayak, 1985, pp. 83–4). To encourage private investment in industries, a tax holiday was introduced in March 1978 in some less developed regions. In addition, concessions on import duties and income taxes were offered, compensatory rebates on the export of some industrial goods introduced and interest rates on fixed investment in industry and agriculture reduced. An export processing zone was also set up to attract foreign investment. Nevertheless, private investment was slow to respond and for several years increased only nominally. In 1978–80, the level of private investment in total gross fixed investment was still less than half of the public sector's investment, compared to 1969–70 when it was twice that of government investment (Ahmed and Amjad, 1984, pp. 100–101).

Under Zia, the ad hoc planning of the Bhutto period was replaced by greater technocracy and the sixth five-year plan was drafted for 1983–88 (*ibid.*, p. 58). This plan emphasised the role of the private sector in industry and identified as its priorities education, rural development, energy development and employment. The plan envisaged an average annual GDP growth rate of 4.5 per cent, which was in fact surpassed (Gilani, 1989, p. 841). In addition, the growth of domestic income was greater than official rates suggested, due to the increase in illegal drug production and remittances from migrants abroad. The annual value of the trade in drugs, which is not included in official statistics, is estimated to be 8 per cent of GNP. In addition, in 1984, remittances from abroad constituted 40 per cent of foreign-exchange earnings, or a further 8 per cent of

GNP. Thus, despite the reversal of the nationalisation of industries and the land reforms of the previous period, distribution of income in this period actually became more equitable (Noman, 1988, pp. 157–65).

However, inflationary pressures persisted, at an average of 8.1 per cent per year in the period 1980–85, and the level of deficit financing remained high, the trade gap continued to widen. More importantly, domestic savings had declined to 5.4 per cent of GDP by 1984 (Ahmed and Amjad, 1984, pp. 99–100).

By 1987, despite a 6.5 per cent growth in GDP, the structural problems of the economy had worsened. The government budget deficit was about 9 per cent of GNP, and military expenditure and the servicing of foreign debt accounted for 26 and 30 per cent respectively of total government expenditure. Transfers from migrant workers were declining and investment was stagnant due to the decrease in savings. In such a situation, the World Bank and the IMF made their loans conditional on fiscal austerity, and the US government suspended its aid package to Pakistan because of Pakistan's refusal to approve the non-proliferation treaty and allow an international body to inspect its nuclear capacity (*Le Monde, Bilan Economique, 1987*, p. 118).

During Benazir Bhutto's premiership the economic situation worsened. The government refused to implement the World Bank and IMF austerity proposals, which led to the freezing of a $200 million loan. However, the US government agreed in principle to renew its aid commitment to Pakistan. In the meantime the budget deficit was again on the rise and the government's development projects became yet more dependent on international finance. GNP growth slowed to 5 per cent while inflation stood at more than 10 per cent. By the end of the 1980s, Pakistan's international debt was more than $15 billion, or 40 per cent of Pakistan's GNP, and debt services constituted 45 per cent of total government expenditure (*Le Monde, Bilan Economique, 1990*, p. 120).

## Islam and the constitution

The debate over whether Pakistan should be an Islamic or secular state has been reflected in the country's constitution.

As noted before, Islamic ideology and symbols were used as a mobilising and unifying force in Pakistan's independence movement, but there was no consensus about their content or application. After independence, two clear tendencies on the role of Islam in the state can be identified. The first advocated a traditional Islamic state based on the *Shari'a* that would apply its laws to all aspects of life. This tendency was supported by the *ulama* and certain groups such as Jama'at-e Islami. The second, represented by the bureaucracy, the military and most of the leaders of the Muslim League, demanded a modern Muslim state, based on Western civil and political rights with a secular content. However, neither tendency had a clear blueprint or a definite model. Thus, the task of drafting a constitution was formidable and the Constituent Assembly, which was charged with its formulation, was very slow in its work.

In 1949, the Assembly came up with the Objective Resolution, a mixture of modern and traditional views. Modernist Muslims saw in the Resolution the sovereignty of the people, while the traditionalists interpreted it as the sovereignty of God. The Resolution laid out the principles on the basis of which the constitution could be drafted. It underlined the Sovereignty of Allah "that will be exercised in Pakistan by the people as His sacred trust"; it stated that "the rights and legitimate interests of the minorities are to be protected and minorities are free to profess and practise their religion"; it asserted that the principles "of democracy, freedom, equality, tolerance and social justice as enunciated by Islam, are to be fully observed" (Mahmood, 1973, p. 25).

However, the 1953 anti-Ahmadiya riots in Punjab encouraged the traditionalists to press for a more Islamic constitution. This eventually led the Assembly to form a committee to study Islamic teachings on constitutional provisions of an Islamic state and to lay down the qualifications of an Islamic head of state.

Finally, in March 1956, the Constitution of Pakistan was approved. It established a parliamentary form of government and a federal Islamic Republic of two provinces, East and West Pakistan. However, the constitution was an eclectic compromise of traditionalist and modernist outlooks. It embodied many aspects of a secular state, but included several Islamic provisions. Islam was not proclaimed the state religion, but people's sovereignty was qualified by subordinating it to that of Allah. The state was to be the Islamic Republic of Pakistan based upon Islamic principles and no law was to be promulgated contrary to the Qur'an and the *Sunna* of the Prophet. There were also clauses in the constitution for the establishment of the proper organisation of the *zakat*, removal of interest rates and bringing all laws in accordance with the Qur'an and the *Sunna*. Pakistan was declared an Islamic Republic, but was not transformed into an "Islamic State" in the strict sense of the term. Thus, according to the Constitution it was not the *Shari'a* and its application by qualified *ulama*, but Parliament that was responsible for legislation.

The traditionalists, such as Maududi, approved the constitution, interpreting it according to their own ideals, while the modernists were content that it was so imprecise about the Islamic character of the state. In short, the constitution reflected the lack of consensus on the Islamic versus the secular nature of the state which still remains an important source of ideological discord.

In June 1962, after obtaining a "mandate" by referendum, Ayub Khan promulgated a new constitution. Ayub Khan wanted a more centralised national government, with more executive and legislative power for the president and a liberal approach to the question of Islam in Pakistan's politics. The new constitution dropped the word "Islamic" from the official name of the republic and omitted the phrase requiring laws to conform with the Qur'an and the *Sunna*. However, in 1963, bowing to public pressure under the leadership of the *ulama*, the 1962 Constitution was amended: the word "Islamic" was restored to Pakistan's official title; the Advisory Council of Islamic Ideology was formally given the function of bringing existing laws into conformity with the Qur'an and the *Sunna*; and the Islamic Research Institute was commissioned to study the role of Islam in modern Pakistan (Mahmood, 1973, pp. 30–31).

In April 1973, Pakistan had a third constitution, approved by all political parties in the National Assembly. However, in drafting the new constitution, the modernists, including Bhutto, capitulated before the *ulama* on several points. Although Bhutto had talked about Islamic socialism when he first came to power, he remained basically a secularist, illustrated by his slogan: "Islam is our faith, Democracy is our policy". The first draft of the new constitution contained the term "Islamic socialism". The *ulama* and all the Islamic parties, including the Jama'at-e Islami of Maududi, vehemently opposed its use. Bhutto capitulated, and the 1973 Constitution declared that Pakistan would be a democratic state based on "social justice, as enunciated by Islam" (quoted in Mahmood, 1973, p. 43). Furthermore, the text of the oath of office for the president and prime minister clearly spelled out the belief that Mohammad was the last messenger of Allah (Esposito, 1980, p. 150).

The 1973 Constitution explicitly declared Islam as the state religion. It also contained more provision than before to ensure the conformity of laws and civil rights with the Qur'an and the *Sunna*. More importantly, a fundamental error from the Islamic point of view regarding the delegation of authority by Allah to Man was corrected in the 1973 Constitution to limit the legislative power of Man: "sovereignty over the entire universe belongs to Almighty Allah alone and the authority to be exercised by the people of Pakistan within the limits prescribed by Him, is a sacred trust ..." (quoted in Mahmood, 1973, p. 43).

The new constitution not only gave the Council of Islamic Ideology the function of giving religious opinion, but also required it to submit a report recommending steps for the implementation of Islamic injunctions, and to make suggestions for bringing all laws into conformity with the *Shari'a* (*ibid.*, pp. 414–16).

As regards the collection and disbursement of *zakat* and the elimination of interest, the new constitution, like the previous ones, was not explicit: it only stated that efforts would be made to realise these objectives (*ibid.*, p. 140).

When Zia came to power, he introduced the idea of completing the Islamisation of Pakistan. In December 1984, when all political parties were banned and the dissidents were silenced, Zia announced a referendum to seek popular approval of his policies and the establishment of an Islamic Order which, despite its approval by the population, was still controversial. In fact, in March 1985, in a speech in the newly elected National Assembly, Zia himself admitted that he had not been able to introduce an Islamic system in the economy and polity of Pakistan (Neinhaus, 1987, p. 42). Thus, after more than four decades in quest of an Islamic society and economy, Pakistan is still in search of them.

# 6. Islamic Economy According to the Saudi-Wahhabi Interpretation

Saudi Arabia is the oldest Islamic fundamentalist state of the modern world. The national flag carries the Islamic *shahada*, the Qur'anic statement of faith, and the sword of the House of Saud, symbolising the religious-political alliance and interdependence of Wahhabi Islam and the polity of the Saud family. This is despite the Sunni belief that kingship and hereditary power are not sanctioned by Islam. The Islam of Abd al-Wahhab has been used as the most important legitimising force for the al-Saud's dynastic rule. However, since the formation of the Saudi Arabian state in 1934, the balance between the House of Saud and the Wahhabi *ulama* has gradually shifted in favour of the al-Saud, even though the *ulama* still enjoy more power and prestige in Saudi Arabia than in any other Sunni country. This long process has gone through different stages associated with different Saudi Kings and their timid reforms, combining ideological conservatism with pragmatism when they have confronted pressure from within and without the kingdom.

## The origin and foundation of the Saudi state

In 1934 much of the tribal society of the Arabian Peninsula was finally united into a single patrimonial monarchy under the rule of King Abdul Aziz al-Saud. However, the origin of the kingdom goes back to an alliance between Shaykh Muhammad-ibn Abd al-Wahhab, spiritual leader, and Muhammad-ibn Saud, a political-military chieftain.

Abd al-Wahhab's Islamic doctrine has been the unifying force that has extended the scope of the Saudi State beyond the narrow confines of a single tribe. In about 1740, Wahhab preached a return to the basic principles of Islam in the Qur'an and the *Sunna*. His teachings were based on the Hanbali Islamic school of law and Ibn Taymiya (Esposito, 1980, p. 132). He was vehemently against mysticism and all signs of polytheism, which he believed to be prevalent in the way Muslims of the day invoked the name of the Prophet in their prayers, and built, visited and worshipped holy shrines. In his opinion, the accepted interpretation of the Qur'an was heretical and he insisted that Muslims observe an extremely strict moral code, which included obligatory public prayers, the payment of *zakat*, and a total ban on smoking, the use of rosary beads and luxuries. He was against all the kinds of communal and mystical Islam that would prevent Islam from becoming a guide for social action in Arabia. He considered that tribal traditions, mores and structures were a restraining factor in this process; his emphasis on God's absoluteness allowed a higher form of authority beyond the tribal association, facilitating the formation of a unified

Islamic society (Islami and Kavoussi, 1984, p. 7). Politically and religiously, he rejected the legitimacy of the Ottoman Sultans. Abd al-Wahhab allied himself with Muhammad-ibn Saud, who ruled in Najd and thus became the temporal defender of the Wahhabi doctrine (Lackner, 1978, pp. 10–11).

The coalition of tribes led by the military power of the al-Saud, armed with the puritanical ideology of Wahhabism, produced a single authority in a large part of the peninsula. The area was divided into twenty regions governed by Wahhabi faithfuls. Each region collected the taxes assessed by the ruler and levied troops. Major decisions were taken by the al-Saud ruler in consultation with the leaders of allied tribes.

The occupation of Hejaz, the site of Mecca and Medina, by al-Saud in the early nineteenth century led to the expedition of the viceroy of Egypt, Muhammad Ali, against the Wahhabis. Muhammad Ali was asked by the Ottoman Sultan to reconquer Hejaz. In 1814 the Egyptians entered Hejaz victoriously and in 1818 the al-Saud ruler was beheaded in Constantinople.

By 1843, Najd was again reunited under al-Saud rule. Even though Najd fell to the al-Saud in 1843, by the end of the nineteenth century the rival al-Rashid family conquered Najd and its capital Riyadh. During this period, Hejaz was under the control of the Ottoman Empire and the rest of the peninsula was under varying degrees of British control. The al-Saud family accepted the protection of Shaykh Mubarak and went into exile in Kuwait (*ibid*., pp. 11–13).

At the beginning of the twentieth century, the Saudi tribe, under the leadership of Abdul Aziz and with the support of the ruler of Kuwait, ruled over the eastern region and Najd. After the First World War, due to the weakness of the Ottoman Empire and subsequent to the withdrawal of British protection from the western regime including Hejaz, the Saudis brought the eastern and western regions under their control. In his rise to power, Abdul Aziz effectively used the service of a political-religious-military force called the Ikhwan (the Brotherhood). The Ikhwan, a force of tens of thousands of warriors, were members of different tribes who were to fight for the purification of Islam under the banner of Wahhabism. Abdul Aziz had urged their settlement in agricultural communities as militia loyal to him. However, their loyalty to the Saudis was not always guaranteed due to their fanatical Wahhabist outlook and their extreme anti-modernist orientation. By the mid-1920s, they were openly disobeying Abdul Aziz because of his conciliatory policy towards the British “infidels”. Their challenge finally led to their complete suppression by 1930 (Esposito, 1980, pp. 124–5).

In 1927, Abdul Aziz was the King of Hejaz and Najd and by 1930 the contemporary borders of Saudi Arabia were defined. Finally, in 1934 Abdul Aziz proclaimed himself King of Saudi Arabia, a state that was named after the ruling family and was conceived as its property. The King ruled in consultation with his advisors. Provinces were ruled separately, not on the basis of a central administration but according to allegiances. Local governors were appointed from the Saudi family or allied families and the structure of local government was based on tribal hierarchies. The Saudi family was the strongest among a large group of tribal leaders, all of whom had become dependent on the King who subsidised them. In fact, since Abdul Aziz had obtained international recognition of his rule in the region, all income of the land was in his hands.

The Qur'an and the other sources of the *Shari'a* were considered as the constitution of the state. The law was interpreted and applied by the Wahhabi *ulama* based on the Hanbali's somewhat rigid school of Islamic law, which adheres to the Qur'an, the *Sunna* and the *hadith*. However, it is flexible concerning issues not covered by these scriptures, for which it accepts *ijtihad*, or independent reasoning, and the rulings of other recognised schools in cases of "public well-being" (*maslaha*). Thus, the Wahhabi *ulama* accepted changes in their interpretation of the law as long as they did not concern something that was expressly forbidden. In 1945, when Saudi Arabia joined the UN, it refused to sign the Universal Declaration of Human Rights on the pretext that the Qur'an was the constitution of the land and covered all rights (Lackner, 1978, p. 89).

The King was regarded as the guardian of Islam and was supposed to maintain Islamic values in the community and throughout the world as a true Wahhabist. However, he had to persuade the *ulama* to accept change and innovation. After all, he needed the *ulama* to give legitimacy to his regime. For example, Abdul Aziz used the Qur'an and traditional texts to justify the use of modern inventions. Photography was accepted by the *ulama* as "the bringing together of light and shadow, both divine creations ... despite the idolatry of pictorial art" (Esposito, 1980, p. 132). The use of radios was legitimised by arranging for a demonstration of reading the Qur'an on air and proving to the *ulama* that it was the faithful transmission of the words of Allah. In 1944, when some of the *ulama* and *shaykhs* were denouncing the King for selling Muslim land to the unbelieving Americans, the King summoned the *ulama* and the dissident brothers to the court and, after citing several cases in which the Prophet employed non-Muslims, asked for, and received, approval of his decision (*ibid*., p. 134).

In the late 1930s, Saudi Arabia's economy was a fragmented one based on nomadism, which dominated, sedentary agriculture, found in the oasis, and trade in a few cities in the western province of Hejaz. There was virtually no physical infrastructure, and industry consisted of only a few traditional handicrafts. Agricultural activity was quite primitive and herding dominated the life of nomads. There were a number of foreign bank offices and trading houses in Jeddah. The trading community in Hejaz was the only local modern sector that had a liberal culture compared to the dominant puritanical Wahhabism of the rest of the country. In fact, Abdul Aziz did not enforce Wahhabi rules on the use of tobacco in Hejaz due to the revenues it brought him (Lackner, 1978, p. 29).

The main problem of King Abdul Aziz was the financial crisis of the 1930s and early 1940s. State income was small. The pilgrimage and trading resources of Hejaz were providing an annual income of only £5 million. However, the world depression in 1931 led to heavy losses in pilgrimage revenues, partly made up by the USSR, which considered the King an anti-imperialist monarch. Considering the total absence of budgeting, the careless spending of the King and the subsistence nature of the economy, something had to be done. Thus, in

1933, the King granted an oil concession to Standard Oil of California (Socal) for a £50,000 gold down payment, which solved the state's immediate problem. Socal received a sixty-year concession for all of Saudi Arabia's oil. The company agreed to build a refinery, supply the government with 200,000 gallons of gasoline and 100,000 gallons of kerosene annually, and advance loans that would be deductible from future royalties. The royalties were fixed at 4 gold shillings per ton of crude oil. In 1933, Texaco acquired a 50 per cent share in Socal and in 1944 the name of the company changed to Arabian-American Oil Company (Aramco). After the Second World War, Aramco's need to increase its capital for new operations led to a new consortium, composed of Socal (30 per cent), Texaco (30 per cent), Standard Oil of New Jersey (30 per cent) and Mobil (10 per cent).

In 1938, the first oil discovery was made and oil production started in the Eastern Province of Saudi Arabia. By 1940, Socal and Texaco were producing 5 million barrels per year (Johany, Berne and Nixon, Jr., 1986, pp. 30–37).

In the latter part of the 1930s, oil exploration had little impact on the Saudi economy. Oil companies imported all they needed from the US and employed locals only rarely, and then on short-term contracts. However, with the expansion of the oil industry after the Second World War, local employment increased and the oil companies set up training programmes under government pressure. Some merchant families became rich by acting as agents for the oil companies (Lackner, 1978, pp. 35 and 118).

During the Second World War, due to the drastic decline in pilgrimage taxes and the fall of oil output, the Saudi Arabian government was again in financial crisis. The King needed $10 million per year and asked for a $6 million advance on royalties from the oil companies. The companies did not want to commit themselves, but persuaded the US government to grant the loan. The US government asked the UK to pay the sum out of its $425 million lend-lease loan (*ibid.*, p. 36). In 1941 and 1942, the British government provided $17 million. However, in 1943, due to the regional rivalry of the US and the British governments, Washington declared that the defence of Saudi Arabia was vital to the defence of the US and Saudi Arabia became eligible for lend-lease aid. By 1947, Abdul Aziz received about $100 in US aid and the US military constructed one of its largest air bases outside the US at Dhahran, near the oil wells (Halliday, 1975, pp. 62–3).

Oil production rose dramatically after the end of the war and by 1950 Aramco was producing about 200 million barrels per year (Johany, Berne and Nixon, Jr., pp. 32–7). The income of the Saudi government rose, but the government had no control over oil operation and production and was only receiving a royalty of 21 cents per barrel. This situation led, in December 1950, to an amendment to the original concession. Now Aramco paid the government one-half of its gross income as a tax so that Aramco could deduct it from its tax payment in the US, which effectively reduced its US tax nearly to zero. As a result, the Saudi government's oil revenues increased from $39.2 million in 1949 to $111.7 million in 1950 (Lackner, 1978, p. 38).

## The period of misrule and profligacy: 1953–64

In 1953, King Abdul Aziz died and his son, Saud, succeeded him. Just like the previous period under King Saud, Saudi Arabia was governed by the tradition of personal rule with the assistance of non-Saudi Arab advisers. However, in this period, a Council of Ministers was established, chaired by the King and vice-chaired by his brother, Faisal, who was also Minister of Foreign Affairs and Crown Prince. The Council had only an advisory role and all its members were appointed by the King.

The King's whim controlled the budget, which was published for the first time in 1954. Saud had an extravagant life style. He built himself several palaces at great cost and generously handed out gifts to tribal leaders during his frequent travels throughout the country in order to retain their support. Besides gifts, tribal leaders' loyalty to the Saudi family was bought by subsidies, themselves financed by the rise in oil revenues. A limited amount of the oil revenues was also spent on infrastructure, especially in the oil industry, and projects such as schools and hospitals.

In the early 1950s, the number of Egyptian professionals and military advisors increased, while many male children of the Saudi family were having their secondary education in Egypt. Thus, Nasserist Arab nationalism spread, and combined with increasing conspicuous consumption by the ruling family, aroused a reaction among the Wahhabi religious authorities. To reduce the worries of the *ulama*, in 1955 Saud issued a decree that forbade sending children to schools abroad. In addition, the role of the Public Morality Committees (religious police) expanded in order to enforce the Wahhabi civil norms.

In the mid-1950s, the kingdom was in the grip of financial crisis and political contradiction. The extravagant and spontaneous expenditures of Saud and his family reduced the gold and foreign currency reserves drastically. The market value of the Saudi Rial dropped to half its official value and the public debt increased. In the meantime, oil revenues were falling since Aramco was reducing its production in Saudi Arabia. Saud asked for advances on royalties and the completion of royal projects by the company. Aramco refused the demand by claiming that the price of oil was falling. The company also persuaded other international institutions not to grant loans to Saudi Arabia. As a result, the government was unable to pay the contractors, and salaries of government employees were paid irregularly. In 1956, oil workers went on strike over work conditions in Dhahran. Strikes and demonstrations that followed the government's renewal of the lease for the US air base in Dhahran interrupted oil operation for several weeks. Saud reacted with force and a large number of workers and Arab nationalists who were involved in the demonstrations were imprisoned. Nevertheless, the unrest forced Aramco to adopt a more conciliatory labour policy and accept some of the demands of the workers. About 60 per cent of the workers, mostly unskilled, were from South Asia, and the intermediate staff from Palestine, India and Pakistan (*ibid.*, p. 95).

Saud's misrule and profligacy and the rise of Nasserism led the more modern-minded factions of the ruling family in the Council of Senior Princes to hand executive power to Saud's more cautious and efficient brother, Amir Faisal. In this move, the Saudi princes had the blessing of the *ulama* and the US government. Faisal became prime minister in 1958.

Faisal's first step was to introduce financial reform and an austerity budget proposed by the International Monetary Fund and the International Bank for Reconstruction and Development. Financial balances were re-established and by the end of 1959 gold and foreign exchange reserves increased, inflation was curbed and the government paid off its debt to the Central Bank.

Faisal also cut part of the allowances of the royal family. King Saud took advantage of this situation and opportunistically allied himself with liberal Arab nationalist princes, like Talal-ibn Abdul Aziz, and discontented tribal leaders. This alliance led to the return of Saud as prime minister in 1960. Talal was appointed to a ministry and a commoner, Tariqi, who played an important role in the formation of OPEC, became minister of finance and petroleum. At first, Saud promised political reform, including a constitution. The proposed Islamic constitution included an elected/appointed parliament; a mixed economy that would recognise the existence of trade unions; equal rights for people; and access to housing, education and health care for all. However, Saud refused to sign the proposed constitution. In September 1961, after months of infighting in the royal family, Talal was dropped from the Council of Ministers. Later, he went into exile in Cairo where for a couple of years he headed the Front for the Liberation of Arabia (*ibid.*, pp. 57–64 and 89–100).

By 1962, Saud was ill and the Council of Senior Princes again appointed Faisal to premiership. Tariqi was dismissed and replaced by Shaykh Zaki Yamani. Prince Khaled headed the National Guard and Prince Fahd became minister of the interior. However, infighting within the royal family once again erupted when in September 1962 the revolution in Yemen overthrew the Sultan. Nasser was politically and militarily supporting the Yemeni republicans, while Faisal backed the Sultan. The political threat to Saudi Arabia was real and, therefore, the ailing Saud had to go. In November 1964, backed by the majority of the ruling family and the *ulama*, Faisal was proclaimed King and Saud was sent into exile. Being an Islamic society, the transfer of power in Saudi Arabia had to be legitimised by the Wahhabi *ulama*. They issued a religious order stating that the transfer of power was for the "public well-being", which can be considered as a *Shari'a* principle (Esposito, 1980, p. 128).

## The period of cautious and gradualist reforms: 1964–75

In the face of Nasserist Arab nationalism from abroad and unrest in the armed forces at home, Faisal intensified the reformist initiatives that had begun during his premiership. His objectives were Saudi Arabia's politico-economic and military consolidation. In this endeavour, he was careful to legitimise his initiatives by the *Shari'a* at home and the encouragement of the pan-Islamic movement abroad.

**Faisal's reforms and politics.**
In November 1964, Faisal announced a Ten Point Programme, the major points of which were:

1. The promise of a constitution and a consultative council according to the Qur'an, tradition of the Prophet and the practice of the first four Caliphs.
2. A new structure for local government based on the establishment of five provinces with an advisory council in each, under the guidance of a governor.
3. The establishment of an independent judiciary and a Ministry of Justice to apply the *Shari'a* and formulate legislation for business and commercial contracts.
4. The establishment of a judicial council consisting of twenty members from the *ulama* and lay jurists.
5. Reforming the notorious Public Morality Committees.
6. A social security law and a labour regulations law.
7. Legislation for economic development and the establishment of a legal framework of foreign and domestic business activities, which gave rise to the Foreign Investment Code.
8. The abolition of slavery in the Kingdom with compensation to the slave owners (Lackner, 1978, pp. 64–6).

Faisal never introduced the promised constitution. The Public Morality Committees were never seriously reformed and the new structure for local governments was only partially introduced. A Ministry of Justice was established in 1970 to apply the *Shari'a* and the social security and labour regulations laws were introduced in 1962 and 1969 respectively. Within the framework of legislation for economic development, the first five-year plan was drafted in 1970.

The programme was the first serious attempt on the part of the royal family for gradual change in Saudi Arabian society. In his reformist efforts, Faisal won the support of the young educated class in the bureaucracy and the business community who could benefit from economic development and a more modern legal economic framework. He introduced price controls, educational grants and health facilities to win popular support. Despite some tensions, Faisal's personal piety, Islamic conservatism and fiscal discipline secured harmonious relations with the *ulama*. He increased the salaries of the *ulama* and made sure that the reforms were formulated within the vocabulary of Islam and were approved by the *ulama*. The innovative royal decrees were called *nizam* (rule or code) rather than *qanoun* (law) to permit legal and social changes without transgressing the fundamentals of the *Shari'a*. The labour regulation code, the mining code and the abolition of slavery were all presented as cases that satisfied the Islamic notion of "public well-being". When the Judicial Council, which was supposed to reconcile the conflicting demands of modern life and traditional teachings, was set up, Faisal was hoping that its legal verdicts would supplement the *Shari'a* by providing new norms. However, not all of Faisal's initiatives won the support of the *ulama*. They opposed the introduction of schooling for women in 1961 and television in 1963, and thus delayed the implementation of such "innovations". Faisal's reaction, dressed in Islamic polemics, was that Islam does not permit the wasting of minds, including women's, and to allay the criticism he placed women's education under the special protection of the Grand Mufti's office. Nevertheless, by 1975 only one-sixth of eligible girls were in elementary school (Esposito, 1980, pp. 129 and 131). Television broadcasting started in 1965, but only after several clashes, one of which even led to the death of a prince opposed to such "innovations'. In this case, too, very strict rules were observed to reduce Islamic opposition (Lackner, 1978, pp. 86–7).

With respect to regional developments, Faisal was anxious about the threat of Arab nationalism and tried to oppose it with pan-Islamism. In 1965 he became active against Nasserist and Ba'athist attacks by encouraging the development of Islamic institutions in the region and holding summits with Muslim leaders. In this he was relatively successful. In fact, after 1967, even Nasser resumed normal relations with the Saudi monarchy. By the end of the 1960s, with the steady rise of oil revenues, better economic performance, Nasser's capitulation and internal repression of the opposition, Saudi Arabia appeared a secure and stable state. Faisal had established himself as an Arab political leader. However, internal security of the regime was to a large extent maintained by the military and the police. In the 1965–71 period, Faisal spent up to one third of oil revenues, i.e. 8–10 per cent of GDP per year, on arms and Western arms contracts. In 1972, Saudi Arabia had a regular army, airforce and a small navy whose members were trained and equipped by the USA and Western European countries. However, internal security remained the responsibility of the National Guard, which was backed by police and paramilitary tribal forces (Halliday, 1975, pp. 69–74). The Saudi family, numbering about 5,000 male princes, is a tribe in itself and due to its size has been a powerful political force in Saudi Arabia. The government bureaucracy and the armed forces under Faisal were loyal to the regime, but were divided along two factions of the Saudi family: the traditionalists and the timid modernists. The traditionalists were concerned about the erosive effect of modern socio-economic development on traditional values and supported the maintenance of Islamic and tribal traditions and good relations with the *ulama*. This faction was led by Khaled, the Crown Prince in Faisal's period, his brother, Prince Mohammed and Prince Abdullah (the commander of the National Guard). The modernist faction was for economic growth. Its leaders were "the Sudairi Seven", all sons of the same mother, and included Prince Fahd and his brothers. Yamani was associated with this trend (*ibid*., p. 73), and Faisal was a balancing force between the two factions.

In March 1975, King Faisal was assassinated by one of the princes of the family. The assassin was the brother of the prince who was killed in 1965 during the clashes over television broadcasting.

### Economic change

Unlike the 1940s and 1950s, when economic development in Saudi Arabia was merely an offshoot of the oil industry, in the 1960s more conscious efforts led to the improvement of the infrastructural and industrial basis of the economy.

The number of airports, seaports and paved roads increased. The construction sector experienced a boom and the number of factories that supplied this sector expanded. In 1962, Petromin was set up. Petromin has the right to search for oil in joint projects both with Saudi Arabian private capital and foreign companies. It has also been responsible for the distribution of oil products in Saudi Arabia since 1967 (Johany, Berne and Nixon, Jr., 1986, pp. 31–3).

Before 1970, the government's industrial policy was not very systematic. Nevertheless, in 1963 the Protection and Encouragement of National Industries ordinance provided the necessary framework for encouraging a local import-substitution industry through generous financial assistance, free land grants and tax concessions. Local food industries, mainly in the eastern regions, developed and a few plants in the construction, clothing and printing industries were set up.

Structural change in the economy was slow but steady, and traders still found commerce and imports more lucrative. By 1968, of 8,174 manufacturing units, 89 per cent — traditional workshops such as tailors, bakers, etc. — employed fewer than four people. Import substitution industries numbered fewer than 200. They were supplying only a small part of the national demand, and. importing all of their machinery and intermediate goods. By 1970–71, non-oil manufacturing was 2.8 per cent of real GDP, or 5.4 per cent of non-oil GDP (El-Mallakh, 1982, pp. 109–13).

Saudi Arabia's agriculture was based on small farms. Most of the land had belonged to the government since confiscation by Abdul Aziz in the 1920s. This land was worked by share-croppers hired by tenants who leased the land from the government. In 1968, the government started a programme of land distribution, but only a few thousand farmers received any.

The nomadic Bedouins, whose culture was based on kinship and tribal ties, started to feel the economic change in this period. Trends towards the dominance of the market economy and the unification of the country upset their nomadic life style. Nevertheless, in the late 1960s there were one million camels and four million sheep and goats, indicating the importance of the pastoral sector in the economy (Halliday, 1975, p. 75).

The absolute value of agricultural output increased in this period, but the relative share of agriculture declined due to the more rapid rate of growth of other sectors, especially that of oil. By 1970–71, agriculture constituted 11.8 per cent of real non-oil GDP and 5.1 per cent of real GDP (El-Mallakh, 1982, pp. 80–85).

The oil sector was, of course, the major contributor to GDP, and by 1970–71 its share of real GDP was 56.6 per cent. In 1971, Saudi Arabia's total oil revenues, mainly from Aramco operations, was $1.9 billion. After the price rise of 1974, oil revenues jumped to $22.6 billion. Oil revenues dominated Saudi Arabia's foreign-exchange earnings and government revenues, and made the most important contribution to growth in the national income, increasing the *rentier* character of the state (*ibid.*, pp. 55 and 66).

In this period the ownership status of Aramco changed radically. In 1973, the government acquired 25 per cent of Aramco ownership. This figure was raised to 60 per cent in 1974, and by 1980, 100 per cent. Aramco is currently the largest oil-producing company in the world, with more than 50,000 employees. It has a substantial effect on the economy of the Eastern Province by procuring 70 per cent of its needs from Saudi vendors (Johany, Berne and Nixon, Jr., 1986, pp. 34–5).

In 1974, the size of the population was about 7 million. About 27 per cent of the population were nomads who made up the majority of the population in many of the provinces. Thirty-nine per cent of the population lived in towns of 30,000 inhabitants or more. Depopulation of the countryside was considerable in the 1960s, but not as rapid as in the 1970s.

In 1975, the work force numbered 1.75 million, 314,000 of whom were expatriate workers. A little more than 1 per cent of women were actively engaged in economic activity and a great part of the labour force was unskilled. The share of the labour force in agriculture, industry (including oil), private services and the government sectors were 39.8, 16.8, 29.3 and 14.1 per cent, respectively (El-Mallakh, 1982, pp. 20–6 and 418).

Numbers of pupils attending school rose from 119,000 in 1960 to 700,000 in 1973 (500,000 boys). However, a great majority were at primary school, taught by non-Saudi Arabs, who constitute half the teaching staff. By 1976 technical training centres could offer only 2,500 places, but even these remained unfilled despite generous financial assistance offered to students, reflecting the general prejudice against manual work. The most respected occupations were in government employment or in the import business, which was an easy source of enrichment. Besides, in a society where satisfactory employment is unrelated to the level of educational achievement, aspiration for educational attainment is low (Lackner, 1978, pp. 79–81).

Between 1963 and 1972, mainly due to the steady rise of oil revenues, GDP increased from 8.7 billion Saudi Rials (SR) to SR 27.3 billion. By 1975, after the sudden increase in the price of oil, GDP rose dramatically to SR 139.6 billion.

The role of the government in the economy increased significantly in the 1960s, despite the government's belief in a private market economic system. Generous subsidies and provision of social services for redistributive purposes expanded dramatically. In 1972, government expenditure, excluding transfer payments, made up 15.7 per cent of GDP. Private consumption, private and public investment, and the net foreign sector constituted 25.4, 9.1 and 49.8 per cent of Gross Domestic Expenditures, respectively (El-Mallakh, 1982, p. 31).

The government influenced the performance of the economy in the 1960s through selective monetary and fiscal policies, participation in investment projects, and financial assistance to the private sector through quasi-governmental financial institutions. The first five-year plan was launched in 1970. Its main objectives were infrastructural investment and defence-related projects (*ibid.*, pp. 145–61).

In this period, the Saudi Arabian Monetary Agency (SAMA) which is the central bank of Saudi Arabia, gained more control over monetary policy. Growing oil revenue made a liberal tax policy possible and ever since this period sales taxes and some custom duties have been abolished. Foreign concerns do pay a low rate of income tax, but Saudi citizens and companies were exempted from taxation on personal and corporate income. In May 1975, a Royal Decree abolished personal income taxes for all foreigners in Saudi Arabia (*ibid.*, pp. 265–6, 416–17 and 428).

## The period of King Khaled and King Fahd

In 1975, the Council of Senior Princes, with the approval of the *ulama*, proclaimed Prince Khaled King and Prince Fahd Crown Prince. Khaled had a good relationship with the tribes and the *ulama*, and was considered the representative of the traditionalist faction in the ruling family. However, Faisal's death and the fast-rising oil revenues required the relaxation of the regime's socio-economic and foreign policies. Khaled's first act of reform, as a sign of the stability of the regime, was to release all political prisoners and allow political exiles to return. He also departed from Faisal's monopolisation of political power by distributing it more evenly among the ruling family. The Sudairi brothers held three ministerial posts: Prince Fahd was first deputy premier, Prince Sultan defence and aviation minister, and Prince Nayef interior minister. Shaykh Yamani kept the ministry of petroleum, and younger princes were appointed to other ministries.

At home, after the death of Faisal, the idea of a consultative council was raised, but nothing came of it. The new king encouraged the development of sporting facilities, though only for men, and in a manner that would not contradict Wahhabi puritanism. Nevertheless, social life remained as restricted as ever and the Islamic judicial code continued to be rigorously enforced.

Internationally, Khaled pursued a more flexible foreign policy. Tension between the Kingdom and other Arab countries was reduced considerably. Khaled pushed Bahrain, Kuwait and the Emirates to develop a more united policy with Saudi Arabia and follow a more conservative national policy. Relations with the then South Yemen improved and Khaled helped bring an end to the fighting among opposing Lebanese factions in 1976. He encouraged a return to the Islamic legal code in Egypt, Pakistan and Sudan.

In the economic field, Khaled did not interfere with the second five-year plan despite the fact that it had been Fahd's brainchild. However, implementation of the plan was constrained by the traditionalist faction's concern about the importation of unIslamic values (Lackner, 1978, pp. 71–3). The oil policy of the Faisal government, i.e. the stabilisation of oil prices contrary to the wishes of OPEC members such as Algeria and Libya, was continued.

In 1979 the regime's stability was to be rocked from within Islam. In the 1960s Nasserists and Ba'athists constituted the main opposition to Saudi Arabia. However, in the 1970s the Arab nationalist movement subsided, to be replaced with Islamic fundamentalism, a more indigenous ideology. One of its earliest appearances can be traced to 1965 when the new Ikhwan movement, led by one of the princes of the Saudi family, opposed Faisal's cautious modernisation. In 1975, the brother of the same prince assassinated Faisal. In the 1970s, fundamentalist ideas were used to challenge the legitimacy of the Wahhabi Islamic state, its institutionalised Islamism and its programme of gradual modernisation. Further, the fundamentalists found increasing conspicuous consumption by the Saudi princes and other rich families, together with the growing American presence, both results of the success of the oil industry, provocative. Opposed to the modernising reforms, they advocated an uncompromising return to the Qur'an and the *Sunna* through a revival of Wahhab and his teachings. Unlike the new Ikhwan movement of the 1960s, which had attracted the young, literate and somewhat urbanised Wahhabists, the new fundamentalist movement was attracting many marginalised groups in Saudi Arabia. The leader of the movement, Juhayman, was from the lower-class Utaba tribe. In November 1979, Juhayman led the siege of the Grand Mosque of Mecca with about 300 followers, some armed. They were mostly poor tribesmen, theology students and petty shopkeepers. Juhayman's programme, announced at the takeover of the Mosque, was the overthrow of the Saudi monarchy since, according to him, Islam did not recognise kings or dynasties. He also rejected the Wahhabi *ulama* and their "incorrect" teachings. His ideal society was based on the establishment of a puritanical Islamic community, which would protect Islam from disbelievers and would not "court foreigners" (quoted in Dekmejian, 1985, p. 142).

King Khaled sought a *fatwa* (religious opinion) from the convened council of *ulama* to attack the rebels in the Grand Mosque. Many on both sides were killed in the attack by the National Guard and those captured were later executed, including Juhayman. At about the same time, riots broke out among the proletarianised Shi'ites in the Eastern Province who were followers of Khomeini. The riots were crushed by the National Guard, but unrest continued into 1980.

In response to these unrests, Prince Fahd, exercising considerable power due to Khaled's illness, promised the establishment of a consultative assembly of 50–70 nominated members, and appointed a committee to draw up a "system of rules" based on Islamic principles (*ibid.*, pp. 145–8). This committee has drafted the promised constitution but Fahd has so far delayed its presentation for debate (Hunter, 1988, p. 110).

The Iraq–Iran War and the Soviet invasion of Afghanistan in the early 1980s gave rise to an increase in Saudi military expenditures. In May 1981, Saudi Arabia joined the five Persian Gulf states in the Gulf Co-operation Council, an economic-military security pact. In the same year, Saudi Arabia mediated the crisis in Lebanon and became active in trying to find a solution to the Arab–Israeli problem and the issue of Palestinian autonomy.

In June 1982 King Khaled died and Crown Prince Fahd was proclaimed king. Fahd's half-brother, Abdullah, became Crown Prince and first deputy prime minister. In the same year, oil prices declined, bringing a slump in government revenues. Despite this, Fahd continued or even increased the supportive loans and donations to other Arab countries, especially Iraq. Partly due to this support, the Iranian-based Islamic Jihad group intensified its terroristic acts, and in 1987 Iranian pilgrims and Saudi security forces clashed in

Mecca, which finally led to a diplomatic break with Iran, which lasted more than three years.

In 1984–85, with Saudi Arabia increasingly concerned that it might be drawn into the Iran-Iraq war, the government approached the US and French governments for an improved military system. However, it refused to give the US access to military bases on its land should there be an escalation of the war. Later, the refusal of the US Congress to sanction a $1 billion arms agreement with Saudi Arabia led instead to an agreement with the UK.

In October 1986, Shaykh Yamani was replaced as minister of petroleum and mineral resources, reflecting Saudi dissatisfaction with its oil policy. At the end of 1985, OPEC adopted a "fair share" policy to regain its lost share of the world market by dropping its system of official quotas for oil production. In December 1986, the new minister, Shaykh Nazer, proposed a return to a fixed reference price for crude oil at $18 per barrel. This OPEC endorsed. In 1988, Nazer became the first Saudi chairman of Aramco, which was by now fully owned by the government (Saudi Arabia, 1989, pp. 717–9).

On 2 August 1990, Iraq invaded Kuwait and King Fahd, after some hesitation, asked that US troops be sent to the kingdom in the context of Article 51 of the UN charter. Ironically, this time the ruler of Kuwait and most members of his government who had fled Kuwait found themselves in exile in the House of Saud. King Fahd's request for foreign military aid also received Islamic approval by a *fatwa* of the religious leader of the country, Ibn Baz (Eilts, 1991, pp. 7–8). Under the auspices of the USA, the UN Security Council had passed a series of resolutions condemning Iraq and finally authorising the use of force against Iraq. By early 1991, 500,000 US troops and about 200,000 soldiers from other nations were in Saudi Arabia. The coalition forces won a quick victory and Iraq conceded a truce on 3 March 1991.

Although Saudi Arabia was not badly damaged by the war, it saw a massive decline in its financial assets. First, there was a loss in anticipated foreign investment in new petrochemical projects of about $10 billion. Second, Saudi banks were confronted with an unprecedented withdrawal of savings, which affected more than 10 per cent of all bank deposits. A crash in the banking sector was only prevented by SAMA providing the system with $4.4 billion. Third, the government had to transfer, house and feed Kuwaiti refugees and Saudi citizens who had fled border towns; cover the cost of US troops and other allied forces, especially those from other Arab countries; and write off these countries' old and non-performing debts or pledge new aid for them. By mid-1991, the total cost to Saudi Arabia was estimated to be between $64 and $80 billion, while the windfall gain from the rise in oil prices during the war was not more than $16 billion. Therefore SAMA's liquid funds were massively decreased and the government had to start to borrow from international banks (Sadowski, 1991, pp. 4–7).

The war ended very soon. However, the presence of so many foreign troops, most of them from the West, in Saudi Arabia for about six months, was to result in changes to the Kingdom's traditional way of life and its relation with the rest of the Arab world.

Until the Gulf crisis, timid reforms in Saudi Arabia, which in an amazing manner had avoided major complications, had slowly created a bipolar society. Economically, the country had been integrated into the world economic system, but had been loyal to Islamic conservatism and political and civil archaism. The Gulf crisis exerted pressure on the system from without and within. It seemed plausible that the role of Saudi Arabia in regional politics would become more closely and openly linked to the interests of the West; however, this time Saudi Arabia was to press more than before for its geo-political interest.

It appears that the Saudi family will continue to base its rule on the same Islamic conservatism that has constituted the pillar of its policies ever since its inception. Nevertheless, the Saudi business community, part of the royal family itself, the bureaucracy and Western governments will continue to press for a certain political liberalisation. In the past the ruling family has shown itself to be cautiously flexible when necessary, and will probably continue to be in the future if not confronted with a major financial or political crisis.

## Islam, government, economic institutions and policy

### The role of Islam in the economy

Islam is the ideological base of the patrimonial Kingdom of Saudi Arabia and the *Shari'a* is the law of the land. The *Shari'a* is interpreted according to the Hanbali school of Islamic law by the Wahhabi *ulama* and is enforced by the Saudi Kings, considered as Imam or leader of the faithful, the *ummah*.

The Hanbali school of law asserts that everything in human affairs is an expression of divine will and that the meaning of all things is to be found in the *Shari'a*. Thus, the *Shari'a* is immutable and holy since only God can legislate. However, the same Hanbali school, which is uncompromising on the social behaviour of the faithful, appears to be one of the most liberal Islamic schools of law on business and economic affairs. In fact, despite its social welfare orientation Saudi Arabia has one of the most laissez-faire economies in the world.

Saudi Arabia is an absolute monarchy. Saudi kings head the government as prime minister in a council of ministers mostly filled with members of the al-Saud family and some descendants of Abd al-Wahhab who are all responsible to the King. However, the King's regulatory or administrative decrees outside the scope of the *Shari'a* must have the approval of the Wahhabi *ulama* under the aegis of the al-Shaykh family (Hunter, 1988, p. 105). Thus, the King issues decrees with the force of law, but only as guardian of the *Shari'a*. Potentially important legislation is first considered by ad hoc ministerial committees and Islamic scholars and then is promulgated as a Royal decree. In cases where the King fears religious opposition, he issues a Royal *order* rather a Royal *decree*. Nevertheless, "Islam and the *Shari'a* notwithstanding, the word of the House of Saud remains paramount" (Wilson, 1991, p. 8). Thus, with no constitution, the Kingdom tries to preserve the interdependence of state and religious authority. The latter provides legitimacy to political power and relies on the state for the implementation of the *Shari'a*. For this reason, all five-year plan objectives start with the principles of maintenance of Islamic values and assurance against foreign cultural influences (Wells, 1976, pp. 112–14).

Trade, commerce and industry are governed by a body of rules and regulations based on the *Shari'a* and its extension by the proclamation of decrees in fields such as labour and commercial codes (see Wilson, 1991, pp. 123–9).

The labour code applies to domestic and expatriate workers, except domestic servants and agricultural employees. The code has provisions for formal labour contracts, paid vacations, working hours, safety standards and medical treatment like many modern labour laws. It also specifies a minimum wage, but this provision is not enforced. The labour code permits the employment of women, but in accordance with the Islamic code of behaviour it requires the separation of women from male employees. Strikes and labour unions are illegal, but labour disputes can be settled by the ministry of labour's special committees, which include religious experts. This procedure also applies to commercial disputes. Therefore Saudi Arabia is not a litigious country by modern standards, and the legal system is badly in need of reform. However, codification of the legal system is strongly resented by the *ulama*.

The commercial code was amended in April 1992, reflecting the expansion of the role of corporate activity in the economy, making directors more responsible for their actions. From an Islamic point of view, the important change is the legitimisation of preferred stock with a predetermined rate of return (MEED, April 1992, p. 24).

In accordance with the *Shari'a*, Saudi law recognises different types of business organisations involving unlimited and limited liability of owners. Foreign individuals or firms are not allowed to operate a business in Saudi Arabia, except for the sale of military equipment, or when a foreign investor is granted a licence or a contract from a ministry. Therefore all foreign firms must have a Saudi citizen participating in the venture, unless the firm is a subcontractor of a Saudi contractor. The establishment of such foreign firms is subject to the foreign investment code. Many firms prefer to operate through a Saudi agent, who is entitled to a maximum of 5 per cent of a contract's value and receives compensation for other services that might be rendered (Johany, Berne and Nixon, Jr., 1986, pp. 101–4). In fact, the operation of a great number of foreign-owned private companies in the Kingdom and the partial involvement of the government and the private sector in many industrial and foreign trade activities makes it difficult to assess the relative size of the foreign/domestic and private/public sectors.

**The role of the government and the private sector in the economy**

The Saudi economy is a mixed market economy. The private non-oil sector operates with little day-to-day government planning or restriction except when its activity is contrary to the *Shari'a*. However, by virtue of oil receipts, the government dominates the economy and influences the private sector considerably by its economic activity. The government is directly and indirectly involved in production, distribution and consumption processes. It initiates almost all domestic development projects and is the main source of funds entering the private sector, much of it consisting of interest-free loans for desired projects and government contracts. The government decides the type of industries to be established, the tempo of the industrialisation process and its own role in it. A number of specialised banks have been established to provide interest-free loans to help meet the objectives of the five-year plans. The most important of these funds are the Saudi Investment Development Fund, the Saudi Arabian Agricultural Bank and the Real Estate Development Fund.

The government's socio-economic objectives are reflected in the five-year plans. The plans' general objectives have been the maintenance of religious values and traditions, improvement of the welfare and security of the country's citizens, and the achievement of social and economic stability. The strategy for the realisation of these objectives has been the acceleration of GDP growth, manpower development and economic diversification.

Since the 1970s the government has avoided price fixing, except under certain conditions. Price fixing is used only for goods and services sold by monopolies under government licence and firms that have received interest-free loans or subsidies, such as air transportation, gasoline and hotel services. If imported inputs are important for the production of a commodity, the price can vary but the government sets the mark-up (*ibid*., p. 106).

Oil revenues greatly dominate government revenues. There is no tax on wages or salaries of Saudi citizens. Saudi nationals and firms pay *zakat* on the total income and capital gains that have been retained for one year or more at the rate of 2.5 per cent of total income as determined by the *Shari'a*. *Zakat* payments are distributed among the poor and the needy. The government also subsidises some sectors, notably agriculture; provides tariff protection for five years and import duties exemption in some activities; provides preferential treatment to encourage local enterprises; and has introduced regulations for consumer protection and the maintenance of environmental standards. Government contracts for small services or large undertakings are numerous. Domestic and foreign firms take part in bidding, and local firms that have foreign partners enjoy preferential treatment.

Subsidies are provided for a large number of goods, such as basic food stuffs, water, utility and gasoline. Housing loans are provided at very generous rates, and an important part of recreational and social programmes is supplied free of charge by the government. Education and health services are also offered by the private sector (Presley, 1984, pp. 122–4). The social-security system is managed by the government. A social insurance scheme exists for employees of the private and public sectors. The system has been developed piecemeal and is operated as a pension fund (Johany, Berne and Nixon, Jr., 1986, pp. 103–4).

However, since the rise in oil revenues in the early 1970s, the government has emphasised its long-term objective of building an economy based on free enterprise and the market, yet within the framework of Islamic values. The first five-year plan stated that:

> The Kingdom's commitment to the free enterprise economy is founded on

> Islamic guidelines and traditions. The Kingdom has concluded that the economy could not exploit fully the opportunities open to it except through the full utilisation of private initiative and by including private enterprises of all sizes and forms to perform the activities which it could perform more efficiently than the government. (Quoted in Looney, 1982, p. 43)

The private sector is dominant in traditional agriculture, modern farming, medium and small manufacturing, mining and quarrying, handicrafts and cottage industries, residential and commercial construction, motor transportation, banking, wholesale and retail trade, importing and exporting, and shipping.

Many merchants are rich, even richer than some members of the Saudi family and in the private sector the spirit of profit-making dominates. The royal family controls many economic activities through front companies and influence over government contracts. Influential princes are behind many wealthy merchants: the merchant runs the business while the prince arranges contracts and eliminates bureaucratic obstacles (Wilson, 1991, pp. 124–35).

The majority of business establishments remain very small. In the late 1970s, of about 77,000 private establishments, over 73,000 employed fewer than ten people and about 69,000 had four employees or less, operating mainly as family units. Only about 400 establishments, mostly government enterprises, employed over 100 employees (Presley, 1984, p. 76).

**The financial sector**

At the top of the structure of the Saudi Arabian financial sector is the Saudi Arabian Monetary Agency (SAMA), the central bank of the Kingdom. Below the SAMA are the commercial banks (Saudi privately owned, joint private-government and Saudi–foreign owned banks), development banks (government owned, joint private government and Saudi–foreign owned banks) and non-banking financial institutions such as insurance companies, money-changers and Islamic financial institutions.

The exceptional growth of the economy since 1970 has not been matched by expansion of the financial system, especially in the private sector. This is due to the restrictive Islamic law against interest payment, which has affected the nature of the private banking institution, and to its unclear position on insurance business in Sunni Islam; the nature of economic growth; and the constraints created by SAMA.

Interest payments have always been prohibited in Saudi Arabia, but banks, private and public, bypass the rule by charging and paying commissions instead of interest. In fact, according to SAMA's charter, the "Agency … shall not act in any manner which conflicts with the teaching of the Islamic Law", which in the charter is identified as paying and receiving interest (El-Mallakh, 1982, p. 336).

In the early 1970s, commissions charged for services varied from 7 to 8.5 per cent, while commissions paid on savings accounts and time deposits varied between 3.5 and 5 per cent (*ibid.*, pp. 294–303). On the whole, the effective rates of interest, including the commissions, charged by commercial banks in early

1980 were as follows: 7.5 to 9 per cent on long-standing facilities for the best customers; 12 to 14 per cent for additional loans; and 17 to 18 per cent for new Saudi and non-Saudi customers (Looney, 1982, pp. 52–3).

Thus, despite the opposition of the *ulama* in recent decades to what they term *riba* (usury) banking, Saudi Arabia's commercial banking system is effectively based on interest. In reality, the government has always favoured a Western-style banking system and has opposed the creation of Islamic banks to the point that even adoption of the prefix "Islamic" for banks is not recommended; on the pretext that it reduces the "Islamic" credibility of other banks. This situation creates a legal quagmire in the case of rising non-performing loans. In the mid-1980s many loans were literally given away to princes and other citizens. By 1985, it was estimated that 25 to 40 per cent of the banks' outstanding advances of more than SR 60 billion were non-performing. In reaction, SAMA prohibited banks from making their records available to any court, including the *Shari'a* courts, since the courts were deducting service charges from debts on the grounds that they constituted illegal interest (Wilson, 1991, pp. 130–37).

The national insurance industry, despite substantial demand by the public and private sectors, is underdeveloped and unregulated. Insurance is viewed as unIslamic among Saudi Sunnites and the courts do not hear insurance cases. Thus, insurance companies formed with Saudi capital and as offshoots of the commercial banks or multinational firms in Saudi Arabia, are incorporated offshore (Presley and Kebbell, 1982, p. 45).

The second reason for the relatively slow growth of the financial sector is that economic growth demanded long-term credit for large-scale projects with heavy risks and small immediate returns. To overcome this problem, the government established several development banks that grant loans free of interest with very low commissions. These banks are for agricultural, industrial, residential and construction industries. Oil revenues have made the operation of these banks possible even though repayments are a major problem for them (Presley, 1984, pp. 110–12).

The third reason for the relatively sluggish growth of the banking sector is the restrictive regulations of SAMA. Commercial banks are required to hold deposits of 15 to 17.5 per cent of their total deposit liabilities and this is in addition to liquid assets that must be maintained at not less than 15 per cent of their deposits. Furthermore, deposit liabilities of banks must not be greater than fifteen times their capital and reserves. If deposits are greater than this ratio, commercial banks must deposit 50 per cent of the excess with SAMA. All these deposits yield no interest (Looney, 1982, p. 51). These rules have limited the volume of loans by banks with relatively low levels of capital and reserve (Presley, 1984, p. 101).

Since 1977, the Saudisation of foreign banks has transformed the majority ownership (60 per cent) of ten former foreign banks to Saudi nationals or the government. However, the two original private Saudi banks, established in 1937 and 1957, control most of the banking business, 70 per cent of total commercial bank assets, 80 per cent of total deposits, and 90 per cent of current accounts in the country (*ibid*., p. 105). Thus the banking sector is largely oligopolistic.

Despite the prohibition on receiving interest, the financial returns of major banks, especially Saudi banks, reflect the high profitability of their operations. The banks' massive deposit bases and the low cost of obtaining funds, especially deposits by government agencies and "commission" on loans, explain this high profitability (Looney, 1982, pp. 57–8).

So far, commercial banks have avoided engagement in Islamic contracts like *muzaraba* or profit-sharing agreements with their depositors and customers; even though these activities could give the banks a fixed percentage of the profits generated by the loan, thus circumventing the interest restriction. However, in the latter part of the 1970s, the Islamic Development Bank, largely capitalised with Saudi money, was established in order to introduce such Islamic innovations in the banking sector. It is hoped that in the future only 20 per cent of its business will be in interest-free loans and that the remainder will be in the form of Islamic partnerships (*ibid*., p. 60).

Financial institutions that call themselves Islamic have been operating in Saudi Arabia since the late 1970s. In reaction to this development, which is not favoured by the government but is strongly supported by the *ulama*, SAMA, rather than prohibiting it, has refused to license them. It is ironic that such institutions have to register in other countries, including the Bahamas, although more than half of their deposits originate in the Kingdom (Wilson, 1991, pp. 179–88).

Another important institution in the financial sector of Saudi Arabia is the unregulated moneychangers. Over the past three decades they have played an important role in financing domestic and foreign trade. They exchange foreign currency notes, cash traveller's cheques, maintain interest-free accounts for the faithful and provide short-term financing. With low operating costs and no SAMA regulation, they have been highly profitable. Since January 1982, moneychangers have been required to divest themselves of their banking activities and submit their books to SAMA for auditing, which has trimmed some of their activities (Johany, Berne and Nixon, Jr., 1986, pp. 160–61). In 1987, one of the largest money changers was transformed into a bank, thereby becoming the third largest bank in Saudi Arabia (*Le Monde, Bilan Economique, 1987*, p. 113).

Until 1987, there was not much reason for a stock market in Saudi Arabia. In 1985, there were more than 1,200 private companies with limited liability, in which founder shareholders had largely maintained their holdings. However, there had been trading in stocks of some 60 companies in unofficial markets. In fact, the Saudi Investment Company used to list the prices of 36 companies in the daily papers (Dalmoak, 1988, p. 49). In 1987, banks under the supervision of SAMA were granted the right to engage in trading of stocks in an official stock market (*Le Monde, Bilan Economique, 1987*, p. 113). According to the stock-exchange decree, all banks could have a brokerage department for trading shares on behalf of both private and corporate clients. In accordance with its long-run objective, the government hopes that with the privatisation of state-owned companies such as the state airline, telecommunication network and many public utilities, their stocks would be floated off. Already, the Saudi Basic

Industries Corporation (SABIC), the Saudi petrochemical giant, has opened seven joint ventures. In 1984–85, 28 per cent of SABIC stock was owned by the private sector (Dalmoak, 1985, p. 45). However, the stock-exchange trading floor was closed after less than a month of trading due to ministerial conflicts and "technical problems with the computers". Apparently the *ulama* had protested about control by the unIslamic banks over the stock-exchange market (Wilson, 1991, p. 161). Later, the problem was circumvented by setting up electronic trading, with no formal trading floor, in which transactions are managed by banks and independent brokers (MEED, 20 March 1992, p. 16).

**Fiscal and monetary policy**

In Saudi Arabia and similar countries such as Libya and Iran, where economic activities depend on oil revenues under government control, the role of government budgetary policy is crucial. Monetary and fiscal policies are closely related and both can affect the level of production, income and expenditures on consumption and investment goods and services. In these countries, money and capital markets are not well developed and the sheer size of the government sector reduces the importance of monetary policy. Nevertheless, inflationary tendencies in these countries, especially in Saudi Arabia, have led to a more active role for monetary policy.

The Saudi government budget has two key features: its enormous size relative to the economy and its almost total reliance on oil revenues. Saudi governments have adhered to the principle of balanced-budget financing for many years, and government deficits, if incurred at all, were very small. However, in the mid-1980s the situation changed.

A decline in oil revenues led to a deficit in the balance of payments, and the government had to modify its liberal tax and expenditure policies. The budget of 1985–86 was balanced by a cut in public expenditure, especially in the construction sector, and an increase in custom taxes (*Le Monde, Bilan Economique, 1985*, p. 108). In 1987, in order to rationalise the local consumption of petrol produced by the state company, its price was increased (*Le Monde, Bilan Economique, 1987*, p. 113). Finally, in 1988, the government introduced an austerity budget cutting public expenditure by 17 per cent. Nevertheless, the budget deficit increased to $10 billion and for the first time the government started to borrow from the public, issuing $8 billion bonds. The issue of the so-called "development bonds" was decreed by King Fahd. The concept of *muzaraba* was used by the government to justify the payment of a yield based on the return of unspecified government projects. At first, some leading *ulama* strongly questioned the Islamic nature of the decision, but soon capitulated.

"Development bonds" have been offered to social insurance and pension fund institutions and commercial banks as balance-sheet entries; to avoid incurring the displeasure of the *ulama* no certificates were issued. Further, to avoid Islamic criticism, banks were forbidden to advertise the resale of bonds to the public in the media (Wilson, 1991, pp. 172–4).

In 1988, the government decided to reimpose income tax on expatriate workers, although many were expelled as projects were abandoned. Agricultural subsidies were reduced to rationalise the cost of production: in 1985–87, the government was paying $400 per ton for Saudi wheat while the international price was only $130 per ton (*Le Monde, Bilan Economique, 1988*, p. 113). However, the invasion of Kuwait by Iraq and the presence of allied forces in Saudi Arabia brought a mini-boom to an economy that in 1990 had a $6 billion budget deficit and a fast declining foreign-exchange reserve (*Le Monde, Bilan Economique, 1990*, p. 114). In addition, the high cost of Desert Storm has forced the Saudi government to economise its lavish use of resources. With a GNP of about $85 billion, Saudi Arabia had already committed $48 billion to the war effort, and government liquid assets, estimated to be only $10 billion, were declining. In early 1991, SAMA negotiated an emergency three-year loan of $4.5 billion with a syndicate of international banks headed by Morgan Guaranty Trust Co., with further loans to be negotiated (*ibid*., 1992, p. 116).

The central bank of Saudi Arabia, SAMA, is a semi-independent institution. It is interesting to note that SAMA is not called the central bank. In 1952, when it was established, the word bank was resented by the *ulama* and represented an unIslamic financial activity; therefore the neutral title Saudi Arabia Monetary Agency was adopted (Wilson, 1991, pp. 27–8).

In the past two decades SAMA has acquired the functions and instruments of traditional central banks, except that due to Islamic constraints it cannot use the discount rate and open market operations as instruments of monetary policy. As in many developing countries, nominal money is mostly created by net government spending which is paid in cash. However, SAMA can to some degree affect the money supply by controlling capital flows in and out of Saudi Arabia. In general, since SAMA cannot normally use rediscount facilities and open market operations, it has a limited ability to stabilise the economy, and changes in money supply largely depend on government spending. The government can control the timing and method of payment of its spending to effect desired changes in the monetary base and these controls have sometimes been used (El-Mallakh, 1982, pp. 287–300). In 1987, the Islamic court accepted the religious legitimacy of arbitrage in the banking sector under the control of SAMA, which has increased the effectiveness of monetary policy (*Le Monde, Bilan Economique, 1987*, p. 113). SAMA had already been authorised to invest foreign exchange reserves of the country in foreign securities, which effectively exempted it from the Islamic prohibition of interest payment (El-Mallakh, 1982, p. 299). Furthermore, with the lifting of the ban on government borrowing by means of issuing bonds in 1988, the effective role of SAMA in the conduct of monetary policy is likely to increase yet further.

**Planning**

Between 1970 and 1990, Saudi Arabia implemented four five-year development plans. The government claims that its economic and social objectives for these plans are derived from the moral principles of Islam: strong preference for private enterprise; the desirability of government intervention in the operation of the economy where the market fails; and the provision for the welfare of Saudis according to Islamic social justice. In addition to this, the defence of the Islamic land and maintenance of internal security and social stability have always been an important objective of the government.

The first plan (1970–75) was drawn up at a time of financial difficulties: a balance of payments deficit in 1973–74 and only a modest increase in oil revenues in 1972–73. In this plan, infrastructural investments, notably defence, social services, transport and communications, urban development and public utilities, respectively, received the largest shares of the planned allocations.

The large increase in oil prices in 1973–74 totally removed the financial constraint of the second plan (1975–80). As a result prices rose rapidly and infrastructural and labour shortages gave rise to serious bottlenecks. Problems concerning the absorptive capacity of the non-oil sector and manpower shortages thus determined the priorities of the plan. In addition, the second plan also emphasised the expansion of agricultural and industrial sectors. Incentives such as credit facilities and subsidies for the private sector were expanded and education and training facilities increased. To reduce the burden of inflation on Saudi citizens, subsidies, interest-free loans for house-building and social security benefits expanded. Thus, despite waste, uneven regional development, rising inequality of income distribution and mismanagement, by the end of the plan infrastructural facilities were improved, absorptive capacity was expanded and favourable growth rates were achieved. Prudent monetary policy and increased imports to satisfy the rising level of aggregate demand reduced the rate of inflation. In addition, social, welfare and financial measures increased the real living standards for significant numbers of Saudi citizens (*ibid*., pp. 138–211).

Improvements in the problem areas led to a shift of priorities in the third plan (1980–85) towards manpower, efficiency and private participation. While ongoing infrastructural projects were being completed, more output-oriented investment by the public and private sector was emphasised. To control the rising inflow of the expatriate labour force, the plan opted for a lower rate of economic growth. However, after two favourable initial years, the decline of the price of oil affected the implementation of the plan. By the end of the third plan there were more than a million expatriate workers, increasing the ratio of expatriate to Saudi workers from 1.03 to 1.49 (*OPEC Bulletin*, 1987, p. 26).

The fourth plan (1985–90) gave priority to economic diversification, emphasising agricultural and industrial development, to reduce dependence on oil, the price of which declined even further during this period. The expatriate labour force continued to decrease in numbers throughout the years of the plan. In addition, the government planned to increase private sector participation through a policy of privatisation of public enterprises (Montagu, 1985, pp. 47 and 51).

By 1986, foreign earnings had dropped by 78 per cent of their 1981 value, when oil revenues had been $110 billion. The deficit in the fourth development budget has been financed by reserves and credit; sharp cuts in expenditure on physical infrastructure and imports; the introduction of an austerity programme with reductions in subsidies; and the partial expulsion of the expatriate workforce. Thus, by 1990 the fourth plan had not realised its targets and the implementation of many projects was delayed. The Saudi economy, like that of many other OPEC countries, turned from a cash to a credit economy. The absolute level of current GDP, all the components of GDP in different sectors, except agriculture, and the components of GDP by expenditure approach — government and private consumption, gross fixed capital formation, exports and imports — all fell during the period 1986–89 ("Saudi Arabia", 1989, p. 731). In 1987, four out of twelve commercial banks recorded a loss due to the domestic recession and "bad debts" (*ibid*., p. 727). A number of major contractors went bankrupt (Montagu, 1985, p. 51). By 1990, oil revenues had risen again, and with them government expenditures, raising the level of GDP. In addition, the Gulf crisis and the consequent increase in the price of oil and the increase in local expenditures of coalition forces boosted the sluggish economy of the kingdom (*Le Monde, Bilan Economique, 1990*, p. 114).

Despite many problems, over the past sixty years the overall economic performance of Saudi Arabia has been positive. The prevailing mixed economic order that has emerged is relatively pragmatic in its socio-economic outlook and practices and has been capable of adapting to new circumstances. The major exception, however, is society and the government's adherence to Islamic restriction with respect to the role of female labour, modern financial instruments and modern civil and political rights. It is not easy to foster modernisation whilst adhering to the tenets of Wahhabism. This contention has been proved by the spasmodic socio-economic development of Saudi society during the past six decades.

# 7. Islamisation of the Iranian Economy at the Behest of the Clergy

Since 1979, Iran has been ruled by the Shi'ite clergy, who came to power under the leadership of Ayatollah Khomeini during the 1979 Revolution. The name of the country was changed to the Islamic Republic of Iran and, ever since, the national flag has carried the Islamic *shahada*, the Qur'anic statement of faith symbolising the Islamic nature of the republic.

Initially, the clergy shared power with Bazargan and then with the Bani-Sadr faction under the leadership of Khomeini. Major economic measures were introduced and implemented to varying degrees. The dismissal of Bani-Sadr from the presidency marked the beginning of a second stage, characterised by full-fledged clerical rule and, paradoxically, a period of open dispute among clerical factions, generally manifested in economic controversies, which has continued in the post-Khomeini period. In this second stage, no major economic measures were introduced and some of the previous ones were endlessly debated and disputed, or even drastically modified. These disputes, the Iran–Iraq war, international sanctions, economic policy and the structural weakness of the Iranian economy adversely affected economic performance. This enhanced the position of the advocates of a more liberal economic policy in the clerical infighting.

## The post-revolutionary polity and economic policy

### Bazargan and the clergy

On 5 February 1979, Khomeini appointed Bazargan as prime minister. This appointment was a step towards the realisation of the Islamic Republic. Bazargan had the support of the majority of the liberal intelligentsia, small and middle-rank entrepreneurs, merchants, the state- and private-sector employees, and officers of the armed forces. The clerical leaders were aware that without the help of the technocracy they could not realise their objectives and gain control over the important levers of the government. The clergy needed to restore law and order in the aftermath of the fall of the Shah. Despite their influence and connections among the masses, they had not created the instruments of power necessary to guarantee their hold on the state apparatus or the destruction of opposition. In fact, they were surprised by the speed with which the revolution had brought them to power. They had to buy time.

Politically, Bazargan was not an advocate of government by the Islamic jurisconsult. However, socially and economically, the clerical leadership and Bazargan's government had many common viewpoints. Both had the interest of small- and medium-sized commercial and industrial capital in mind. Nevertheless, the clergy was more sensitive to the necessity of paying lip service to the dispossessed, who formed their principal political base in the struggle for the realisation of an Islamic Republic. The economic objective of the Bazargan government was to restore the confidence of the owners of capital and embark on economic reconstruction. Bazargan, himself an industrial entrepreneur, had always recognised the importance of the private sector as the agent of change and growth in the national economy. He argued for gradual reforms. However, the deteriorating state of the economy and the mood of the masses in the urban and rural areas did not lend themselves to gradualism and a time-consuming policy of change. The clerical leadership, with its eye fixed on full-fledged clerical rule, was ready to react to the mood of the movement in a populist manner.

The urban economy was in serious difficulties due to months of strikes or go-slows and the shortage of raw material and intermediary goods. Many owners and senior managers of the largest industrial enterprises, private banks and insurance companies had left the country and those who remained had lost confidence. The banking system was facing a crisis caused by massive withdrawals in the latter part of 1978. A further aggravating factor was the heavy debts owed by large industries to the banks.

Immediately after the revolution, white- and blue-collar workers were organising employees' and workers' councils, demanding a purge of "informers" and "collaborators", higher wages and benefits and more control over the running of the factories and offices. They were supported in their demands by the leftist forces, certain young clerics and radical Muslims. Further lay-offs and lockouts in industry led to the demand for more control over managerial functions. Major government industrial complexes, such as steel mills, petrochemical plants, nuclear reactors, construction projects, ports and military bases were left unfinished and idle. Workers employed by private contractors on government projects were being made redundant on a massive scale. The level of unemployment and underemployment increased to three million, about 30 per cent of the labour force. The political organisations of the left and their cadres in factories, offices, educational institutions and the mass media were demanding nationalisation of large industries, the banking system, arable and urban lands and empty dwellings.

The rural sector was not affected by the political turmoil that had gripped the cities before the revolution. However, after the insurrection, confrontation between landlords and peasants became widespread and violent. Some of the land seizures were carried out by landlords who had lost land during the Shah's land reform, especially in less developed provinces, with their tribal traditions and semi-feudal relationships. In almost all provinces, landless peasants and rural farm labourers also participated in land seizures.

The flight of capital was intensified in the second half of 1978 and in 1979, pushing up the price of foreign currencies against the rial in the black market (Rahnema and Nomani, 1990, pp. 237–9).

**Major economic measures in the first year of the revolution**

Against such a background, the Revolutionary Council and provisional government moved slowly and cautiously. The economic measures that were gradually approved were a mixed bag of philanthropic and spontaneously populist and radical measures. As long as the radical measures affected only the property of the royal family and the top echelons of the *ancien régime,* nobody objected. Trouble started when some of these measures touched the sensitive issue of property rights and property distribution.

On 28 February 1979, Khomeini authorised the Revolutionary Council to confiscate the mobile and immobile properties of the Pahlavi dynasty and their close associates. The Foundation for the Disinherited was established to administer these properties. The immobile properties of the Pahlavi family included two hundred large factories, farms, banks, hotels and trading companies.

On 5 March 1979, the National Iranian Oil Company took over all the activities of the oil and gas industries. On 20 March 1979, the anniversary of the nationalisation of the oil industry in 1951, the government cancelled its agreements with the international consortium. The government also changed the oil-production target, reducing it from 6 million barrels a day (MBD) to 4 MBD, with an export target of 3.4 MBD.

Certain routine and partly philanthropic measures were introduced to reduce the problems of industry and the banking system and to prevent further economic stagnation. For example, the central bank liberalised import regulations and allocated funds to the Chamber of Industries and Mines to improve cash flow in industry and very low interest housing loans were provided to government employees. However, more substantial changes were inevitable. In the summer of 1979, certain important measures were approved by the Revolutionary Council that greatly increased the government's role and ownership in the economy.

*Major nationalisations*

On 7 June 1979, the Revolutionary Council nationalised twenty-seven privately owned banks, of which thirteen were joint ventures with foreign share holdings, and on 25 June, fifteen privately owned insurance companies were nationalised. According to the government, the justification for nationalisation was the heavy domestic and foreign trade debts of some of the banks, especially the development banks, the possibility of bankruptcy of others and the risk of capital flight. In the Revolutionary Council's ruling, there was no reference to Islamic banking, but the head of the Planning and Budget Organisation announced that the decision was an important step towards usury-free banking. Four years later, in August 1983, a new Law of the Interest-free Banking System "eliminated" interest and forbade banks to charge it. As early as 1979, the nationalised banks started to substitute the words "service charge" and "profit" for "interest rate".

At the end of summer 1979, thirty-six government and newly nationalised banks were reorganised and integrated into ten banks: the central bank; three specialised banks in the fields of industry and mines, housing and construction and agriculture; and six commercial banks.

In the large industrial establishments, government supervision became increasingly inevitable, due to the exodus of owners, managers and foreign technicians, outstanding debts, and increasing dependence on government funds. On 14 June, the Revolutionary Council approved a measure for the appointment of one or more managers to all companies whose owners were absent. This also applied to companies that had closed or were unable to continue their operations and had asked the government for help. The law also obliged the government to determine the ownership of those industries within the "framework of Islamic law".

The next major step was taken in July. On 5 July, the Revolutionary Council approved the Law for the Protection and Expansion of Iranian Industry which nationalised three categories of private industry: strategic industries, such as metals, chemicals, ship building, aircraft manufacture and mining; industries belonging to fifty-three individuals and families who were close associates of the Pahlavi dynasty; industries whose liabilities exceeded their net assets and those which, despite their solvency, were indebted to the government. The enterprises in the last two categories were to be nationalised without compensation. The owners of enterprises in the first category could receive compensation according to their net assets, if their companies were not included in either of the other categories. The government was to partly own enterprises whose assets were greater than their liabilities, in proportion to the value of the debts to the banking system.

It is interesting to note that two days after the nationalisation of large enterprises, Khomeini tried to reduce the anxiety of merchants and traders. In an audience with them, he indicated that the objective of the Islamic economy was not to eliminate private economic activity, but to reduce the concentration of wealth.

### *Housing, urban and rural land measures*

One of the populist moves of the clerical leadership was a series of abortive housing measures, introduced in the period 1979–80. In March 1979, Khomeini promised homes for poor families. Thus, agitation for the seizure and distribution of empty houses, apartments, extra dwellings and urban land began. The Housing Foundation was established and identified 200,000 empty dwellings that were to be confiscated or bought. However, no appropriate measures were ever approved.

In June 1979, the Revolutionary Council nationalised almost all dead or underdeveloped land in urban areas. Despite circumvention of the law, by early 1983 twenty million square metres of private urban land was transferred to government ownership.

The reaction of the Revolutionary Council to the rural or agricultural land problem was slower and more conservative. Despite the confiscation decrees issued by the revolutionary courts in Tehran and other major cities, agricultural land was not officially subjected to nationalisation or land reform. However, the provisional government proposed a limited land reform concerning the distribution of state arable lands and dead lands, which was revised by the Revolutionary Council after the resignation of Bazargan on 6 November 1979.

**Bani-Sadr and the clergy**

On 25 January 1980, Bani-Sadr was elected president by an overwhelming majority. Bani-Sadr's ideological position combined Islamic pluralism and socio-economics with Western analytical tools. In his book on Islamic economics published before the revolution, Bani-Sadr espoused social justice, the equitable distribution of wealth and state regulation of the economy. However, as his explanation did not rely on the arguments of Islamic jurisconsults, it was not considered very persuasive by the clergy.

In his campaign for the presidency, Bani-Sadr advocated the uprooting of Iran's dependent socio-economic structure without specifying any replacement programme. He was not against the nationalisation of the banking system and large dependent industries or land reform. However, he was against any concentration of decision-making in the hands either of the state or of an unspecified entity which he called "capital", which for him was the source of all types of exploitation. For this reason, he was also opposed to the idea of the absolute power of the *faqih*, which was Khomeini's ideal Islamic state. He spoke against the increasingly monopolising role of the clergy in state politics, calling them "a fistful of fascist clerics".

Bani-Sadr, as president, never sought to implement his egalitarian ideas. However, he did not oppose the adoption of economic measures that adversely affected the interests of the traditional merchants *(bazaris)* and undermined the confidence of the property-owning classes. His mind appeared fixed on the question of state power. Thus, in the period of his presidency, Bani-Sadr viewed law and order as a prerequisite for the elimination of the clergy's control of the state apparatus. He advocated a return to normality and a moderate central authority. Such a state of affairs required the repression of the Hezbollah, which constantly threatened the social and political peace of the country. For the clerics, however, law and order was the continuation of the August 1979 crackdown on anything unIslamic in the political, cultural and economic spheres (*ibid.*, pp. 239–46).

*Major economic measures in the second year of the revolution*

After the resignation of Bazargan, the Revolutionary Council's communiqué, despite its rhetoric, specified only two measures for solving the pressing land and housing problems. However, the radical mood of the country after the occupation of the US embassy and approval of the Islamic Constitution hastened approval of the economic bills of this period. The Islamic Constitution was approved in December 1979 and its articles on social and economic justice raised the expectations of the lower middle classes, peasants and the poor. In general terms, the economic and financial articles of the Constitution ruled out exploitation of labour, monopoly, hoarding and usury. It defined the forms of ownership of the economy as state, co-operative and private and stated that these sectors were "to be based upon systematic and sound planning" (Article 44). The state sector included "all large-scale and mother industries, foreign trade, major minerals, banking, insurance, power generation, dams and large-scale irrigation networks, radio and television, post, telegraph and telephone services, aviation, shipping, roads, railways and the like" (*ibid.*). Private ownership, "legitimately acquired", was to be respected and the private sector could engage in all kinds of economic activities "that supplement the economic activities of the state and co-operative sectors" (*ibid.*). However, there were also clauses concerning ownership that could lend themselves to different interpretations. Article 44 of the Constitution stipulated that, "in each of these three sectors [ownership] is protected by the laws of the Islamic Republic, in so far as this ownership ... does not go beyond the bounds of Islamic law, contributes to economic growth and progress ... and does not harm society"(*ibid.*).

Article 4 of the Constitution also had an important implication for future economic measures. It stated that all "civil, penal, financial, economic, administrative, cultural, military, political and other laws and regulations must be based on Islamic criteria" (Article 4), and made it clear that this principle "applies absolutely and generally to all articles of the Constitution as well as to other laws and regulations and the *foqaha* [jurisconsults] of the Guardianship Council are judges in this matter" (*ibid.*)

*Housing and rural land measures*

In early 1980, the Revolutionary Council approved a series of measures concerning the rent or resale to the public of empty dwellings, which caused considerable unrest. These measures were all lifted by June 1981 or by 1983, at which time the government's control over housing transactions had ceased completely.

Another important measure approved by the Revolutionary Council in the period of Bani-Sadr's presidency, was the land distribution bill of March 1980 which permitted the division of large estates, without compensation. However, the first draft of the bill provoked the opposition of prominent conservative ayatollahs, such as Qumi of Mashhad who condemned expropriation of private property as unIslamic. The council revised the law and, to appease the opposition of the conservative clergy, Khomeini asked ayatollahs Montazeri, Beheshti and Meshkini to judge whether or not the bill was in accordance with Islamic law. They reviewed the bill and did not find anything unIslamic in it. Nevertheless, they introduced minor changes. The bill approved the distribution of land to landless and land-poor peasants, high-school and agricultural-college graduates, civil servants and others who desired to cultivate the land. The size of each plot was not to exceed three times the accepted average in each district for the maintenance of one peasant family. Absentee landlords who had no other source of income were limited to twice this plot size. Mechanised farms were exempted from the break-up yet they had to be administered co-operatively and were to join existing co-operatives. Landlords were to be compensated net of their debts to the government and any outstanding religious dues. Distribution of land at the village level was the responsibility of the seven-man local land transfer committees comprising government representatives, revolutionary agencies, local religious judges and local villagers.

The committees presented themselves as champions of the peasant cause. In response, the landlords became active, protesting against the work of the committees by lobbying members of parliament and religious leaders. They also managed to obtain some *fatwas* (formal religious proclamations) from some *motjaheds* (Islamic jurists) against land distribution, and even resorted to a *fatwa* of Khomeini against the usurpation of private land.

In May 1980, landlords published a resolution which drew the attention of the *motjaheds* and Khomeini to the unIslamic nature and unconstitutionality of the denial of ownership and violation of property rights. Ayatollah Rouhani sent a telegram to Bani-Sadr stating that the law was in gross violation of Islamic law and the Constitution and that it was not approved by the newly created Guardianship Council. Others, such as ayatollahs Mahallati, Shirazi and Qumi, reiterated the same point and, finally, the seminary teachers' society at Qum warned against bills presented in the name of Islam under the pretext of helping the oppressed, and deplored the ruinous effect of the land distribution law on agricultural output. Finally, in November 1980, Khomeini ordered the suspension of Articles 3 and 4 of the law concerning the distribution of private lands and, eventually, in 1981, left the final decision on distribution and other property issues to parliament. Peasants reacted in a defensive manner by sending representatives and petitions to parliament and Tehran newspapers. Some clerics and members of the committees sided with them, accusing other clerics of being pro-landlord and following an "American Islamic line". The dispute continued and the problem was left unresolved. After 1981, the struggle was mostly shifted to debate between members of parliament and the Guardianship Council.

### *Islamisation of the labour movement*

If peasants veered towards a defensive struggle at the end of 1980, workers and salaried employees had been pushed in that direction after the crackdown of August 1979. Workers and employees' organisations were steadily being purged of non-Islamic elements. Workers were also threatened by rising unemployment, a result of the deteriorating economic situation. Nevertheless, after the fall of Bazargan's government, workers intensified their demands for control of the work place and self-management. However, this new wave of struggle coincided with the intensification of the power struggle between Bani-Sadr and the clergy and later with the Iran–Iraq war. The clergy in the Islamic Republic party and Prime Minister Rajaee created their own *shouras* (councils) in factories, offices and ministries. Gradually, Islamic associations were established in factories and governmental institutions and Islamic managers replaced liberal managers of state-owned factories, most of whom had been appointed by the Bazargan government.

The clerics launched an anti-professional campaign, arguing that the country was in need of dedicated Islamic managers, and not the Western-trained unIslamic type of experts that Bani-Sadr supported. The political dispute that was being fought in the economic realm was gradually being won by the clergy. Islamic associations and managers replaced the independent *shouras* and liberal managers. Labour House, an independent headquarters for workers' assemblies, was turned into a centre for pro-Islamic Republic *shouras* and Islamic associations. In the same period, between August 1979 and the dismissal of Bani-Sadr in June 1981, labour unrest dropped mainly due to national campaigns of intimidation, repression and the cultural revolution, the forced establishment of Islamic associations in factories and offices, and the Iran–Iraq war. Labour's radical demands were reduced to immediate economic ones. No new labour law replaced the restrictive and undemocratic labour law of the *ancien régime* and even some of the perks of the profit-sharing scheme of the former regime were abolished.

*Foreign and domestic trade measures*

In May 1980, the Revolutionary Council approved the implementation of a government monopoly over the importation of goods for which control was desirable. This was not really necessary, since a similar law had empowered the government with the same monopolistic right over foreign trade in 1930. However, the council, the left and the bazaar talked about the decision as if a radical new law had been approved.

Article 44 of the Constitution explicitly placed foreign trade under state control. The freeze on about $12 billion of Iranian assets, trade sanctions against Iran by the US government during the hostage crisis, and the subsequent rise in the price of imported goods in the national market hastened the government's intervention in foreign trade. Nevertheless, the impracticality of complete nationalisation of foreign trade in those days and the anticipated negative reaction of the merchants, who were regarded as an ally of the revolution, prevented the council from imposing a full government monopoly over foreign trade. Furthermore, the outbreak of war between Iraq and Iran, in September 1980, necessitated the extension of government control to domestic trade.

In 1980, the ministry of trade officially established a government monopoly over many imported goods, including machinery, metals, paper, wood, essential food and textiles. Thirteen procurement and distribution centres were set up to handle importation and domestic distribution of these goods, and soon they were handling 40 per cent of the total value of imports. Private traders could still import individually, but they were obliged to use a licensing system implemented by the *ancien régime*. However, since trading in imports was much more profitable than industrial activities, such practices as favouritism in the allocation of licences increased. Importers were required to hand over 30 per cent of the volume of each consignment to the government and to sell the remainder at predetermined prices.

The outbreak of war and the shortage of foreign exchange due to the decline in oil revenues forced the Islamic government to impose rationing on petrol and fuel. Rationing was soon extended to essential goods, such as sugar, meat, vegetable oil and cloth. The Foundation for Economic Mobilisation was established to administer rationing, and local mosques distributed ration cards. This policy improved the distribution of essential goods.

*Foreign capital and the Islamic government*

The Iranian revolution affected key international economic relationships, especially those between the United States and Iran. After the revolution, the central banks in the major capital cities of the world, including the Federal Reserve Bank of New York, honoured payment instructions from the Central Bank of Iran and other Western banks followed suit. However, some foreign economic contracts and agreements, such as the Consortium Agreement, were cancelled by the Iranian government. It was increasingly difficult to honour other contracts, while others, though not cancelled, were officially stopped, such as the $9 billion contract for the purchase of armaments from the United States. Foreign companies operating in Iran adopted a wait-and-see attitude. Iran honoured debt payments and the Law for Attraction and Protection of Foreign Investments was not rescinded. Nevertheless, the long-term security of such investments was uncertain. After the nationalisation of all private banking institutions and large industries, including those with mixed ownership, foreign owners started negotiations with the government authorities over compensation. The outcome of these negotiations has never been announced in Iran. However, as trade has continued between Iran and the rest of the world, one could conclude that foreign owners of nationalised banks and industries may have been compensated.

Another major turning point in the strained economic relationship between Iran and the Western world, particularly the United States, took place in the period after the November 1979 occupation of the US embassy. In this period, the US government imposed its most comprehensive sanctions on any country in the twentieth century. A comprehensive trade embargo, banning the flow of physical goods between the United State and Iran, was imposed in April 1980. A ban on Iranian oil imports had been adopted immediately after the US embassy occupation. After April 1980, nearly all trade between the two countries stopped. The reaction of US allies to the US government's demand for the imposition of a similar embargo was not exactly wholehearted. But in December 1979, they agreed to the following limited trade sanctions: a ban on the sale of military equipment to Iran (Iran bought military supplies on the black market at higher prices); a ban on paying premiums for Iranian oil (the increase to $45 per barrel made them reluctant to increase demand); a ban on opening new deposit facilities; a restriction on the increase in existing dollar balances relative to non-dollar reserves; and a ban on the extension of new credit (after the revolution no one was eager to grant any loans to Iran).

The effect of these trade sanctions on the Iranian economy was felt slowly, but surely. Initially, oil revenues did not drop, due to the increase in the price of oil. However, over time, oil revenues fell steadily, putting a strain on an economy much dependent on oil for its growth and development.

The start of the Iran–Iraq war, in October 1980, undoubtedly exacerbated the situation. It forced the closure of some oil fields and facilities and scared off prospective buyers. The combined effect of sanctions and the war increased the cost of imports, and led to changes in import routes and a fundamental restructuring of Iran's foreign trade. The largest Iranian port, Khoramshahr, was lost early in the war and this forced a rerouting of imports through overland routes via Turkey and the Soviet Union.

By late autumn 1980, the Iranian government was hard pressed for foreign exchange. Reserves were falling, due to the decline in oil revenues and non-oil exports, and military purchases abroad were rising. The only source of relief was the unblocking of $12 billion of Iranian government assets by the US government. In fact, the most effective US sanction proved to be its financial freeze of Iranian assets imposed on 14 November 1979. All holders of Iranian government assets in the United States, or of those under control of US entities overseas, were instructed to hold them as they then were. Any form of disposition was prohibited, without permission from the US government.

The Islamic government's reaction to the freeze was to start litigation and demand the intervention of local banking authorities in Europe. However, Iran only managed to recover its assets in stages. Some $4 billion held in the United States was to be transferred to the Bank of England within six months. It was to be placed in a trust account pending settlement of legal disputes with Iran. Another $7.9 billion was transferred to an escrow account with the Algerian Central Bank. When the balance reached $7.9 billion, hostages were released and the money was transferred to an Iranian account. The $7.9 billion comprised: $3.67 billion in outstanding syndicated loans with United States and foreign banks, which was entirely paid off, much to the surprise of the US government; $14.2 billion which was put in an escrow account to be used to pay off Iran's debt to US banks, and $2.88 billion which was sent to Iran.

In sum, during the hostage-crisis period, Iran suffered from its loss of access to about $12 billion in assets, paid off its outstanding debts to US banks and accepted a claim-settlement procedure that favoured the claimants. The assets of the Shah and his family were not returned to Iran and the cost of imported goods greatly increased due to black-market purchases and the increased role of middlemen (Rahnema and Nomani, 1990, pp. 246–55).

**The clergy versus the clergy**

After the dismissal of Bani-Sadr, the Islamic Republic party (IRP), under the control of the clergy, emerged stronger than ever. In the second half of 1981, all important governmental positions were held either by the clergy or by their secular followers, representing different factions of the clerical leadership. To preserve its power, the clergy adopted heavily repressive measures. A new mood of Islamic pragmatism set in. Although this did not mean civil and political liberalism or tolerance, it did herald a return to economic and administrative "normality", which was further manifested in a conditional reconciliation with Iran's European and Japanese trade partners. Encouraged by the relative upturn in economic activity in 1981–82, and the position of the Guardianship Council against economic measures that tampered with the institution of private property and trade, representatives of the bazaar demanded more security and further expansion of private economic activity. The government was plagued by lack of discipline and uncoordinated decision-making. The Hezbollah's intimidation campaign against experts had added to the paucity of trained technocrats, the majority of whom had emigrated. These conditions led to the demoralisation of the remaining efficiency-conscious technocrats and government managers. In December 1982, the ruling clerical coalition received an eight-point decree from Khomeini, ordering them to curb the excesses and semi-anarchy of the Islamic courts, committees and the IRP.

Khomeini's eight-point decree strengthened the position of the pragmatic clergy and those government members who were conscious of the importance of rebuilding the crisis-ridden economy. Its emphasis on the security of property and social peace provided the pragmatists with a justification to call for an improvement in the Islamic Republic's relation with Europe and Japan. Tehran's empty hotels were gradually filling with foreign businessmen and journalists. Nabavi, the minister of heavy industries and a former Islamic populist, reflected the new pragmatic mood. He criticised himself and others for being under the spell of the left in adhering to "anti-dependency" and "isolationist" economic policies, for underestimating the importance of managerial skills in factories and plants, and for undermining the role of the private sector. Rafsanjani, the powerful patron of the pragmatic faction, referred to those who had left the country and announced that "people are prepared to forgive the fugitives' past record" (*ibid.*, pp. 255–6).

In February 1984, on the fifth anniversary of the revolution, Khomeini pointed out three crucial problems facing the Islamic Republic: the war with Iraq, the deepening economic crisis, and the factional disputes among the ruling clerics. All these problems had weakened the unity and stability of the Islamic regime. To solve the first problem, Khomeini stubbornly insisted on "war, war, till victory". He did not propose any concrete solutions for the second problem, but he did invite all factions to come to their senses and realise the threat their infighting posed to the preservation of the regime.

One can identify two principal factions with respect to the economic issues: the interventionists and the non-interventionists. The advocates of intervention were of the opinion that the Islamic government should play a greater role in the market economy of Iran, in order to improve the economy's crisis-ridden performance. They argued for social justice, preservation of the government sector, more government control over foreign trade, income policies, including price and wage control, and more government planning. They believed that "traditional Islamic jurisprudence" was outdated and unable to provide all the answers to the complex problems of the present. They insisted that the jurisconsult, in other words, Khomeini, should introduce new rulings or overrule former ones, as he saw fit. They referred to their ideal economic system as a "mixed Islamic economy" and insisted that it was quite different from either capitalism or socialism.

The non-interventionist view was that an unregulated "Islamic" market economy, relying almost entirely on the private sector, could best achieve the goals of growth, employment, price stability and economic justice; government intervention should only be necessary under abnormal conditions and as a temporary measure; and minimal direct intervention should be the rule. They called for a strong Islamic government, but only in the political and ideological realm. For them, Islamic government should supervise the functioning of the market, ensuring observance of Islamic economic regulations, and providing a stable and secure environment for the functioning of the private sector. They criticised the interventionists for ignorance of "traditional jurisprudence" and for not adhering strongly enough to Islamic principles on the functioning of the economy. They called the other faction "leftist", "eclectist" and "statist".

The interventionist faction argued that such an approach was at best naïve in the face of war, deep recession and the profiteering attitude of merchants and traders. They dubbed the supporters of the non-interventionist view "capitalist roaders" and "reactionaries". Mir-Hossein Moussavi, who was prime minister from 1981–89, essentially represented the "statist" faction, which claimed that it represented the general interests of the dispossessed.

In 1982–83, Moussavi's cabinet consisted of a coalition of outspoken non-interventionist, pro-bazaar ministers and advocates of a mixed Islamic economy. Following months of behind-the-scenes intra-government disputes, the cabinet was finally reshuffled in Summer 1983 and two important pro-bazaar ministers, Asgaroladi and Tavakoli, were dismissed.

The non-interventionist faction waited until early 1984 to attack the government. This time, the conflict shifted to parliament and spread to Friday congregational prayers and Islamic newspapers. In the debate over the government budget, the non-interventionist tendency criticised the wastefulness, inefficient policies and eclectic views of the Moussavi government. They blamed it for inflation and recession and the expanded bureaucracy. The government faction responded by accusing the Guardianship Council of being obstructive (*ibid.*, pp. 257–8).

In Autumn 1985, the internal power struggle centred on the choice of a new prime minister and the issue was resolved by Khomeini's personal intervention in favour of Moussavi and against President Khamenei. However, Khomeini's position on the issue of a mixed economy was more moderate than the interventionists'. In a meeting with the president and Moussavi's cabinet, he reiterated the importance of Islamic unity, then said: "Do not follow the policy of turning everything into state [control and ownership]. No, this has its limits ... let people and the bazaar participate [in economic activity]" (*Keyhan*, 11 Aban 1364).

Before Khomeini's ordinance of 7 December 1987, which reiterated his power to change his own ordinances in favour of new ones, supporters of the Moussavi faction could only try to intimidate their opponents by accusing them of being "employees of the Godless capitalists and millionaires" (*Keyhan*, 6 Azar 1364). However, the prominent advocates of "traditional jurisprudence" were not intimidated by such name calling. For example, Khazali, an outspoken clergyman in the Guardianship Council and an appointee of Khomeini, in a speech before the bazaar supporters, reminded the other faction that they must follow the orthodox and conservative rulings of Khomeini in *Tahrir al-Vasileh*:

"I hereby announce that whenever the Guardianship Council rejects a bill passed by parliament, God is disapproving it and as long as you [deputies] have not submitted [to God's will], we [the Council] will not retreat. God's ordinances must be executed" (*Resalat*, 29 Shahrivar 1366).

Apparently, he was ignoring the fact that in the "Government of God" interpreted by Khomeini, the grand jurisconsult could overrule the Council when he found it necessary, despite his occasional support. By late 1987, the Council was taking its role all too seriously and its veto of important economic bills proposed by the "statist" controlled parliament had made the parliament look like a barren institution in the eyes of the devoted followers of the Islamic Republic.

According to the Islamic Constitution, the Council had the right to judge whether "civil, penal, financial, administrative, cultural, military, political and other laws and regulations" were based on the *Shari'a* or not. There were three general reasons that rejected major laws passed by parliament: the laws were not really in response to "overriding necessary conditions"; they encroached on the "sphere of primary rulings", which did not come under parliament's authority, and the laws had a universal bearing, whereas their application should have remained restricted. Such vetoed or modified bills include: the bill on full nationalisation of foreign trade, which was vetoed on the grounds that it was universal in scope and thus contrary to the *Shari'a*'s rulings on free trade; the bills on the nationalisation of mines and utilised lands which were drastically modified by the Council; the bill for the provision and distribution of certain necessities; and the land reform bills of 1982 and 1985 (Rahnema and Nomani, 1990, pp. 260–66).

Such statements led the ministers of the Moussavi government to ask for the Imam's direct rulings on certain economic issues in late 1987. Their questions finally led to Khomeini's now famous reiteration of the idea of the absolute power of the government of the "Prophet of Allah" and to the curbing of the power of the Guardianship Council.

In December 1987, after several years of debate over the Islamic interpretation of labour codes, parliament approved a labour law. One of the major articles provided an Islamic justification for government intervention in "Islamic contracts" between employees and employers that would bind the companies to observe regulations concerning insurance, minimum working age, hours of work and so on. The Guardianship Council, however, found the law unIslamic and unconstitutional on the grounds that, in Islam such contracts were voluntary bonds between individuals and that the government had no right to impose conditions. However, based on a question of the minister of labour, Khomeini as "vicegerent of God" issued a religious ruling granting the government the right to legislate in certain cases related to government intervention in the contracts between two parties. He also created a new institution, the Council for the Determination of Exigencies (CDE), comprising clerical members of the Guardianship Council, certain other ruling clerics, the prime minister and the minister involved. This board was supposed to identify urgent matters of state and reduce the obstructive role of the Council (*ibid*., pp. 266–9). Khomeini's son, Ahmed, was to participate in the deliberations of the new Council without the right of vote.

In 1987, Khomeini also agreed to the dissolution of the Islamic Republic Party (IRP) which had become polarised by infighting between interventionists and non-interventionists. After purging society of all parties that stood in its way, the IRP bowed out of the political scene, leaving behind a handful of Islamic political groups essentially representing two major factions. The non-interventionist faction combined forces around the *Ruhaniyat Mobarez* (militant clergy), the interventionists around the newly created *Ruhaniyoun Mobarez* (militant clerics) which had splintered from the militant clergy with the blessings of Khomeini (*ibid.*, pp. 215–18).

On 20 August 1988, after repeated defeats on the battlefield, Khomeini approved the ceasefire between Iran and Iraq and, thus, a protracted war that had greatly weakened the position of the Islamic government politically and economically came to an end (*Keyhan*, airmail weekly, 5 Mordad 1367). A Council of Policy Making for Reconstruction (CPMR) was set up to design reconstruction policies. This council has effectively become the highest policy-making institution for formulating economic policies; it is comprised of heads of the three organs of state and the minister concerned with the issue in question. Khomeini also spelled out the general guidelines of reconstruction policies: strengthening defence capabilities, reconstruction of industry and increasing agricultural production. He also asserted that foreign and domestic trade should be opened to the public and that rich traders' monopolistic powers should be curbed. The Council drafted a blueprint that urged the decentralisation of decision-making, increased privatisation of the economy and government support for agriculture, mining and industry. It called for the sale of shares in non-strategic state-owned enterprises through the stock exchange. However, priority in this ownership scheme was given to employees of the enterprises concerned, the former fighters on the battlefields and to families of the martyrs. The government was also required to prepare laws that would guarantee the security of private investment. The blueprint also permitted foreign loans and assistance as a last resort if they did not jeopardise national independence. With respect to foreign trade, the CPMR freed imports of goods by the private sector at a free market rate for foreign exchange (*ibid.*, 27 Ordibehest 1368). The interventionist faction criticised the private-sector-orientation of the CPMR guidelines, but could not prevent the approval of the five-year development plan that incorporated these guidelines into law.

## The economic structure and institutions

The present economic structure and institutions are the end product of the pre-revolutionary period and, to some extent, of the changes since the revolution.

### Population structure and the labour force

The population of Iran was estimated to be 58.5 million in 1990, representing an annual average increase of 3.1 per cent in the period 1986–90 (*Keyhan*, 12 Tir 1370). This rapid growth has given rise to a very young population, 45 per cent being under 15 years of age in 1986. With such an age structure, the proportion of youth (under 10 years of age) to economically active adults was high. In 1986, 22.3 per cent of the population were employed and this work force had to support the rest of the population. Of the labour force, 20 per cent were women, mostly employed in civil services.

Considering that the economy has been in crisis since 1976 and the relative increase of the dependent population in the last decade, it will be more difficult for those in work to support those who are not. Nevertheless, before the ceasefire between Iran and Iraq, the reaction of the authorities of the Islamic Republic to these facts was amazingly militaristic: more people meant that more could be mobilised for the war effort (Rahnema and Nomani, 1990, pp. 273–4). However, after the ceasefire, the pressure of economic hardships had forced the leaders of the Islamic Republic to advocate birth control, which had been criticised by the same clergy in the pre-revolution period. Nevertheless, in 1983, about 23 per cent of married women of child-bearing age were using contraception; included in this percentage are women whose husbands practised contraception (The World Bank, 1987, p. 259). This figure increased to 28 per cent by 1988. The government has now started to distribute contraceptives and has terminated family aid and benefits for the fourth child of the households (*Keyhan*, airmail weekly, 2 Mordad 1370 and 23 Mordad 1370).

The 11.1 million people who were considered as employed in the 1986 population census came from 5.6 million urban and 4.2 million rural households. The breakdown of the employed labour force indicates a relative decline in agricultural and industrial employment and a very rapid growth in the service sector. This is mainly due to the prolonged economic crisis and the drastic rise in government employment. In 1986, the employed labour force was distributed as follows: 30 per cent in agriculture, 26.5 per cent in industry and 43.5 per cent in services. In the urban community, 56.5 per cent of the employed work force was in the private sector and 43.5 per cent in the public sector. In the rural community 82 per cent was employed in the private sector and 18 per cent in the public sector (Rahnema and Nomani, 1990, pp. 274–5).

The development of Iran from the pre-revolutionary period onwards, has been constrained by a shortage of skilled middle-level and high-level workers. However, the share of skilled labour in the work force as a whole is below the pre-revolution figure and the situation is not improving, as the number of students in vocational training and higher education is also far below the pre-revolution figure (see *Keyhan*, airmail weekly, 12 Tir, 1370). Of more than 65,000 Iranian students who are studying abroad, only about 5 per cent return to Iran each year, which is lower than the pre-revolution rate. In addition, up until 1990, a great majority of skilled people who left Iran after the revolution, whether voluntarily or not, did not come back.

The social-security system in Iran is quite underdeveloped. Less than 4 per cent of the employed labour force benefits from retirement pay and less than 23 per cent of them are insured. Since 1987, an unemployment benefit scheme has been introduced. However, given the restrictive conditions attached to the payment of unemployment benefits, the majority of the unemployed labour force does not qualify for this payment which is based on a minimum wage rate.

Despite the long history of labour unions in Iran, since the 1960s labour has not had independent unions. Anti-labour and anti-union policies of the Iranian governments since the Constitutional Revolution of 1906, along with the peasant origins of many of the unions, have adversely affected the continuity and militancy of the union movement. The main features of the Iranian working class are that it is based on migration, especially migration to Tehran Province, and that most workers are young. In addition, a relatively important proportion of workers are employed in traditional small industries. At present, the state-run Islamic labour councils and Islamic societies constitute the only legal labour organisations. All non-Islamic unions and councils created before and immediately after the revolution have been banned and liquidated.

The controversial and recently adopted Islamic Labour Law is not much different from the Labour Law of 1959, with the exception of improvements in provision for paid leave and the reinstatement of laid-off workers, and new restrictions imposed on the work and weekly working hours of women. The Islamic Law, like its predecessor, applies only to large workshops which employ ten or more workers. According to the law, workers are denied the right to join any union except the Islamic labour councils and do not have the right to strike.

**The role of the government and the private sector in the economy**

The government has played an important role in the Iranian economy since the 1930s. However, since 1979, due to nationalisation and the confiscation of industries, banks and farms once owned by the royal family or business people closely associated with the former regime, the government's share of aggregate supply has increased. In 1986, 68.4 per cent of the employed population worked in the private sector, with the rest in the public sector (Rahnema and Nomani, 1990, pp. 273–8).

The public sector in Iran includes both financial and non-financial sectors. The non-financial sector includes general government, the nationalised industries and the Islamic foundations. The size of the nationalised industries, the foundations (the former Foundation for the Disinherited, now called the Foundation of Life-Sacrificers, the Martyrs Foundation and the Housing Foundation) and public and nationalised banks, is important in terms of their share of aggregate demand expenditures. However, Iranian national-income accounting places investment in nationalised enterprises in the private sector, while it really belongs in the public sector. In 1989, private consumption of goods and services accounted for 50.4 per cent of real gross national product. The private and public sectors' demand for investment goods — inventories and fixed investment in plants, equipment and construction — made up 13.4 per cent of real GNP. In the same year, the government's consumption of goods and services constituted 10.4 per cent of real GNP (*Gozaresh-e Eqtesadi*, 1369, pp. 41–2).

According to official statistics, in the first four years after the revolution, the private sector and the government's share in the total value of imports were 59 and 41 per cent respectively, compared with 49.7 and 50.3 per cent in the last four years of the former regime. The government share in foreign trade may have increased in the second half of the 1980s. However, inasmuch as the private sector controls non-oil exports, which have increased since 1983, the role of the private sector in foreign trade is still considerable.

In 1984, there were 6,596 workshops in the industrial sector. They were considered "large" enterprises because each employed more than 10 people. However, the majority were actually small: in fact, 68.5 per cent of them employed fewer than 50 people. Large enterprises employed 594,000 people of whom 519,000 were wage earners and 75,000 salary earners. Only 6.2 per cent of the labour force in large enterprises were women, compared with 6.8 per cent in 1976. In 1983, 986 industrial establishments (excluding the oil and gas industries) were owned by the Islamic government and state foundations. These produced 68.8 per cent of the value added, employed 67.2 per cent of the workforce and provided for 55.5 per cent of wage and salary payments of large enterprises. The very large enterprises constituted the modern industrial sector of the economy. Most were established before the revolution, mainly through licensing agreements and, to some extent, through foreign investment.

Due to the nature of licensing agreements and direct foreign investment in the pre-revolution period, poor communication between different sectors and the continuation of the industrial strategy of the former regime, a large proportion of industrial input continues to be imported (see Rahnema and Nomani, 1990, p. 278).

The industrial sector is protected by tariffs, quantitative restrictions, pricing policies and foreign-exchange allocations. The prices of public sector inputs and outputs are set on a cost-plus basis under government control. These companies receive foreign exchange at a much overvalued official exchange rate and their commodities' distribution margins are also pre-determined by the government. As a result, managers of these companies do not have an incentive to reduce costs and become more efficient.

The major industrial policy of the government, as in the pre-revolutionary period, is import-substitution industrialisation and export promotion. In addition, as we saw before, the Rafsanjani government is gradually reducing administrative regulations and procedures for private investment and plans to sell many non-strategic public enterprises to the private sector. Thus, the government is trying to introduce more liberal trade and price policies. To ensure more reliable oil revenues, the government is also moderating its demand for high oil prices at OPEC meetings.

The agricultural sector, which includes fisheries and forestry, employs 30 per cent of the labour force spread over almost three million small and large plots of arable land. In 1989 the contribution of the agricultural sector to real GDP was 21.7 per cent (*Gozaresh-e Eqtesadi*, 1369, p. 41). Over half of the country's land is uncultivable, 12 per cent is under cultivation, and up to 18 per cent comprises natural pastures and forests.

The Islamic government's major agricultural policy has been to promote self-sufficiency in basic staples, through a whole range of incentive policies.

These include subsidisation at the producer (output and input prices) and consumer levels.

Guaranteed prices are set by the government on basic staples — meat, sugar beets, cotton and oil seeds. These prices are based on production cost, inflation and input prices. In addition, there are other incentives: for instance, farmers may use a percentage of the money they receive from the government for their wheat to purchase consumer goods or tractors at official prices, far below market prices. The government also buys part of the farm's surplus staple produce and milk, thus limiting the role of the private sector in marketing, especially in the wheat market.

The Islamic government has also subsidised agricultural inputs, e.g. fertilisers and pesticides. At consumer level, basic staples (except rice) are subsidised, their prices controlled and there is two-tier pricing with the use of ration coupons. Wheat is heavily subsidised. The ratio of the purchasing price from the farmers to the selling price to flour mills has been around one to five. There is a dual market for meat: the controlled price of meat that is rationed, and the free market. Milk is bought by the government at a high price, and consumers buy it either at a lower price with ration coupons, or at a free market price.

Subsidies currently constitute less than 5 per cent of government budget deficits. Since the fall in oil revenues in the second half of the 1980s, the level of subsidies has decreased due to the change in government policy on subsidies and inflation.

On the whole, the government's agricultural support policy has distorted relative prices, and has introduced changes in production and consumption patterns in agricultural trade vis-à-vis manufacturing.

The service sector, private and public, modern and traditional, grew to be the largest economic sector in the Islamic Republic. In 1989 it accounted for 46.7 per cent of the real GDP and about 47 per cent of the labour force, compared with 31 per cent in 1977 (*ibid.*, pp. 41 and 44).

Despite the expansion of the Islamic government's role in domestic trade, the private sector's role prevails in services. After the revolution, the government's role in domestic trade expanded in reaction to the US embargo of 1980 and the disrupting effect of the Iran–Iraq war in September 1980, which gave rise to shortages of foreign-exchange reserves and imported commodities, and rising prices and hoarding. However, the government expanded its role in domestic trade, mainly by supervising the distribution of staple commodities through a limited number of co-operatives and procurement and distribution centres. Coupon rationing was imposed on certain commodities. As one would expect, a thriving black market developed, which the Islamic government allowed to flourish. In fact to some extent this market was an "official" black market, sanctioning a system which supplied high-income groups with goods unavailable to the rest of the population. However, after the ceasefire, and especially when Rafsanjani became president, rationing has been gradually phased out.

**The Islamic banking system and financial institutions**

Contrary to the noticeable growth in wholesale and retail trade in the period

1977–84, the share of financial and monetary institutions in the service sector has been in continuous decline. In 1984, the value added of the financial and monetary subsector, of which banking and insurance are the two major activities, represented 2 per cent of real GDP. The banking system and insurance companies were nationalised in 1979 and the Law of Usury-Free Banking was approved by parliament in August 1983. According to this law, banks perform the function of a profit-sharing institution. They can accept two kinds of deposits: *qarz al-hassana* (interest-free) deposits (both current and savings); and term-investment deposits. A *qarz al-hassana* current account is similar to conventional current accounts. *Qarz al-hassana* savings accounts are interest-free savings accounts. However, banks can attract deposits through: non-fixed bonuses in cash; exempting depositors from payment of commissions and fees; or by granting priority to depositors in the use of banking facilities.

Term-investment deposits are of two kinds: short-term (3 months) with a minimum amount of 2,000 rials, and long-term (1 year) with a minimum of 50,000 rials. Banks can use their resources in investment projects, sharing the profit (or loss) with the depositors' funds, in which case a commission is charged by the banks. In principle, the profits earned as a result of the banks' investment are to be divided among depositors, after deduction of the banks' fees. The return is calculated in proportion to the total value of investment deposits, excluding the required reserves. In any case, the return of the principal of these deposits is guaranteed by the banks, which makes the operation questionable from a strictly Islamic point of view. In addition, banks must announce their profit rate every six months, when the depositors' share of profits is due to be paid. Of course, if deposits are withdrawn before the minimum time required or reduced below the required minimum, no profit will be earned. Term-investment funds can be used by banks in accordance with Islamic contracts, such as *muzaraba*, *musharaka*, direct investment, hire-purchase, forward transactions, credit sale in industrial, agricultural and the service sectors. Consumers can receive *qarz al-hassana* loans and enter into credit sale contracts for consumption purposes.

*Muzaraba* and *musharaka* are two kinds of partnership wherein the bank provides cash capital and the other party provides entrepreneurship, or funds are provided by both parties and profit is divided between them at the end of the term of contract. Hire-purchase is a leasing contract and forward transaction (*salaf*) is the cash purchase of products beforehand at a fixed price. Credit sale is sale by instalment wherein the bank may acquire a commodity and sell it to applicants in instalments.

The implementation of the law, as in Pakistan, has been mainly limited to the liabilities of the banks. So far, banks have been able to convert their liabilities into Islamic deposits and the government has implicitly guaranteed a return on savings accounts which is well below the rate of inflation. However, banks have not been very successful in converting their assets into Islamic contracts. According to the balance sheet of the banking system in March 1985, at the end of the first year of operation of the new system, 39.2 per cent of private-sector deposits had been transferred into *qarz al-hassana* and term-investment deposits; the rest were in the form of sight, non-sight, savings and time deposits (*ibid.*, pp. 277–81 and 283–5). *Qarz al-hassana* deposits are considered simply as demand deposits and can be withdrawn at will, even though from a strictly Islamic point of view they must be considered as loans to banks. As one would expect, due to a positive nominal return on term deposits, the growth in these deposits has been much higher than that in *qarz al-hassana* (Khan and Mirakhor, 1990, pp. 361–2).

On the asset side, in March 1985 only 16.8 per cent of new credits to the private sector were in new Islamic facilities; of these 78.4 per cent were allocated from term investment deposits and the rest from *qarz al-hassana* deposits. In the same year, 73.3 per cent of new banking facilities were allocated to short-term commercial activities, rather than long-term production investment.

At present, as in Pakistan, the rate of profit on term-investment accounts is determined by the Central Bank on the basis of the overall profits of the banking system. In 1985–87, the official "rates of profit" (or interest rates) for the short- and long-term investment accounts were 6 per cent and 8.5 per cent respectively. Of course, in real terms, i.e. after adjusting for inflation, these rates were negative. In 1987, the cash bonus, or prize, on *qarz al-hassana* savings accounts was 1.5 to 2 per cent of the value of deposits.

Banks charge a commission on loans granted to borrowers, the lowest rate being on housing loans. Some banks have now been ordered by the Central Bank to finance government projects (Rahnema and Nomani, 1990, pp. 281–2).

The uncertainty about the role of the private sector in the economy, despite the interventions of the Rafsanjani government, is a major reason for the slow move toward greater use of profit-sharing schemes in the banking system. The private sector needs clear-cut guidelines and legislation to clarify its role. In addition, the six existing nationalised commercial banks, unlike the three specialised banks, lack the skill of project analysis and monitoring, which is important in Islamic banking. However, the specialised banks are not allowed to receive private-sector deposits, and so they rely on the Central Bank and government deposits, which leads to a shortage of funds for the specialised banks. The commercial banks lend their excess liquidity to one another on a fixed rate of return, which is unIslamic, but they are reluctant to engage in profit-sharing schemes with the specialised banks on the basis of an unknown rate of return. Moreover, Islamic banking requires that owners of funds must be able to assess in advance the risks they are taking. However, without balance sheets and profit and loss accounts from both banks and the individual companies, this if often not possible (Khan and Mirakhor, 1990, pp. 363–4).

As far as interest-free banking is concerned, there is a device that facilitates evasion of Islamic practices: discounting. Of course, the "purchase of debt", or discounting, is legitimate in Shi'ite banking law in Iran. However, whatever one calls the discount rate, the difference between the purchase price and the redemption value of a financial document represents an interest return on the purchase. In addition, interest is charged in the large, but amorphous, and uncontrolled money markets of the bazaar, catering to the financial needs of small- and medium-sized companies and individuals. In this market, interest rates are very high. Attempts to increase the number of small private *qarz al-hassana* funds and the use of Islamic contracts such as *muzaraba* for financing trade in order to cut down usurious and unIslamic practices, have not been promising. Many of the small "interest-free" funds and *muzaraba* agents have become bankrupt or their managers have embezzled funds. In fact, litigations against such establishments have been increasing and in May 1988 the establishment of new private *qarz al-hassana* funds was forbidden. Another motivation for this action was to prevent the withdrawal of money from the nationalised banking system. After all, the rate of profit was much higher in private *muzaraba* contracts than in the banks.

The largest and economically most powerful private enterprise in Iran at present is the Islamic Economic Organisation (IEO). The IEO was originally established under the auspices of powerful clergies, immediately after the revolution, to work as an interest-free loan fund, accepting deposits and granting loans. Initially it was called the Islamic Bank. After the nationalisation of all private banks, Khomeini personally exempted the Islamic Bank from nationalisation. Nevertheless, it soon changed its name to IEO to avoid controversy. Since then, it has extended its banking activities and, at present, has more than eight hundred affiliated funds and controls more than 2 per cent of the private sector's liquidity. The IEO, as a "non-profit" oriented enterprise, is not under the control of the Central Bank. In fact, it competes with the nationalised banking system and does not always co-ordinate its policy with the government's monetary policy. It has expanded its activity to cover trade, construction, and imports and exports, in order to increase its capital.

Most Shi'i jurisconsults find insurance business and stock exchange activities legitimate. Until 1988, of the twelve nationalised Iranian insurance companies and the state-owned Iran Insurance Company (IIC), only three (the IIC and two formerly private companies) have been able to expand and continue their operation.

Immediately after the revolution, transactions in corporate shares and government bonds on the Tehran Stock Exchange came to a standstill. The private banks, insurance companies and industries nationalised in 1979 were no longer quoted. However, by mid-1991, the total value of transactions in nominal terms had climbed back to 84 per cent of their 1978 value and the shares of about 48 industrial companies were traded (*ibid.*, p. 282–3. *Keyhan*, airmail weekly, 12 Tir 1370). The National Iranian Industries Organisation has already offered the shares of 18 nationalised industrial units on the stock exchange and plans to offer those of 77 other industrial unit by the spring of 1992, for about 120 billion rials (*ibid.*, 30 Mordad 1370).

**Monetary and fiscal policies**

All conventional instruments of monetary and fiscal policy are used to influence the performance of the economy, in accordance with the objectives of the Islamic government. Fiscal policy is reflected in the government's budgetary policy. Government receipts include income taxes, government and private taxes, inheritance and capital gains taxes, indirect taxes (import taxes, sale and consumption taxes) and oil revenues. The government's expenditures are divided into development and current expenditures.

Monetary policy is formally the responsibility of the Central Bank of the Islamic Republic of Iran. In accordance with the Islamic principle that precludes the use of interest rates by the Central Bank, monetary policy cannot formally use the application of fixed interest rates. However, reserve requirements for various types of bank deposits, direct credit control (bank-by-bank credit ceilings on aggregate and sectoral credit), moral suasion, limited buying and selling of government bonds to and from commercial banks and re-discounting financial documents are used to determine the level of liquidity. In addition, as in Pakistan and Saudi Arabia, the Central Bank intervenes in and supervises the banking system's operation in various ways. It fixes minimum or maximum rates of profit for banks in their joint venture and *muzaraba* contracts; minimum expected rates of return for various investment and partnership projects; and minimum and maximum profit margins, for instalment and hire-purchase transactions. The Central Bank determines maximum and minimum rates of commission for banking services and fees charged on investment accounts; it determines the types, amount, and minimum and maximum bonuses paid to depositors.

Certain structural constraints greatly reduce the effectiveness of monetary and fiscal policy. The Iranian economy is a fragmented market economy, in which modern and traditional structures and institutions coexist. Since 1982, whenever oil revenues have fallen, the government has decreased its development expenditure and has raised sales, consumption and, to some extent, business taxes. In the 1980s, the government allocated an ever-increasing proportion of resources for priority sectors, notably agriculture and heavy industry and war-related expenses. On balance, the official budget deficit has been large, though it has been underestimated by the government because its budget excludes a significant proportion of the revenues and expenditures of the non-financial public sector, such as nationalised industries, the foundations and the war and military expenses. This deficit has been financed by borrowing from the Central Bank and the banking system. Thus, monetary policy has been ineffective in the sense that it has been subservient to the borrowing requirements of the public sector and has lacked instruments for controlling monetary expansion.

In 1983–85, oil revenues accounted for 48.2 per cent of total government revenue. With the fall in oil revenues since 1984, this ratio had fallen to about 23 per cent by 1986. In 1982, sales and consumption taxes accounted for 16.4 per cent of total receipts. By 1988 this had reached 31.8 per cent. The ratio of the deficit to total expenditure which had been 29.2 and 21.4 per cent in 1983 and 1984 respectively, rose to 39.3 per cent and 50.2 per cent in 1987 and 1988 respectively (*Gozaresh-e Eqtesadi*, 1369, p. 47).

The ups and downs of oil revenues not only affect the level of composition of government revenues, expenditures and deficit, but, together with the budgetary deficit, determine the monetary base of the economy. In 1988, net foreign assets, Central Bank claims against the government and against the nationalised banking system, constituted 3.0, 56.7 and 40.3 per cent of the monetary base respectively (*ibid.*, p. 45). Increasing reliance on Central Bank credits to finance the deficit has hampered the implementation of monetary policies for specific macro- or microeconomic objectives. In fact, in spite of the decline of real GDP in 1984–89, the growth of private-sector liquidity has always been higher than that intended by the government. Moreover, despite the government's official policy of restricting the growth of commercial credit in favour of industrial and agricultural credit, it is commercial credit that has enjoyed the highest growth. In addition, poor management, the dependence on imports of intermediate and capital goods, and the overall lack of coordination within the industrial sector gave rise to structural problems such as low elasticity of supply. Budgetary deficits, which increase demand for goods and services, combined with rigidity in structural supply, lead to chronic excess demand, which merely pushes up prices, and leads to higher inflation. In the 1980s, this problem was aggravated by the fall in output, which gave rise to unprecedented stagflation. Nevertheless, the rate of inflation was lower than in many underdeveloped economies, mainly due to the fact that the increase in the level of liquidity was partly held back through price controls by the private sector. The high level of liquidity, however, indicates that there was a high inflationary potential during the recovery and reconstruction period (Rahnema and Nomani, 1990, pp. 286–7).

The rapid expansion of the monetary base, which was used to finance public-sector borrowing, has also led to a transfer of resources from the private to the public sector, mainly for consumption purposes. This was brought about through an inflation tax on currency holders and on investors with low-yield deposits. Moreover, the Central Bank increased reserve requirements and set credit ceilings to provide additional sources for government deficit financing. The banking system was also used to direct resources to the public sector. In fact, most of the increase in private liquidity was diverted to the public sector since the increase in credit here exceeded the expansion in private sector liquidity. This is due to the fact that the main cause of the expansion of the monetary base was public sector borrowing. Thus, the Central Bank was not able to control the growth of nominal aggregate demand since the instruments of monetary policy were used to facilitate public sector borrowing. The expansion of the monetary base and rising prices led to a depreciation of the rial in the free market, which made the free market exchange rate an important outlet for private sector savings. The inability to control the money supply and give stability to the currency were major factors in the change of economic policy of the Rafsanjani government.

## Planning

Despite the experiences gained in planning from the 1950s onwards, the Islamic government was unable to draft or implement a medium- or long-term economic plan in the period 1979–89. This was mainly due to factional disputes over the orientation of the "Islamic economy" among the rulers of the Islamic Republic. In 1982, a five-year plan was tabled before parliament. This plan envisaged parallel growth in both the agricultural and industrial sectors, emphasising economic independence, inter-sectoral linkages, the growth of capital goods industries at the expense of consumer goods industries, and self-sufficiency. However, the plan was, at best, unrealistic; it assumed that the oil sector would expand by 16 per cent annually and that the price of oil would be $33.25 per barrel in constant 1982–83 prices with exports rising to about 3 million BPD by 1987. Moreover, it did not take into consideration the effect of the war on the economy.

An intense dispute over the plan's objectives, the long-term economic orientation of the country, the government's sources of income, the plan's unrealistic assumptions about oil export revenues — indeed over the need for a plan at all — led to the plan being crossed off the parliamentary agenda in early 1983. The government presented a revised version to parliament in January 1986. This time, the plan emphasised war mobilisation. It did not set any growth targets or promise any structural or institutional changes. In fact it was little more than an annual government budget. It envisaged the encouragement of private sector investment in non-service activities by means of credit policies and tax relief programmes, and avoided major new investments by the government. The plan was approved by parliament in January 1986 (*ibid.*, pp. 285–6). However, in early 1989, the government tabled the Law on the First Plan of the Socio-Economic and Cultural Development for 1989–93 in parliament. The Plan was approved by parliament in early 1990. Its main objectives were: to reduce the budget deficit by curbing expenditure and raising tax revenues; to increase public investment and stimulate private investment by curbing government and private consumption; and to increase the utilisation of existing capacity. It set a target of 8.1 per cent real growth in GDP.

In June 1990, the International Monetary Fund completed its first economic consultation with the Islamic Republic of Iran in twelve years. It suggested certain reforms as an extension of the five-year plan. If these reforms were implemented, the IMF report asserts, they would eliminate macroeconomic disequilibria, improve economic incentives and increase the private sector's share in the economy. The main proposals involve drastic devaluation of the rial, removal of multiple currency practices and price controls, reduction of subsidies, privatisation of nationalised industries, and determination of relative prices by the market (*IMF Survey*, 1990, pp. 226–9). Despite some resistance and opposition on the part of the interventionist faction, the government has proceeded with a timid, but steady and gradual implementation of the IMF's proposals (see, for example, the critical evaluation of the IMF report and the government's economic policy in "Assar-e Mokhareb-e Tazief-e Arzesh-e Rial", 1369, pp. 54–6; "Seminar-e Moasseseh-e Tahqiqat-e Iqtesadi", 1369, p. 59; "Vaqeiiathay-e Nagofteh", 1369, p. 51).

To conclude, the economic performance of Iran in the 1980s was affected by: political, institutional and policy changes in the aftermath of the revolution; political crisis and intra-governmental conflicts; the disastrous eight-year Iran–Iraq war; the fluctuation of oil-export revenues due to price and production changes; and international trade and financial sanctions against the country. All these factors, in addition to structural weaknesses of the Iranian economy, i.e. one-sided economic dependence upon the world-market system and its distorted and fragmentary nature, gave rise to stagnation in production of industrial goods, many services and some agricultural commodities, disruption of the distribution process, rising inflation and unemployment, a decline in real per-capita income, the standard of living, and growing poverty (see *Keyhan*, airmail weekly, 23 and 30 Mordad 1370).

Revolution led to the migration of many business people and skilled workers, and increase in government ownership of production and distribution. The war, and trade and financial sanctions, increased government control and led to new regulations on price, distribution and the external sector. This in turn led to further migration. Factional infighting prevented the implementation of a clear economic policy and further undermined business confidence (Rahnema and Nomani, 1990, pp. 289–96).

## The post-Khomeini period

On 3 June 1989, Ayatollah Khomeini died and the Assembly of Experts elected Ayatollah Khamenei as the new leader of the Islamic Republic (*Keyhan*, airmail weekly, 24 Khordad 1368). Later, the Constitution Review Council (CRC) came up with a series of amendments to the constitution that would increase the power of the leader of the Islamic Republic, by abolishing the office of prime minister and substituting it with the office of president. The CRC was written into the constitution as a board of advisers to the leader, appointed by him. The constitutional amendments were voted for in a referendum and on 28 July 1989, Hojatolislam Rafsanjani was elected fourth president of the Islamic Republic. Rafsanjani's cabinet included many centrists, and excluded hard-liners of the interventionist factions. Ever since, there has been a marked, but gradual, change of policy in the national and international orientation of the Islamic Republic. However, the new government has also benefited from the end of the Iran–Iraq war, the relative rise in the price of oil since 1989, and the lifting of most international trade sanctions against Iran. Politically, Rafsanjani has strengthened his authority within the regime with the support of Khamenei and has, so far, been able to maintain his policy of non-intervention in the economy and normalisation of political and economic relations with the West and the Persian Gulf states. His "statist" opponents have so far been unable to muster the support of the discontented public for an effective offensive against the government. Nevertheless, the risks of losing religious legitimacy and of failure of his gradual liberal economic policies remain.

The government's key economic objective is to restore the private sector's confidence and trust, and increase its role in economic activities. The government explains the interventionist policies of the 1980s by the constraints of the war and the human and financial capital migration. Now, ministers and non-interventionists assert that Islam favours the private sector and its development (*Resalat*, 11 Shahrivar 1370). However, it is claimed that to realise this objective, the austerity programmes and government controls of the Moussavi government that gave rise to all kinds of distortions, must be replaced by macro- and microeconomic balances (*Keyhan*, airmail weekly, 30 Aban 1369).

The five-year plan Law explicitly asserts that: "the change in price policy for goods and services is in such a way that gradually equilibrium prices are achieved for economic resources and in this process, prices are determined ... based on ... demand and supply" (*ibid.*). From a macroeconomic point of view, this policy requires the reduction of the government budget deficit and a gradual unification of different foreign-exchange rates.

On the whole, therefore, the government has been reducing subsidies; dismantling price controls; rationing and administrative distribution of essential goods; freeing private participation in imports; encouraging private and foreign investment; setting up free industrial trade zones; reforming multiple currency practices; increasing indirect taxes and selling government enterprises (*ibid.*).

Subsidies on vegetable oil and meat have been eliminated, while those on fertilisers, sugar, wheat and milk are gradually being reduced. However, the government is planning to eliminate subsidies to consumers and replace them with a plan that would directly provide help to "vulnerable social groups", a term coined by the World Bank and currently employed in Iran instead of the term "dispossessed" (*Mostazafin*).

All centres for the provision and distribution of essential goods have been officially closed and price controls for many producer and consumer goods have been lifted (*Keyhan*, airmail weekly, 26 Tir 1370; *Resalat*, 17 Mordad 1370). However, the effectiveness of the latter policy depends on exchange rate policy. The exchange rate varies according to the type of imports, so the final price of a product depends on who the producer is and how inputs have been purchased.

In a country that largely depends on foreign inputs for the production of many commodities, homogenisation of exchange rates is very important. In January 1991, the government reduced the number of preferential foreign exchange rates from six to three: a floating rate which reflects free market demand and supply; a competitive rate; and the government rate for imports of basic goods and large national projects. The immediate result of this policy was an increase in the government's revenues, which together with increased oil revenues in 1990–91, reduced the budget deficit. However, without a continuous rise in oil revenues and with a strong domestic demand for dollars, the rial has remained weak and volatile against foreign currencies, allowing for speculation on the exchange rate, and requiring ongoing subsidies amounting to around $3 billion.

By 1995, some 400 state companies are to be sold to their employees (up to 33 per cent of total shares) and the private sector on the stock exchange. These are nationalised industries belonging to nationalised banks and the National Organisation for industries. In addition, the government announced that 1,000 state mines will be leased to the private sector and that forests by the Caspian Sea will be leased to private applicants for commercial exploitation (*ibid.*, 22 Farvardin and 26 Tir 1370). However, only a small number of such companies have yet been sold through the stock market (*ibid.*, 5 Tir and 30 Mordad 1370).

The private sector is still hesitant and is awaiting a final political settlement of differences between the two opposing factions.

The government has also tried to attract foreign investment for its $27 billion industrial development programme in the fields of automotive, petrochemical and shipbuilding industries, construction materials and infrastructural facilities. Some ministers and the governor of the Central Bank have been sent abroad to present the government's moderate and pragmatic policy to foreign investors and exiled Iranian entrepreneurs, despite loud criticism by the interventionists of the return of "fugitive capitalists" (*ibid.*, 25 Ordibehest, 1 Khordad and 8 Khordad 1370). Many Western companies, banks and governments, including France, Germany, Japan and Canada, have agreed to commit themselves to different projects, but most have yet to materialise.

Another important measure for the encouragement of the private sector and foreign investment is the creation of free industrial-trade zones. This was envisaged in the five-year plan Law and the government has already selected two islands in the Persian Gulf, Kish and Qeshm, for this purpose. These islands will enjoy special rights in terms of trade, tax holidays and customs duties. The government is planning to set up the plants of the buy-back deals in these islands and the private sector has been asked to participate. Imports from the islands to the mainland are granted generous commercial tax cuts; while their exports would allow merchants to import goods up to 60 per cent of the value of the exports (*ibid.*, 3 Aban 1368, 5 Tir and 12 Tir 1370). It is interesting to note that the interventionist faction tried to block the creation of these zones on the pretext that the law of the islands would not be the Islamic law of the land, but they did not succeed in convincing the majority of members of the parliament on this matter (*Resalat*, 20 Khordad 1370).

However, despite all the above measures, the extent of state ownership and state control does not look likely to change drastically in the near future. This is due to the sheer size of the public sector and unresolved problems in the social and economic structure of the country. The five-year plan emphasises much higher investment and growth of strategic industries, such as the hydrocarbon sector and the intermediate and capital goods sectors. Finally, if the $15 billion buy-back deal envisaged by the plan should materialise, it can only lead to an increase in the government's share in non-oil exports, which have traditionally been dominated by the private sector.

# 8. The Islamic Socialism of Qadhafi in Libya

On 1 September 1969, a group of young officers, the so-called Unionist Free Officers, overthrew the Libyan monarchy in a military coup. The new ruling group, under the leadership of Qadhafi, were devout Arab nationalists of the Nasserist type as well as practising Muslims. Islam and Arab nationalism united them against the monarchy and its Sanussi interpretation of Islam. Once in power, differing interpretations of Islam and Arab nationalism led to dissent among the officers.

## Independence of Libya and the Sanussi rule: 1951–69

King Idris had ruled Libya since independence in December 1951. By the time of independence, Libya had experienced three decades of Italian colonialism, and a decade of British and French administrative rule on a care and maintenance basis in the period 1942–52. The UN decree of independence created a united kingdom, uniting the distinct provinces of Cyrenaica, Tripolitania and Fezzan within the framework of a federal constitution under King Idris. The King, the former Amir Idris al-Mahdi al-Sanussi, leader of the resistance against the Italian occupation, was nominally a constitutional monarch in a representative democracy with limited male suffrage. In practice he was a religious leader with autocratic temporal powers. Backed by the British and the United States, his authority was based on his leadership of the Sanussi Order. He was simultaneously a dynastic ruler and, as Grand Sanussi, the supreme religious and spiritual guide. His principal source of political legitimacy was religion. However, the Sanussi Order, a sufi sect of Sunni Islam, was dominant only in Cyrenaica. By itself, the Order could not impose a unitary state structure; a federal constitution seemed more plausible. Local autonomy which delegated power to native families reflected the state of Libyan politics.

At the time of independence, the indigenous population numbered little more than one million, mainly Libyan Arabs. There were about 47,000 Italian settlers and a smaller number of Greek immigrants. The urban population, mainly in small cities on the northern coast, constituted one-fifth of the total. One third of the population led a nomadic or semi-sedentary life. In Cyrenaica and the central part of Tripolitania, nomads predominated, while in the rest of Tripolitania and in Fezzan province, sedentary agriculturists made up the largest section of the population (Bearman, 1986, pp. 1–4).

Cyrenaica (called Eastern Province in 1969) was basically a tribal society, united by adherence to the Sanussi Order. Tripolitania (called Western Province in 1969), the most populated and urbanised part of the country, was divided by geographical and family rivalries, reflecting the political parties created during the British administration. Fezzan (called the Southern Province in 1969) was populated by different tiny ethnic groups (Allan, 1982, pp. 121–2). The Arabic language and Islam, both introduced first in the seventh and then in the ninth and tenth centuries A.D. by large-scale immigrations of Arabic speaking Sunnite tribes, formed the main mechanism of integration in Libya (Fisher, 1988, p. 626).

Monetary and financial institutions were quite underdeveloped. There were two foreign banks, with only a handful of Libyan customers. State revenue for 1949–50 was about £1.8 million and the level of public expenditure was lower than revenue (Sayigh, 1978, pp. 423–4). Industry was confined to a few small Italian factories and a few hundred small-scale workshops. Some eight hundred very small industrial units were producing goods for consumption in four cities. Four out of five industrial units were owned by Italians. The major exports were esparto grass and the scrap metal of Second World War battlefields, neither of which was enough to offset post-war imports (Allan, 1982, p. 56).

During the Second World War, Libya was devastated by successive military operations; wells were blocked up, buildings ruined and agricultural lands mined. After 1945, Western aid was indispensable; the British, US and French governments provided money and technical assistance. In exchange, the British and Americans were allotted military bases, paid for by subsidies to the Libyan budget.

The increased economic activity, due mainly to greater government expenditure and financed largely by foreign aid, led to an increase in the monetisation of the economy and the expansion of market activities. Oil companies started to search for oil, employing the local population and paying for goods and services. They also imported goods through local merchants. The combined effect of foreign aid, expenditure by oil companies and increased tax receipts led to higher investment in the 1950s. By 1958–59, agriculture contributed about one quarter of GDP, services made up over half, with the rest coming from the industrial sector (including petroleum prospecting). Nevertheless, the country was still very poor (Fisher, 1989, pp. 627–8).

In 1961, Libya began to export oil. During 1953–60, 65 per cent of the land area of the country had been divided into concession areas which were being explored by twenty international oil companies (Allan, 1982, pp. 37–8). Oil output increased considerably in the period 1962–69 and government revenue from oil rose from 14.2 to 419.7 million Libyan Dinars (LD) in the same period. GDP increased rapidly from 61 million LD in 1960 to 1,223 million LD in 1969 (Sayigh, 1978, pp. 440 and 453). The initial rapid development of the oil industry was helped by political stability; King Idris allowed neither an organised opposition nor a free press and political institutions were reduced to mere instruments of a pro-western policy. The closure of the Suez Canal, proximity to West European markets and the high quality of Libyan oil were major factors (Fisher, 1989, pp. 628 and 639). By 1972, the oil sector was contributing 62.7 per cent of GDP and the ratio of oil revenue to GNP was even higher. Oil income trickled through the economy via government expenditures. The first five-year plan was launched in 1963 and the government allocated 70 per cent of its oil revenues to investment projects. The plan emphasised the development of the country's infrastructure and, despite waste due to poor planning, it created the basis of Libya's future development. The second plan started in 1969, but after five months its operation, except for pipeline projects, was suspended by the new regime (Sayigh, 1978, pp. 443–5).

By 1968, 32.5 per cent of the active labour force was employed in agriculture, 26.2 per cent in industry and 41.3 per cent in the service sector. However, less than one third of the population was participating in the labour force and Libya had already started to import labour at an increasing rate.

Thanks to the oil sector, the compound growth rate of GDP per year was about 20 per cent between 1962 and 1971. With the rise in oil revenues, the role of the government in the economy expanded drastically. The government followed a basically non-interventionist economic policy, with little concern for state-sponsored industrialisation. A very small part of the development budget was allocated to industry, and industrial growth was concentrated in private small-scale investments mainly in the form of workshops related to construction. However, oil revenues allowed the government to become relatively independent of socio-economic groups and it began to see itself as non-accountable to the people for its actions. Participation in the main economic activities was limited and the relationship between domestic production and distribution processes declined as oil revenues increased. This trend led to the emergence of a *rentier* attitude in Libya which by 1970 had become an affluent society in the midst of poverty. Shortage of skilled and semi-skilled labour was serious, while government employment hid increased unemployment. As early as the end of the 1960s, 40 per cent of labour was imported.

The rising income of a few cities led to shortage of labour in the rural areas. Tripoli and Benghazi absorbed about 80 per cent of immigrants from rural areas. The migrant population, in nomadic or semi-nomadic kinship groups, settled in tent-cities and shantytowns around the few big cities which were benefiting from the oil-income boom. Between 1954 and 1964, 56 per cent of the population had migrated from rural to urban areas (Bearman, 1986, p. 38).

The increase in the supply of goods and services was not enough to satisfy the large increase in aggregate demand for public and private consumption and investment. This led to three main economic problems: the expansion of imports of consumer and producer goods and services; inflation; and rising inequalities in income distribution. Imports absorbed an increasing proportion of the growing aggregate demand, due to the meagreness of local resources. Many of the opportunities generated by the large expansion of the economic infrastructure, credit facilities and aggregate demand remained inadequately exploited by the private sector. This situation gave rise to a stronger merchant capital class.

However, large increases in imports did not create foreign-exchange shortages in this period since foreign-exchange resources were rising faster than imports. Nor did the increase in imports prevent prices from rising, since the wholesale import sector had an oligopolistic structure which was mainly controlled by Italians until 1967, when a Libyanisation law provided for the transfer of ownership to Libyans within two years. Nevertheless, between 1955 and 1972, prices rose by about 300 per cent (Sayigh, 1978, pp. 458–60).

The economy was reliant on indirect taxes and the economic plan favoured the oil sector and services. Thus, with the rise in oil income and the government's concomitant higher level of expenditure in infrastructural investment, distribution of income deteriorated yet further, and the few big cities were benefiting more than the rest of the country from the economic boom (Khader, 1987, pp. 61–2).

The growth of the market, the flourishing economy and the prospect of oil revenues led King Idris to replace the federal constitution with a unitary one. In December 1962, the king abolished the political status of the provinces and changed them into administrative units (Allan, 1982, pp. 124–5). With controlled parliamentary elections and suppression of opposition movements, he was able to balance the power of various political elements outside and inside the government and pursue his national and pro-Western international policies. However, the slow spread of education, urbanisation, the socio-economic consequences of oil revenues, the rise of Nasserian Arab nationalism and the growth of the doctrinaire parties in the Arab world changed the situation. Arab nationalism was gaining ground among young Libyans and loyalty to the king's government was drastically eroded by the government's preferential treatment of Cyrenaica. Islam, too, seemed to many Libyans to be devalued by the corruption of the king's associates and by the lopsided favouritism towards the Sanussi religious establishment which was alienating the orthodox Sunni *ulama*. All the above changes and developments reduced the credibility of the regime and shook the power base of the traditional political élite. Eventually, in September 1969, the monarchy was overthrown and a new political leadership with a different, but evolving, interpretation of Islamic imperatives replaced it.

## The Arab Libyan Republic: 1969–73

Arab Nationalism inspired by Nasser provided the ideological force guiding the policies of the new regime, under the leadership of Qadhafi. The new constitution, which was presented shortly after the "revolution" by the Revolutionary Command Council (RCC), was literally taken from the Egyptian National Charter. It emphasised the Nasserist slogan "liberty, socialism and unity", rather than the Ba'athist slogan "unity, socialism and liberty". It sought to gain freedom by opposing Western dominance, socialism by extending the role and power of the government in the economy, and unity by the creation of a single Arab nation (Joffe, 1988, p. 621).

Initially, during the period 1969–73, Qadhafi and the RCC paid only lip service to the socialist element of the Constitutional Communiqué which proclaimed the goal of the state to be the realisation of socialism through social justice and peaceful resolution of class differences. After all, agrarian reform was not very relevant in an underpopulated society. Nationalisation of the economy was not very important either, since, except for the oil industry, there were few large industrial enterprises in Libya. With respect to class-based political parties, Qadhafi and the RCC were of the opinion that in Libya class differences were not significant enough to justify their existence. Thus, in the Constitutional Communiqué which reserved the supreme power in the hand of the RCC, there was no mention of a general election or national assembly and it continued the former regime's ban on political parties. In fact, in December 1969, the RCC decreed as a criminal offence any activity against the state, any incitement based on class hatred, and participation in strikes or demonstrations (Bearman, 1986, pp. 65–9). However, an important difference between the RCC and Nasserism was Qadhafi's and the RCC's stress on Islam. Article 2 of the Constitution declared Islam the national religion and stated that all laws should be based on the values of the Islamic-Arab heritage. Thus, Qadhafi tried to appear as the champion of Islam, constantly referring to his attachment to Islamic ideas and practices. Yet he was against the Muslim Brotherhood because of their rejection of Arab nationalism and socialism. Qadhafi's ultimate goal, as stated in his initial speeches, was to reconcile "religion and progressivism" (Allan, 1982, p. 141). In spite of his personal belief in Islam, Qadhafi was also aware of the need for the new regime to legitimise itself before Libyans, who were practising Sunni Muslims following the Shafi'i school of law, or supporters of the Sanussi Order. Thus, Islam was explicitly used by the new regime against its opponents to encourage people's participation in the political process. For this reason the new regime banned the use of alcoholic beverages and the *ulama* were appointed to legal administrative positions. The RCC encouraged Islamic missionary activity in Africa and promised a revision of the legal code in accordance with the *Shari'a* (which implied no practical changes) (Joffe, 1988, pp. 621–2; Allan, 1982, p. 141).

The deposition of the monarchy was welcomed by most sections of Libyan society, with the notable exception of Sanussi tribal sheiks and very rich merchant families who had close relations with the court. This was reflected in the absence of initial opposition, virtually no armed resistance, relatively few arrests and no deaths.

The initial issues raised in the RCC's programme were: first, the promotion of Arabism, which was linked to anti-Israeli actions; second, nationalisation of foreign property in Libya and the removal of US and British military bases; and third, the expansion of Libya's role in the oil industry.

To consolidate the power of the RCC, individuals associated with the new forces replaced elements of the former regime, whose bank accounts were then frozen. Officers above the rank of major were retired or posted abroad. The King's guard was integrated into the regular army and the salary of the lower ranks was raised by 200 per cent. Comprehensive national conscription replaced the favoured recruitment from Cyrenaica, and Egyptian military intelligence officers replaced the British and American advisors and technicians. The *zawiya*, the religious institutional basis of Sanussi control, was dissolved. The Islamic University established by Idris was closed and Crown lands were expropriated and held for redistribution. The key personalities of the old order were tried and imprisoned.

In accordance with the RCC's assertion of Islam and Arabism, the precedence of the Arabic over the Latin alphabet was reinstated, Italian names were changed to Arabic, and Christian churches closed (Bearman, 1986, pp. 70–73). In addition to these measures, the RCC's economic policies consisted of restrictions imposed on foreign firms and individuals. The RCC annulled the 1956 Italo-Libyan Treaty which guaranteed the property rights of Italian immigrants in Libya. This led to the confiscation of land, agricultural equipment, livestock and farm holdings of Italian settlers, with no compensation, and the expulsion of 20,000 Italians. The confiscated lands (37,000 hectares) were leased to farmers subsidised by the government (El-Khawas, 1986, p. 65). The transfer of funds by foreign residents was limited to 60 per cent of their income and various restrictions were imposed on foreign commercial firms, which were mostly Italian. In 1969, of the 189 large industrial plants employing more than twenty workers 70 per cent were Italian owned. These industries included tobacco, tanning, leather, textiles and units for canning sardines and tomatoes. These foreign-owned industries were all taken over by the government (Deeb, 1987, p. 3).

In November 1969, intensifying the process of Libyanisation that had started during the former regime, foreign banks, mainly British and Italian, were asked to choose between converting into joint-stock companies or pulling out. At the time there were eight commercial foreign banks and two Libyan banks. First, the RCC decided to take over 51 per cent of the capital of foreign banks and, later, all foreign ownership in the banking sector was nationalised and a limit of 5,000 LD set on private Libyan shareholding. By the end of 1970, after the reorganisation of the banking sector, two commercial banks were state-controlled and three state-owned (Khader, 1987, p. 184). All the insurance companies were nationalised by 1971 and merged into two. Basic infrastructural units were nationalised and the National Organisation for the Supply of Commodities was set up by the government for the import of certain consumer goods (Deeb, 1987, p. 3).

In December 1971, the currency was changed from pounds to dinars and Libya left the sterling bloc. The Libyan Dinar was revalued twice and in February 1972 the rate of exchange was LD 1 = $3.04 (Khader, 1987, p. 183).

In July 1970, the RCC nationalised all petroleum distribution facilities in Libya and in April 1971 long negotiations with the oil companies led to a five-year agreement, increasing the posted price for Libyan crude oil to $3.447 per barrel. In the final stage of these negotiations, the Libyan government was also representing the interests of the governments of Algeria, Iraq and Saudi Arabia (Fisher, 1988, p. 629).

In December 1971, in retaliation against the UK's support of the Iranian occupation of the Tumbs and Abu Musa islands in the Persian Gulf, the RCC nationalised the assets of the British Petroleum Company. By September 1973, the Libyan government had succeeded in participating in the activities of almost all foreign oil companies in Libya and had acquired up to 51 per cent or more of the shares of these companies' Libyan activities. Since then the licensing system has been abolished and foreign oil companies now operate under product-sharing agreements (Khader, 1987, p. 196). Of course, in these agreements Libya benefited from competition between major and independent oil companies for the European market, the continued closure of the Suez Canal, and threats of an embargo on the export of oil by OPEC.

Finally, in accordance with Arab nationalist feelings, the British and US governments were asked to remove their bases from Libya. These bases were turned over to the Libyan government in March and June of 1970.

In the field of economic development, the new government, unlike the former regime, viewed itself as an agent of change. Thus, more emphasis was laid on the development of public sector projects. The National Public Organisation for Industrialisation (NPOI) was set up to plan and implement state investment. When the five-year plans were resumed, the share of industrial investment in the annual development budget increased from an average of 3 per cent in the 1960s to 15 per cent in 1970–71 (Allan, 1982, p. 57). The NPOI commissioned most of its large industrial projects from French, West German and Spanish companies (Bearman, 1986, pp. 76–9 and 123).

Despite the government's emphasis on the leading role of the public sector, the RCC's attitude towards the private sector was positive. To encourage Libyan businesses, the role of the Industrial Bank was expanded and the Bank participated in small private-sector projects in the food processing and construction industries and granted generous loans to finance commercial enterprises. The number of licences for retail trade establishments increased dramatically, as did the private sector investment in manufacturing. This trend was later reversed when local entrepreneurs became antagonistic towards the RCC's negative attitude to the private sector in 1972.

Initially, the RCC did not have a clear strategy for the agricultural sector. For almost two years, the agricultural policies of the former regime largely continued to be implemented. In 1972, the government endorsed the small-farm land settlement approach of the 1960s to prevent the acceleration of migration from the land. In fact, in the early years of the revolution, Qadhafi insisted that Libyans work their own farms, and that service workers in cities return to rural areas (Khader, 1987, p. 160). However, the expansion of the land settlement projects soon lost its vigour, the.government was unable to slow down migration from rural areas and was thus forced to increase the number of state farms, and foreign labour became an important part of the labour force in the agricultural sector in western and southern Libya.

Rising demand for foodstuffs and a drastic increase in the budget allocation for private agricultural activities in the form of expenditures on soil and water preservation, interest-free credits and generous subsidies led to the expansion of private farming and animal husbandry. However, the negative attitude of the government towards private activity in the late 1970s led to its decline and to its replacement by the dominance of state farms (Allan, 1982, pp. 15–19).

In this period, rising oil revenues removed the constraint on the accumulation of capital. However, manpower shortages and the dependence of small-scale private activities on cheap government loans and subsidies were growing. The government became the chief owner and administrator of a large number of enterprises and the major investor in the economy. Small-scale activities prospered and the economy became more diversified. However, the existence of thousands of small, understaffed, inefficient and high-cost operations, dependent on government loans, subsidies and foreign workers, reduced the incentives of Libyans to rely on their own resources.

In 1973, the indigenous Libyan active labour force was 432,700 in a population of over two million. Most were employed in the government or low-productivity private services. Between 1970 and 1975, the number of foreign workers grew from 50,000 to 323,000. Fifty-eight per cent of the professional and managerial labour force and 41 per cent of the non-skilled labour force were non-Libyans. For a long time Libya did not have any difficulty in financing the outflow of foreign exchange due to remittances by migrant workers. In 1970–74, Libyan gold and foreign exchange reserves increased from LD 576 million to 1,110 million. However, dependence on imported labour, despite the RCC's objective of self-sufficiency in labour, led to the withdrawal of Libyans from the industrial and agricultural sectors (Khader, 1987, pp. 58–67).In the light of the above changes and structural developments and without the introduction of Islamic contracts and economic institutions such as *zakat* or the abolition of interest in the banking system, Qadhafi was ready to label the Libyan economy as a socialist variant of Islam:

> I declare that the Arab nation is honoured by being the precursor of socialism, since socialist principles are found in the Qur'an. Neither Marx nor Lenin, nor other theoreticians and philosophers have succeeded in devising a better system than Islam in the economic, social and moral fields. (Quoted in Allan, 1982, p. 143)

However, despite its economic dominance, the state that was shaped by the RCC lacked the same degree of authority in politics and was in need of a mass ideological following. Thus in May 1970 the RCC, under the guidance of Qadhafi, convened a series of seminars with participants such as the Mufti of Tripoli and "revolutionary intellectuals". The objective of the seminars was to come up with a definition of the working forces of the revolution. The participants identified the "crushed" classes as the pillars of the revolution, yet at the same time rejected the notion of class domination. Following the model of the Egyptian Arab Socialist Union, the Libyan Arab Socialist Union (LASU) was formed on 11 June 1971, consisting of "crushed" classes: intellectuals, farmers, soldiers, workers and "non-exploitative capitalists". With the creation of LASU, the formation of political parties and independent trade unions was ruled out. According to Qadhafi, LASU was a popular political organisation and "trade unions had nothing to do with politics — at no time and at no place" (quoted in Bearman, 1986, p. 137). Of course, at that time there were no independent unions since all had been banned in 1969 and a government-sponsored union had replaced them to perform, according to Qadhafi, "ordinary administrative duties" (*ibid.*, p. 138).

The RCC was at the top of the LASU pyramid of organisation. LASU had a membership of 300,000 by 1972. However, very soon the LASU came under the control of officials who, in collusion with local businessmen and other sectors of the "crushed" classes, tried to gain power and wealth by controlling different sectors of the government and political apparatus. The "pecuniary lust" of officials and businessmen and their lack of zeal for Qadhafi's ideals led to his resignation from premiership in July 1972, even though he continued to occupy the Presidency and the Command of the Armed Forces. By the beginning of 1972, the disenchanted Qadhafi called for a "popular and cultural revolution" against what he called the bureaucratic-business alliance. His new initiative was against liberal nationalists on the one hand and the Muslim Brotherhood, the Islamic Liberation Movement, the Ba'ath Socialist movement and the Marxists on the other hand. The liberal nationalists had supported the new government's initial adherence to the Arab nationalist cause and independence from the West in political and economic matters. They were in favour of a market economy, which they believed would flourish with government help. However, they were against Qadhafi's pan-Arab military orientation, and his intervention in the internal affairs of other Arab countries. They were also against excessive nationalisation of enterprises and the minimisation of the role of the private sector in the development of the country. The RCC leaders of this trend were eventually forced into exile in Cairo in 1975–76, and in 1979 they founded the Libyan Front against Qadhafi's regime in exile (Anderson, 1986, p. 230).

## The transitional stage to *Jamahiriya*: 1973–75

The deviation of the RCC from the path of conventional Arab nationalism and Nasserism took place in 1973, three years after Nasser's death in September 1970. Criticising the influence of "the bourgeoisie and the bureaucrats" who, according to Qadhafi, had penetrated the LASU and the institutions of the government, the Libyan leader tried to undermine their power and purify the revolutionary movement by launching a "popular and cultural revolution". At the same time, Qadhafi was on the verge of a definite break with the Egyptian president, Sadat. Libya was about to enter the transitional period to domestic radicalisation and regional isolation.

On 15 April 1973, Qadhafi called for the liquidation of those who prevented the allegiance of the masses to his leadership. To eliminate the threats to his revolution and eradicate all forms of political allegiances, except that between the people and his leadership, he offered a five-point programme:

1. the replacement of all existing laws by revolutionary procedures;
2. purging the politically "unhealthy";
3. civil liberties only for "the masses of common people";
4. the replacement of the existing administration by popular committees;
5. cultural revolution against all the "reactionary", "poisonous foreign ideas" that would mislead young people's minds (El-Khawas, 1986, p. 49).

The response to Qadhafi's call for the establishment of popular committees was slow, and so Qadhafi turned to the students who, at his instigation, had set up the first committee at the Faculty of Law, Qar Younis University in Benghazi (*ibid.*, p. 50). These university committees revised curricula and censored politically "poisonous" books that propagated communism, atheism and capitalism. The students also brought the cultural revolution to government offices, harbours, factories and the countryside, dismissing local administrators and managers, and tried to lead peasants and workers in a campaign to increase output. The only branches of the government that were saved from the intrusion of the student zealots were the army, the ministries of the central government and the oil fields. This was because the committees were never a spontaneous and independent movement.

By August 1973, about 2,000 committees had been set up. These committees were legally institutionalised within the national government in October 1973 and charged with the supervision of local services, state-run companies and the distribution network. However, due to the passive response of the population and their low level of participation, the former administrators, managers and local notables soon reasserted their influence on committees. This led Qadhafi to the next stage of his experimentation with the *Jamahiriya* (literally "the state of the masses" ) and the popular militia (Bearman, 1986, pp. 100–102).

In 1973–75, in spite of political changes and the disregard for professionalism associated with the mood of "cultural revolution", the economic policy of the previous period was continued. In 1973, the first three-year plan, for the period 1973–75, was launched. The implicit objectives of the plan were: to consolidate the power of the state by expanding its popular base of support, to reduce the dependency of the economy on the oil sector, and finally, to achieve "self-sufficiency" by diversifying the economic structure. To realise the first objective, the service sector received the largest share of the development budget. Housing, health, education, transport, electricity and water and public services constituted 67.3 per cent of the total plan expenditure (Deeb, 1987, p. 3).

To make people "master in their own castles", the housing shortages had to be resolved. In 1969–75, more than 100,000 housing units were built by the private and public sectors. Shanty houses were destroyed and the last hut was symbolically burnt in 1976. These units were either sold to Libyans with generous state loans or distributed free of charge to tent dwellers (El-Khawas, 1986, pp. 69–70).

In response to the dock workers' strike of 1972, the RCC introduced new measures. First, strikes and all forms of workplace disruption were completely forbidden. Later, in mid-1973, a profit-sharing scheme was introduced in many workplaces, and in larger enterprises joint worker-management councils established (Bearman, 1986, p. 138).

In agriculture, the plan emphasised massive government irrigation projects to make Libya self-sufficient in cereals and meat. In the industrial sector, the government opted for capital intensive industrialisation. By 1977, about ninety new plants and factories had been set up, a third in food-processing industries (El-Khawas, 1986, pp. 69–77). Many privately owned small industries were exempted from tax and custom duties on imports (Deeb, 1987, p. 4).

Imports of goods and services were under the control of the state and private sectors and there appeared to be no financial constraints. Oil revenues rose from $1.35 billion in 1970 to $5 billion in 1975 and the current account had a surplus despite the rapid rise of imports — from $555 million in 1970 to $3.5 billion in 1975. Libya's major foreign trade partners were Western European countries, the US, Canada and Japan (Khader, 1987, pp. 65 and 201).

However, there were serious problems associated with the first plan. Rising government and private sector expenditures led to a sharp rise in the import of labour. In the agricultural sector, many projects were confronted with lack of infrastructural facilities, and shortages of water and labour. Farmers were not induced to remain on their farms and the land settlement policy was not successful. Labour shortages and high-cost industrial projects created waste in the industrial sector.

Socially, the middle class was on the rise. However, Libyan entrepreneurs, who relied on government aid, subsidies and contracts, were investing part of their profits abroad. In fact, far from becoming a new class of small businessmen supportive of the populism of Qadhafi and the RCC, they were increasingly challenging his power. Qadhafi had exhausted his usefulness for this upcoming class with its liberal nationalistic orientation, represented in the RCC by the minister of planning, Muhayeshi. Muhayeshi was in favour of national industrial development with the help of the state and the private sector. However, Qadhafi, backed by the majority of the RCC, who had initially supported the role of "non-exploitative capitalists" in the revolution, was gradually leaning towards Islamic socialist development. The "cultural revolution" had not been able to resolve the conflict between liberal nationalists and the Qadhafi faction, and the continuing coexistence of these two tendencies within the RCC was no longer possible. The first open confrontation took place in May 1975, brought about by a drastic drop in 1974 oil revenues of about $1 billion (Khader, 1987, p. 201). This required a change in government expenditure priorities. Muhayeshi and a few other RCC members demanded major reductions in military spending in order to maintain development programmes. Qadhafi's supporters, including Jalloud, favoured a decrease in domestic consumption and a state monopoly of foreign trade. Qadhafi won the dispute and foreign trade became a state monopoly in the summer of 1975. The third congress of LASU, purged of Qadhafi's opponents, approved Qadhafi's position and endorsed the state monopoly of foreign trade and introduced rent control in urban areas. Unrest among businessmen increased and Muhayeshi tried to organise an underground opposition within the armed forces and the administration. However, his secret organisation was discovered and he fled to Tunisia in August 1975. By the end of 1975, the original twelve members of the RCC had been reduced to five. The RCC itself was becoming obsolete and power was increasingly concentrated in the hands of Qadhafi (Bearman, 1986, pp. 145–8).

Supporters of Muhayeshi, especially among the students, reacted to these changes, and in January 1976 ten anti-Qadhafi students were killed in demonstrations. To eliminate "the reactionary elements", Qadhafi urged his followers to form "revolutionary student committees" and seize control of the student councils. Since the *ulama* were also becoming critical of Qadhafi's unorthodox interpretation of Islam and were tacitly siding with businessmen, the "revolutionary students" closed down all private Islamic institutions and the Islamic Library in Tripoli. Several students were arrested and executed. Thus, the transitional period of 1973–75 culminated in the political crisis of 1975–76. Qadhafi emerged victorious. As he became more secure and powerful, he embarked on his experimentation with the *Jamahiriya*, based on the Islamic social, political and economic thoughts expressed in his *Green Book* (*ibid.*, pp. 148–9).

## *Jamahiriya* as expressed in Qadhafi's *Green Book*

The three slim volumes of the *Green Book* were finally published in their complete form in 1976–78. The first volume presents Qadhafi's solution to the problem of democracy, the second his solution to the economic problem, and the third describes the social basis of his theory. All three volumes are the expression of his Islamic ideas although without explicit reference to Islamic sources or the Qur'an. Their main intellectual source, besides some Western theories, notably Marxism, are Islamic and Bedouin egalitarian ideas. On the whole, they are supposed to explain Qadhafi's Third Universal Theory. This is his interpretation of Islam as a superior general theory vis-à-vis capitalism or communism. The Third Universal Theory presents his general socio-economic theory and its application to the Libyan case.

In the three volumes, Qadhafi criticises what he sees as the oppressive political, economic and social systems of capitalism and communism. Their fault is represented by their failure to place "instruments of government" such as wealth and social laws (part 3) in the hands of people. Capitalism and communism are accused of creating artificial social systems and the usurpation of the people's power (*Green Book*, part 1, p. 7; part 2).

His solution to the political problem is "direct democracy" by people's committees and popular congresses formed at local (Basic Popular Congress), regional (Municipality People's Congress) and national (General People's Congress) levels. At all three levels, representatives from unions, syndicates and professional associations will be elected by their constituencies. Qadhafi asserts that parliaments misrepresent people and representation is a denial of participation. The party system eliminates democracy and the formation of parties would split society (*Green Book*, part 1, pp. 1–7). Class-based parties and systems, he argues, are as bad as tribal and sectarian systems since "class dominates society in the same way that a party, tribe or sect does" (*ibid.*, p. 18). Plebiscites are also rejected as "the most cruel and oppressive dictatorial system" (*ibid.*, p. 23).

Parallel to the problem of the instrument of government is the problem of drafting, amending and abrogating laws for society. "The genuine law of any society is either tradition (custom) or religion" (*ibid.*, p. 31). Any other forms of law, including constitutions, are "invalid and illogical", since they are man-made. The only legitimate sacred law is natural law. Freedom is threatened unless society has natural laws "based on stable rules which are not subject to change or substitution by any instrument of 'government'" (*ibid.*, p. 33).

Society has to be safeguarded against any deviation from its natural law by people's rule through people's committees and people's congresses. What about the role of the press in the democratic process? Qadhafi's solution is a press controlled by popular committee. The press, therefore, cannot be owned by individuals, groups or classes (*ibid.*, pp. 38–40).

Qadhafi accepts that his presentation of true democracy is theoretical, but concludes that realistically, "the stronger part in society is the one that rules" (*ibid.*, p. 41). As regards the economic problem, Qadhafi sees neither capitalism nor communism as a solution. For him, both models deny wealth to the majority, either by concentrating it in the hands of a few or in the hands of the state. Thus, both models are considered exploitative of wage workers who "are a type of slave, however improved their wages may be" (*Green Book*, part 2, p. 9).

In Qadhafi's ideal system the only acceptable categories of property ownership are "personal property" and "socialist property". The former is that which satisfies a person's needs without his having to employ others; the latter is the property that is owned by individuals as partners. Thus, he asserts, the wage system must be abolished and societies return to "the natural law which defined relationships before the emergence of classes, forms of government and man-made laws" (*ibid.*, pp. 8–10). This is because "natural law has led to natural socialism based on equity of the economic factors of production" (*ibid.*, p. 10).

In Qadhafi's system, based on partnership in the ownership of the means of production, workers would receive a share of the output according to their contribution to production. Thus, if the factors of production are divided into labour, raw material and machinery, each would receive one-third of the output. This is because the "natural law of equality is that each of the factors has a share in the production ... Each factor has an essential role in the process ... [and] they are equal ..., they all should be equal in their right to what is produced ..." (*ibid.*, p. 11). What this amounts to is that two-thirds of the output goes back to the "general budget of the society" which also belongs to the people in the final analysis. The same principle also applies to the agricultural sector in which the three elements of production are the farmer, the land and the machine. If, however, land is worked by the farmer and his family without hiring other people, he would be entitled to one-third of the output. Thus, land is the collective property of all the people and farmers are allowed to use as much as they can with the toil of their own family. The same conception of land ownership applies to housing. Everyone would be entitled to a house for his own family use, but the house must not be offered for rent. Of course, in the early stages of this ideal society, money and income differences will exist, but in its final stages they will all disappear (*ibid.*, pp. 18–28).

Qadhafi's social programme is even more simplistic and controversial. Again it is influenced by his Bedouin culture and Islamic faith. Society is based on a natural model and the only authentic natural social link is considered to be one of blood. The individual is linked to others by family. Tribalism is originally based on family ties and naturalism is a form of tribalism. Individuals without family are merely vagabonds or rootless and the tribe is the healthiest unit of society. Nations rise and disappear, but religion solidifies national unity if it is compatible with nationalism. Religion provides for the relationship between God and man and between people and society. When religion is effectively followed, exploitation will fade away (*Green Book*, part 3, pp. 1–23). Qadhafi does not advocate Islam for all existing societies, but he asserts that Islam and the Qur'an have the answers to all the problems of man (El-Khawas, 1986, pp. 34–5). However, since Islam began with the Arabs, he believes that it can be renewed only by the Arabs. Therefore, the resurgence of Arab nationalism must culminate in the *Jamahiriya*, which provides the conditions for the renewal of Islam (Bearman, 1986, p. 161).

To illustrate his natural theory, Qadhafi discusses specific issues such as the rights and status of women. According to Qadhafi, due to biological differences, women have a "natural function", motherhood. "The West regards her as a commodity for buying and selling, while the East does not recognise her femininity" (*Green Book*, part 3, p. 39). Therefore, he recommends a revolution against all conditions that hinder women from performing their "natural role" and force them "to carry out men's duties in order to be equal in rights" (*ibid.*, p. 41). Of course society must provide work for all, "but on condition that each individual should work in the field that suits him ..." (*ibid.*, p. 41)

This, on the whole, is the gist of the political, economic and social components of Qadhafi's Third Universal Theory. However, it is interesting to note that he does not quote from the Qur'an. In the *Green Book* Qadhafi talks of religions in general, for his intention is to create a universal socio-economic and political model. However, his position on economic issues and his hatred towards the monopolisation of religious learning and spread of what he considers to be erroneous information about religion by the *ulama* of traditional Sunni Islam and the Sanussi Order, was bound to intensify his conflict with them. Qadhafi's conflict with the *ulama* was more important than his conflict with the Sanussi Order since the latter had lost its influence in Libya except in the Eastern Province. The majority of Libyans are Sunni Muslims, accepting the Qur'an and the *Sunna* as the primary sources of the Islamic faith. In fact until 1973, Qadhafi had always paid lip service to the *Shari'a* as the law of the land. Later, he explicitly criticised Islamic law (*fiqh*) and the various Islamic schools of jurisprudence. He called for an Islamic position which would "transcend sectarianism by going back to the origin" (quoted in El-Khawas, 1986, p. 87). His emphasis on the Qur'an and his rejection of the necessity of any mediation between God and man indicated an implicit rejection of the *Sunna*. This forced the *ulama* to decide whether or not to submit to a political power who was rejecting the fundamental sources of Islamic law. Islam does not distinguish between the spiritual and the temporal, so any conflict between the two is political. Thus, the leading *ulama* complained that the *Green Book* mocked the *Sunna*, was inspired by Marxism and was therefore incompatible with Islam. Qadhafi warned the *ulama* against forming an alliance with reactionaries and the exploitative classes. He denounced them for "propagating heretical stories elaborated over the course of centuries of decadence and conducting a reactionary campaign against the progressive, egalitarian, socialist concepts of the regime" (quoted in Bearman, 1986, p. 163). Later, in a debate with a group of *ulama,* he argued against accepting the *hadith* as a source of Islamic faith. In fact, he even defended Ataturk. According to Qadhafi, the Turkish leader was forced to abandon Islam in favour of Western secularism in reaction to the fanatical *ulama* who "have been [a] disaster for Islam" (quoted in Ayoub, 1987, p. 82).

Thus, in order to quieten the *ulama*, in May 1978 Qadhafi declared an "Islamic Revolution". He called on the *jamahir* (masses), who according to him could interpret Islam better than the *ulama*, to seize the mosques and liberate them from the mediaeval specialists of Islamic law (*fiqh*). Later, he asserted that the *Green Book* was based only on the Qur'an, because the *Sunna*, *qias* and *ijma'* were all unnecessary components of Sunni Islam, for they, unlike the Qur'an, introduced man-made laws (Joffe, 1988, pp. 623–4). He also asserted that the Third Universal Theory was an example of *ijtihad* or the exercise of independent judgement in relation to the Qur'an, and that he would not accept the mediation of the *ulama*. By invoking individual *ijtihad*, Qadhafi intended to proceed to apply the *Green Book* to Libya, which according to the *ulama* would have been in violation of Islam. To reiterate his point, he invoked *ijtihad* with respect to certain Islamic practices. In November 1978, he recommended that the Islamic date which had its origin in the migration of the Prophet from Mecca to Medina, be changed to the death of the Prophet. This was because he believed that the Prophet's death signified the cessation of revelations and was therefore more important for Muslims. Qadhafi's recommendation was adopted by the Libyan government in 1979 (Ayoub, 1987, pp. 91–2). He also declared that the *zakat* rate can be varied and is not to be fixed as in the *Shari'a*. In Libya, however, *zakat* is not imposed, nor is there an institution responsible for its application. Qadhafi is also of the opinion that the amputation of the hand or foot as the Islamic penalty for theft has only symbolic rather than literal interpretation (Bearman, 1986, p. 163).

Qadhafi's version of Islam was duly condemned by the orthodox *ulama* as heretical. The Muslim World League's journal accused Qadhafi of heretical beliefs on several accounts: his alleged rejection of the *Sunna*; his denial of the authenticity of the *hadith* and his doubts about the correctness of certain Qur'anic texts; his rejection of polygamy, which is sanctioned in the Qur'an; and his decision to change the traditional Muslim calendar (Ayoub, 1987, p. 136). Thus, on the eve of the application of the *Green Book* to Libyan society, Qadhafi had managed to alienate not only middle-class businessmen, professionals and technocrats, but also the *ulama* and the believers of orthodox Sunni Islam. Religious figures who had opposed Qadhafi's doctrine either disappeared or were forced into silence, and the role of the mosque in the social and political life of Libya was eliminated. However, the diversified Islamic opposition, many of whose members were imprisoned or executed, still has its followers inside and outside Libya and represents a potential threat to the regime. The opposition includes the Muslim Brotherhood and the Islamic Salvation party, both of which have been opposing Qadhafi since 1970. The Islamic Jihad Organisation and the Lebanese Shi'a Movement can also be added to the Islamic opponents of Qadhafi's brand of Islam (Joffe, 1988, pp. 628–31). In fact, the fundamentalist

Islamic movement is the greatest concern of Qadhafi's regime; it accuses the regime of heresy; and for its part has claimed responsibility for various acts of sabotage in Libya (Vandewalle, 1991, pp. 220–21).

## The application of the *Green Book*

In the first General People's Congress (GPC) in November 1976, Qadhafi announced his intention to introduce constitutional changes; these were finally endorsed by the GPC in March 1977. The official name of the country was changed to the Socialist People's Libyan Arab Jamahiriya. The RCC was abolished and a General Secretariat of the GPC, with Qadhafi as Secretary General, was set up. In 1979, Qadhafi resigned from this position to devote his time to "revolutionary work". The General People's Committee replaced the Council of Ministers, and People's Committees were established at a local level.

However, the new system of direct democracy did not arouse widespread enthusiasm, and low attendance and abstentionism were on the rise. Some representatives criticised the *Green Book* and its application. Thus, in 1978, Qadhafi called on the ideologically committed, i.e. young male adults and students who had been carefully screened by Qadhafi's office, to ensure the success of the revolution by imposing Qadhafi's will on the People's Committees. Thus, "Revolutionary Committees" (RCs) were formed to eradicate political and economic corruption. The RCs quickly assumed certain administrative functions and received more power to execute their decisions. In March 1979, the GPC gave the RCs the right to supervise selection procedures within the Basic People's Congresses (BPC) with a right to nominate and veto candidates who were not desirable in the eyes of the new revolutionary elites of the RCs. The RCs also acquired the right to arrest and detain and to hold revolutionary tribunals, thereby becoming part of the judiciary, propaganda, security and police apparatus of the state. Their members had political immunity and benefited from frequent visits abroad. The committees had no structural links among themselves, yet all formed part of the highly centralised command of Qadhafi who resided in the "Lion's Den" in Tripoli.

After the "Islamic Revolution" and the "Political Revolution", Qadhafi launched the "Producers' Revolutions". In September 1978, he called on the RCs to establish workers' committees and set up "Producers' Partnership" in large enterprises, private and public, except the oil industry. By the end of 1978, there were 180 state farms, commercial enterprises and factories administered by the employees and supervised by elected committees. In the case of private enterprises, financial indemnities were granted to compensate their former owners. The functions of management were given to a people's committee chosen by members of the Vocational People's Congress within each work place. Other enterprises, i.e. the self-employed units, were left intact.

Despite some degree of workers' control over economic decisions, workers' partnerships were constrained by the government planning agency, which was charged with the implementation of the overall development plan. Each productive unit was to compete for inputs and resources, although these remained subordinated to the political priorities of the *Jamahiriya*. These partnerships are confined to Libyans working in the non-oil sectors. Thus, half of the labour force remained outside the scheme (Bearman, 1986, pp. 187–95).

Foreign trade also came under the complete monopoly of the state and public corporations replaced 45,000 merchants who were considered as "non-productive Libyans" (Deeb, 1987, p. 5).

Private agricultural ownerships employing workers were spared from expropriation until 1985. Since 1985, all forms of private land ownership, other than single proprietorship, have been eliminated and the RCs have burned land-ownership records at the Land Registry in Tripoli. In addition to single proprietorships, 420 self-sufficiency farms were organised, selling their output to the state (Bearman, 1986, p. 275).

In the distribution sector all enterprises, except individual or family proprietorships, were turned into state-sponsored distribution agencies, controlled by vocational People's Economic Committees. Then, in 1981, all the retail outlets, including the markets (*souks*), grocers, butchers, shoe and household appliance shops were closed and turned into partnerships. The government built 158 market places and consumers' centres in various regions. Five supermarkets were built in Tripoli and Benghazi and a General Marketing Company was set up to supply "people's supermarkets" with goods heavily subsidised by the government. All private firms engaged in business with the government were consolidated into national firms. To prevent businessmen from keeping their assets in cash, the government changed the bank notes and the banks were instructed to permit the withdrawal of no more than LD 100 (*ibid.*, pp. 195–6 and Deeb, 1987, p. 5).

As a result, even small traders who had long backed Qadhafi joined the silent opposition, alongside the Sanussis, technocrats, professionals, businessmen and the *ulama*. Capital and skill were withdrawn from the market and over time even left the country. A number of merchants were arrested and tried and some dissenting *ulama* and preachers disappeared. However, with the drastic expansion of the role of the government in all economic sectors, foreign companies benefited from contracts granted to them by the government. In addition, the number of administrative personnel increased to 186,000 in 1979, in a country with a population of 3 million (*ibid.*, p. 6).

## The decade of crisis and mellowing of ideals: the 1980s

Due to its basic dependence on oil revenues, Libya has had an economic crisis since 1980. By 1980, demand for OPEC oil started to decline because of economic recession in the industrialised countries and the measures introduced there to economise on oil consumption. Libya's oil production fell from 2 million barrels a day (MBD) in 1979, to 1.1 MBD in 1981 and 1.017 MBD in 1982. At the same time, the market price of crude oil fell to $10.5 below the price prevailing in January 1981. Libya's income from oil decreased from $22.527 billion in 1980, to $14.350 billion in 1982, and to less than $10 billion in 1983 (Khader, 1987, p. 67). The decline continued until 1986, when Libya received only some $5 billion (*Le Monde, Bilan Economique, 1987*, p. 111). The decline in oil revenues, which accounted for 99 per cent of foreign exchange earnings and more than 50 per cent of GDP, led to a drastic decrease in trade surplus and the current account balance was in deficit by 1984, giving rise to a continuous deficit in the remaining years of the 1980s. As a result of this deficit, Libya's foreign-exchange reserves also decreased. In March 1982, US President Reagan imposed trade sanctions on Libya. A trade ban was imposed on imports of Libyan crude oil to the US, which had accounted for 35 per cent of Libyan oil exports, and on US exports to Libya except food and medical supplies (Bearman, 1986, p. 268).

The loss of oil revenues forced the government to change its economic policy in 1982. The GPC opted for a new general policy of "maximum production and minimum consumption". Austerity measures, especially in consumption, were introduced. Certain commodities were declared unnecessary and their import banned. In 1983, developmental expenditures favoured heavy industries at the expense of light industries, and some projects were either postponed or cancelled (Fisher, 1988, p. 641). In the agricultural sector, the land of farmers who employed workers was expropriated and land-ownership records were destroyed (Bearman, 1986, p. 275). The government, however, continued its $25 billion project of "the great man-made river", a pipeline of 1,990 kilometres, which is designed to carry two million cubic metres of water a day from an underground reservoir in the south-east of Libya to the north of the country (Khader, 1987, p. 68). Several US companies were involved in the first phase of this project. However, after President Reagan's ban, South Korean contractors replaced the US companies. To help further with the financing of the project, taxes were imposed on certain goods (Deeb, 1987, p. 7).

In general, since the early 1980s, expenditures were successively reduced each year (Khader, 1987, pp. 206–7). This led to a decline in GDP from $35.5 billion to $24 billion in 1986, the latest year for which government data are available. In the same period, per-capita income fell from $10,900 to $6,404. The government budget deficit and the balance of payments have been covered by drawing on foreign-exchange reserves, which in 1984 were estimated to be between $1 and 4 billion. On the whole, foreign debt, mostly in the form of delayed payment to foreign contractors, increased in this period, though money supply increased only slowly (Deeb, 1987, p. 6). In order to absorb liquidity outside the banks and take the pressure off the market, all interest rates paid on savings, notice and fixed deposits were raised in April 1980. Saving deposit rates rose from 4.5 to 38.5 per cent, notice deposit rates from 4.75 to 35.7 per cent, and the rate on three-year fixed deposits was changed from 8 to 100 per cent to encourage investors to keep their deposits for a longer period (Khader, 1987, pp. 186–90). Due to balance-of-payments and investment difficulties in summer 1985, many foreign Arab workers were expelled; some were replaced by Asian, non-Arab workers, mainly Indians, Pakistanis or South Koreans, who were more apolitical than the Arab workers (Deeb, 1987, p. 7).

In 1985, relations with the US worsened due to Libya's involvement in Chad and its alleged association with international terrorism. In January 1986, President Reagan froze Libyan assets in the US, estimated to be only several hundred million dollars, and banned all trade between the two countries (Fisher, 1989, p. 637). US companies, including oil companies, were asked to leave Libya. Libya now had to sell its oil directly to European refineries, competing with Algeria and Nigeria (Deeb, 1987, p. 6). However, the Libyan government did not nationalise the assets of US oil companies in Libya; they then signed agreements with Libya that gave them the right to negotiate their return in the future. Finally, in June 1986, the US government banned the export to third countries of goods and technology destined for the Libyan oil industry (Fisher, 1989, p. 637). By 1989, the price of oil had declined further, drawing down Libya's oil revenues to $7 billion, intensifying the economic problems in the country *(Le Monde, Bilan Economique, 1990,* p. 112).

The imposition of restrictions on imports and the state monopolisation of foreign trade in the late 1970s created severe shortages and led to Libyans circumvening government rules and regulations. Farmers sold part of their output to middlemen "who then managed to sell them to consumers at higher prices than those in the government's cooperatives" (Deeb, 1987, p. 7). Black markets spread for goods that could not be bought from government supermarkets and retail stores. Some subsidised goods, such as oil, rice and tea, were smuggled to neighbouring countries. Even the housing sector experienced shortages in the mid-1980s, due to cuts in the housing budget (Fisher, 1988, p. 644. *Le Monde, Bilan Economique, 1987*, p. 111).

The continuous decline of GDP, shortages of basic commodities, increasing dissatisfaction with internal political repression and the external assassination of members of the opposition, and regional and international political isolation finally led Qadhafi to reconsider his policies, and forced him to accept a more pragmatic approach to his Islamic socialism.

In February 1987, rising tension between the Islamists and the regime after the assassination of a prominent member of the RC, led to the execution of six civilians, allegedly members of the Islamic Jihad, and three military "traitors". At the same time, delegates at the General People's Congress raised their voice against the excesses of the RCs' involvement in Chad and economic hardships. In response, Qadhafi came out for a "Revolution within the Revolution". He admitted his foreign policy mistake in Chad after the defeat of the Libyan forces in 1987 and toned down his plans for union with other countries. He stated his opposition to terrorism and accused his own RCs of assassinating his political opponents. The RCs lost their right to arrest and imprison people, and in May 1988 a new secretariat was set up to monitor and supervise them. In March 1988, the People's Court and the People's Prosecution Bureau replaced the notorious revolutionary courts. Hundreds of political prisoners were released and Qadhafi personally took part in the demolition of Tripoli's central prison and the destruction of the files of the four existing security organisations. Libyans were granted freedom to travel abroad; and Qadhafi personally supervised the elimination of the border post with Tunisia. In 1988, Tunisia received one million Libyans who were provided generous hard-currency allowances. At the same time, Qadhafi called on Libyan exiles to return without fear of persecution, and met with some of the non-Islamist opposition leaders "in an attempt at conciliation" (Vandewalle, 1991, p. 221). Finally, in June 1988, a Great Green Charter of Human Rights, condemning violence and advocating legality, accountability, freedom and human rights, yet disallowing free press, political parties and strikes, was approved by the GPC.

The Green Charter is heavily based on the ideas formulated in the three volumes of the *Green Book*. The charter envisages a society without discord in which the concept of individual civil liberties is absent. It calls private property "sacred and protected", but "concludes that it can be circumscribed by the public interest without specifying what the public interest entails". It asserts that all Libyans have "the right to legal counsel and to an independent judiciary ...but offers no real guarantees" (*ibid.*, p. 225). It states that every Libyan is under the protection of the "Qur'anic *Shari'a*", but immediately emphasises the equal rights of men and women, stating that the unequal right between men and women "is a blatant injustice that nothing can justify". It recognises the freedom of opinion, but the means for the realisation of this right and the judicial protection for it are not pronounced. Direct democracy under the rule of the people is advocated, but Qadhafi and his entourage are given an exclusive and infallible right to leadership (Djaziri, 1990, p. 631). The Green Charter recognises the right to hold religious beliefs but denies any religious hierarchy the right to act as intermediary on behalf of the creator. It also condemns the use of Islam for political ends, "conspiracy or parasitic activities" (quoted in *ibid.*, p. 632). In fact, the Green Charter has a definite political character and provides a legal foundation for the repression exercised against the opposition (especially the Islamic opposition).

With respect to economic reforms, Qadhafi, in 1987–88, in a retroactive move, advocated economic liberalisation: privatisation and open-door economic policies. He justified this move by arguing that his new policies were against the bureaucratisation of the economy by the state as expressed in the *Green Book*: that the revolution was completed and the economy could be shaped by what we have called "plan-then-market" (see Chapter 3). He cynically stated that people were now free to live like the bourgeoisie in their "ivory tower" (quoted in Vandewalle, 1991, p. 226).

In this new programme Qadhafi called for the elimination of customs and immigration posts with neighbouring countries. Thus, along the border with Tunisia, a free zone was set up where Libyans could buy goods unavailable in their own country (*Le Monde, Bilan Economique, 1990*, p. 112). More importantly, Qadhafi advocated expansion of the role of the private sector, reopening of private retail trade, abolition of state monopoly of foreign trade, and an opening up to foreign investment. He also recommended the establishment of worker cooperatives based on the idea of producers' partnership (the so-called *tasharukiyya* principle). His new policy was justified by the need to increase efficiency, and enter a new phase in the revolution, since "the previous phase was only an exceptional one in order to settle scores with the *ancien* generation who had squandered everything" (quoted in Djaziri, 1990, p. 640). Duly, the

Ministry of Industry came up with a two-year timetable for the privatisation of small and medium-sized enterprises in the agricultural sector, restaurants and hotels, retail trade, transport, textile, construction and consumer goods industries, based on *tasharukiyya* and single proprietorship. According to the *tasharukiyya* scheme, as an employee one would receive a salary based on one's work, productivity, education and responsibility; as a partner, one would receive an equal share of the net revenue of the enterprise. Net revenue was defined as gross revenue minus all costs and the amortisation rate of the value of the enterprise (8 per cent of gross revenue). By August 1988, 141 small factories were turned over to their employees and the lifting of injunctions against private retail trade and private medical clinics fostered the development of private initiatives. The *souks* (markets) in the cities were reopened and the import of consumer goods improved the distribution system. In addition, the rise of oil revenues in 1990 and during the Persian Gulf crisis enabled the financing of imports and government development projects (*ibid.*, pp. 639 and 641). However, after two decades of experimentation with what Qadhafi calls "Islamic scientific socialism", the Libyan economy still suffers from the typical imbalances of a developing, single-commodity economy. Libya remains dependent on oil revenues, foreign supply of goods and services, and immigrant labour (see International Colloquium, 1979, p. 201). The oil sector contributes to more than half of GDP; it provides over 99 per cent of export earnings and financing of development projects. Efforts to diversify exports by producing chemicals has not been successful in an already glutted and highly competitive world market. Libya is still not able to produce enough capital goods, consumer goods and foodstuffs to satisfy its rising population. Continuous labour shortages (skilled and unskilled) due to the wide gap between the level of investment financed by oil revenues and the locally available labour force has been a real dilemma for the economy. Today, more than ever before, Libyans are relying on foreign labour expertise and know-how in their economic activities. Responsibility for production and distribution has been shifted to the state, which hires immigrant, skilled and unskilled workers, giving rise to high cost, low incentives and a lack of local initiatives.

Ideological and political experimentation within Libyan society has constituted a serious constraint on the country's development. The economy is burdened by a large, non-productive and highly ideological government sector. Despite major achievements in housing, education, transport and communication that could also have been achieved through other less costly means than the *Jamahiriya*, Libya remains a lopsided, dependent economy. Nevertheless, Libya today is very different compared to the early 1970s, although the new economic structure and its political and economic institutions remain transitional and fragile.

Qadhafi calls the Libyan economy an Islamic socialist system. This is based on his unorthodox interpretation of the *Shari'a* which consists only of the Qur'an: "The Glorious Koran is the *Shari'a* of our new socialist society" (International Colloquium, 1979, p. 199). However, the system is very much based on Qadhafi's eclectic combination of religion, nationalism and populism.

Whether or not it is based on the Qur'an is not a fruitful discussion. But by the mid-1980s it had become clear that many Libyans remained unconvinced by his vision and the success of his practices. The state created by Qadhafi has become increasingly independent of the social forces, due to oil revenue and state ownership. The *Al-Fatih* revolution in Libya started by relying on all potential constituencies, but has alienated itself from the Libyan *jamahir*, and beyond, and has had to rely increasingly on repression. Of course, Islam and Islamic sentiments will continue to play a role in the future of Libyan development. It is ironic that today the success of Qadhafi's Islamically inspired political and economic liberalisation process depends on the outcome of the conflict between him and the Islamic fundamentalist opposition, which Qadhafi has branded as "more dangerous than AIDS" (Mattes, 1991, p. 80).

# Bibliography


Abu Yusaf. *Kitab-Ul-Kharaj*. Lahore: Islamic Book Center. 1979.

Afzal-ur-Rahman, M. *Economic Doctrines of Islam*. Vols 1–3, Lahore: Islamic Publications. 1980.

Afzal-ur-Rahman, M. *Economic Doctrines of Islam*. Vol.4, Lahore: Islamic Publications. 1982.

Afzal-ur-Rahman, M. *Islam, Ideology and the Way of Life*. London: Seerah Foundation, 1988.

Afzal-ur-Rahman, M. *Encyclopedia of Seerah*. Vol.7. London: Seerah Foundation. 1989.

Ahmad, K. (ed.) *Studies in Islamic Economics*. Leicester: The Islamic Foundation. 1981.

Ahmad, K. (ed.) *Islam, its meaning and message*. Leicester: The Islamic Foundation. 1988.

Ahmadi-Mianji, A. *Usul-e Malekiyat dar Islam*. Vols 1 and 2. Tehran: Daftar-e Entesharat-e Eslami. 1363.

Ahmed, V., and R. Amjad. *The Management of Pakistan's Economy: 1947–82*. Karachi: Oxford University Press. 1984.

Ahmed, Z., M. Iqbal and M. Fahim Khan. *Money and Banking in Islam*. Islamabad: Institute of Policy studies. 1983.

Akhavi, S. *Religion and Politics in Contemporary Iran*. Albany: SUNY. 1980.

Ali, A.Y. *The Holy Qur'an*. Maryland: Amana. 1989.

Alkazaz, A. "The Islamisation of Banking and Finance in Pakistan and its Effect on Savings and Investment". *Economics*, vol. 36, 1987.

Allan, J.A. (ed.) *Libya since Independence*. London: Croom Helm. 1982.

Anderson, L. "Gadhafi and His Opposition", *The Middle East Journal*, vol. 40, no. 2, 1986.

Ayoub, M. M. *Islam and the Third Universal theory: The Religious Thought of Mu'ammar al-Qadhafi*. London: KPI. 1987.

Behdad, S. "Property Rights in Contemporary Islamic Economic Thought; A Critical Perspective". *Review of Social Economy*, vol. 47, no. 2. Summer 1989.

Bani-Sadr, A. *Iqtisad-e Towhidi*. n.p., n.d.

Bazargan, M. *Bazyabi-e Arzeshha*. Tehran: n.p. 3 vols, 1361.

Bearman, J. *Qadhafi's Libya*. London: Zed Books. 1986.

Beheshti, M. *Iqtisad-e Eslami*, Tehran: Daftar-e Nashr-e Farhangh-e Eslami. 1363.

Biazar-e Shirazi, A. K. *Resaleh-e Novin, Masel-e Iqtisadi*. Tehran: Daftar-e Nashr-e Farhangh-e Eslami. 1366.

Biazar-e Shirazi, A. K. *Nezam-e Iqtesade Eslami*. Tehran: Daftar-e Nashr-e Farhangh-e Eslami. 1368.

Binder, L. *Religion and Politics in Pakistan*. L.A: University of California Press. 1961.

Bornstein, M. *Comparative Economic Systems: Models and Cases*. Illinois: Irwin. 1979.

Burki, S. J. and R. Laporte, Jr. *Pakistan's Development Priorities*. Karachi: Oxford University press. 1986.

Cameron, A.J. *Hazrat Abu Dhar al-ghifari*. Lahore: Islamic Publishers. 1982.

Chapra, M.U. *Objectives of the Islamic Economic Order.* London: Islamic Council of Europe. 1975.

Choudhury, M.A. *Contributions to Islamic Economic Theory*. London: Macmillan. 1986.

Coulson, N.J. *A History of Islamic Law*. Edinburgh: University Press. 1990.

Curtis, M. (ed.) *The Great Political Theories*. Vol. 2. N.Y: Avon Books. 1962.

Daftar-e Hamkariy-e Howzeh va Daneshgah (D.H.H.v.D.), *Daramad-i bar Iqtisad-e Eslami*. Tehran: Chape Salman-e Farsi.1363.

Dalmoak, M. "Boost from privatisation". *The Banker*. April 1985.

Deeb, M.J. "Libya's Economic Development, 1961–1986: Social and Political Implications". *The Maghreb Review*. vol.12, no. 1–2, 1987.

Dekmejian, R.H. *Islam in Revolution: Fundamentalism in the Arab World*. Syracuse: Syracuse University Press. 1985.

Djaziri, M. "Chronique Libeyenne". *Annuaire de l'Afrique du Nord*, vol.XXVII. 1990.

Doi, A.R.I. *Shari'ah: The Islamic Law*. London: Ta Ha Publishers. 1984.

Eilts, H.F. "The Persian Gulf Crisis: Perspectives and Prospects". *The Middle East Journal*, vol. 45, no. 1. 1991.

El-Khawas, M. *Qadhafi: His Ideology in Theory and Practice*. Vermont: Amana Books. 1986.

El-Mallakh, R. *Saudi Arabia: Rush to Development*. Baltimore: The Johns Hopkins University Press. 1982.

Enayat, H. *Modern Islamic Political Thought*. London: Macmillan Education. 1982.

Esposito, J.L. (ed.) *Islam and Development: Religion and Socio-political Change*. New York: Syracuse University Press. 1980.

Fisher, W.B. "Libya". *The Middle East and North Africa*. 1989. London: Europa Publications. 1988.

Freyer, E. "Islamic and Western Investment Companies". *Economics*, vol. 36. 1987.

Gardezi, H. and J. Rashid (ed.) *Pakistan: The Roots of Dictatorship*. London: Zed Books. 1983.

Gerami, M.A. *Darbare'e Malekiyat Khosousi dar Islam*, Qum: Entesharat-e Rouh. n.d.

al-Ghazali, M. *Ihya' Ulum al-Din*, Vol.3, Beirut: Dar al Nodvat al-Jadidah. 1974.

Ghazali, A. and S. Omar. *Readings in the Concept and Methodology of Islamic Economics*. Malaysia: Pelanduk Publications. 1989.

Gilani, I. "Pakistan: Economy". *The Far East and Australia, 1989*. London: Europa Publications. 1989.

Gregory, P. R., and R. C. Stuart. *Comparative Economic Systems*. Houghton Mifflin. 1985.

*Gozaresh-e Iqtesadi-e Sal-e 1367*. Tehran: Sazman-e Barnameh va Budgeh. 1369.

Halliday, F. *Arabia without Sultans*. New York: Vintage Books. 1975.

Haeri, K. *Bonyan Hokumat dar Eslam*, Tehran: Vezarat-e Irshad-e Eslami. 1364.

Hashemi-e Rafsanjani, A.A. *Idalat-e Ejtema'i*. Vol.4. Tehran: Chape Sarv. 1362.

al-Hassani, B. *Iqtisad, The Islamic Alternative for Economics*. MD: IMAMIA. 1988.

Hassan-uz-Zaman, S. M. *The Economic Functions of the Early Islamic State*. Karachi: International Islamic Publishers,1981

Heilbroner, R. *The Making of Economic Society*. N.J.: Prentice-Hall. 1985.

Helli, Mohaqeq. *Sharae'al-Eslam*. vols 1–4. Tehran: Entesharat-e Daneshgah. 1364.

Hosseni, H. "Islamic Economics in Iran and other Muslim Countries: Is a New Economic Paradigm in the Making?" *Journal of South Asian and Middle Eastern Studies*, vol. 12, no. 2. Winter 1988.

Hunter, S.T. (ed.) *The Politics of Islamic Revivalism*. Bloomington: Indiana University Press. 1988.

Ibn Taymiya. *Public Duties in Islam*. Leicester: The Islamic Foundation. 1983.

International Colloquium in Benghazi: The Green Book. 1–3 October. Vol. II. Tripoli: Foreign Liaison Office. 1979.

International Monetary Fund. "Islamic Republic of Iran Undergoes Profound Institutional, Structural Change". 30 July 1990.

Iqbal, M. (ed.) *Distributive Justice and Need Fulfilment in an Islamic Economy*. Leicester: The Islamic foundation. 1988.

Islami, A.R.S., and R.M. Kavoussi. *The Political Economy of Saudi Arabia*. Seattle: University of Washington Press. 1984.

Islahi, A.A. *Economic concepts of Ibn Taimiyah*. Leicester: The Islamic Foundation. 1988.

Jensen, H.E. "Are there Institutionalist Signposts in the Economics of Alfred Marshall?" *Journal of Economic Issues*, vol. 24, no. 2. (June 1990).

Joffe, G. "Islamic Opposition in Libya". *Third World Quarterly*, vol.10, no. 2. 1988.

Johany, A.D., M. Berne and J. W. Nixon, Jr. *The Saudi Arabian Economy*. Baltimore: The Johns Hopkins University Press. 1986.

Kamali, M.H. *Principles of Islamic Jurisprudence*. Cambridge: Islamic Texts Society. 1991.

Karpat, K.H. (ed.) *Political and Social Thought in the Contemporary Middle East*. N.Y: Praeger Publishers. 1982.

Karsten, I. "Islam and Financial Intermediation". *IMF Staff Papers*, vol. 29. March 1982.

Keddie, N.R. *An Islamic response to Imperialism*. Berkeley: University of California Press. 1983.

Khader, B. and B. El-Witati (ed.) *The Economic Development of Libya*. London: Croom Helm. 1987.

Khan, M.A. *Islamic Economics*. Leicester: The Islamic Foundation. 1983.

Khan, M.S. and A. Mirakhor. "Islamic Banking: Experiences in the Islamic Republic of Iran and Pakistan". *Economic Development and Change*, vol. 38, no. 2. January 1990.

Khan, M.S. and A. Mirakhor (ed.) *Theoretical Studies in Islamic Banking and Finance*. Houston: The Institute for Research and Islamic Studies. 1987.

Khomeini, R. *Tahrir al-Wasileh*, Vol.2. n.p., n.d.

Khomeini, R. *Resalah*, n.p., n.d.

Khoshneviss, J. *Khotoute Koliy-e Iqtesad dar Qur'an va Ravayat*. Isfahan: Ketabkhaneh-e Omoumiy-e Imam Amir al-Momenin Aleyhasalam. n.d.

Klein, F.A. *The Religion of Islam*. London: Curzon Press. 1985.

Lackner, H. *A House Built on Sand: A Political Economy of Saudi Arabia*. London: Ithaca Press. 1978.

*Law of the First Plan of the Socio-economic and Cultural Development of The Islamic Republic of Iran*. Tehran: Sazeman-e Barnameh va Budgeh. 1990.

Looney, R.E. *Saudi Arabia's Development Potential*. Lexington: Lexington Books. 1982.

Mahmasani, S. *Falsafe-e Ghanoongozari dar Eslam*. Tehran: Amir Kabir. 1358.

Mahmood, M. *The Constitution of The Islamic Republic of Pakistan:1973*. Lahore: Pakistan Law Times Publication. 1973.

Majles-e Shouray-e Eslami. *Sourat-e Mashrouh-e Mozakerat-e Majles-e Barrasiy-e Nahai'y-e Qanoun-e Asasi*. Tehran: Chapkhaneh-e Majles. 1364.

Makarem-e Shirazi, N. *Khotoot-e Asli-e Iqtisad-e Eslami*. Qum: Entesharat-e Hadaf. n.d.

Malik ibn Anas, Imam. *Al-Muwatta*. London : Kegan Paul International.1989.

Mannan, M.A. *The Making of Islamic Economic Society*. Cairo: International Association of Islamic Banks. 1984.

Mannan, M.A. *Islamic Economics: Theory and Practice*. Cambridge: Hodder and Stoughton. 1986.

Mannan, M.A. *Economic Development and Social Peace in Islam*. London: Ta Ha Publishers. 1990.

Mashkour, M.J. *Dictionary of Islamic Sects*. Mashhad: Astan Quds Razavi. 1989.

Mattes, H. “Libya: The Desert Experience”. *The European Journal of International Affairs*, vol.12, no.2. 1991.

Maududi, A.A. *First Principles of the Islamic State*. Lahore: Islamic Publications. 1983.

Maududi, A.A. *Economic Systems of Islam*. Lahore: Islamic Publications. 1984.

Maududi, A.A. *The Islamic way of life*. Leicester: The Islamic Foundation. 1986.

MEED, April 1992.

Moasesehe Motale‘at va Pajouheshhaye Bazargani (M.M.v.P.B.), *Nazari Ejmali bar usul va Mabani Masraf dar Eslam*. Tehran: Moasesehe Motale‘at va Pajouheshhaye Bazargani. 1368.

Montagu, C. “Saudi Arabia Tries to Diversify”. *The Banker*. April 1985.

Motahhari, M. *‘Adl-e Elahi*, Tehran: Entesharat-e Sadra. n.d.

Motahhari, M. *Bist Goftar*, Tehran: Entesharat-e Sadra. n.d.

Motahhari, M. *Nazari be Nezam-e Iqtisadi-e Islam*. Tehran: Entesharat-e Sadra. 1361.

Moussavi-e Isfahani, J. *Payamhaye Iqtesadi-e Qur’an*. Tehran : Markaz-e Nashr-e Farhang-e Eslami. 1368.

al-Mujahid, S. “Pakistan: History”, *The Far East and Australia, 1989*. London: Europa Publications. 1989.

Muslehuddin, M. *Philosophy of Islamic Law and the Orientalists*. New Delhi: Taj Printers. 1986.

Nahjul Balagha. Sermons, *Letters and Sayings of Imam Ali*. Rome: European Islamic Cultural Center. 1984.

Naqvi, N.H. *Ethics and Economics: An Islamic Synthesis*. Leicester: The Islamic Foundation. 1981.

Nayak, p. (ed.) *Pakistan: Dilemma of a Developing State*. Jaipur, India: Aelekeh Publishers. 1985.

Neinhaus, V. “The Pakistan Economy on the way to Re-Islamisation: Problems and Perspectives”. *Economics*, vol. 37. 1987.

Noman, O. *The Political Economy of Pakistan: 1947–85*. London: KPI. 1988.

Paydar, H. *Malekiyat, Kar, va Sarmayeh az Didgah-e Islam*. Tehran: Daftar-e Nashr-e Farhang-e Eslami. 1357.

Presley, J.R. *A Guide to the Saudi Arabian Economy*. London: Macmillan Press. 1984.

Presley, J.R., and M. Kebbell. “Saudi Arabia’s Financial System”. *The Banker*. April 1982.

Proceedings of the Third East Coast Regional Conference of the Muslim Students’ Association of the US and Canada. *Contemporary Aspects of*

*Economic Thinking in Islam*. Indianapolis: American Trust Publications. 1976.

al-Qadhafi, M. *The Green Book, part One: The Solution of the Problem of Democracy*. London: Martin Brian & O'Keefe. 1976.

al-Qadhafi, M. *The Green Book, part Two: The Solution of the Economic Problem*. London: Martin Brian & O'Keefe. 1976.

al-Qadhafi, M. *The Green Book, part Three: The Social Basis of the Third Universal Theory*. Runcom, England: Astmoor Litho. n.d.

Qadri, A.A. *Islamic Jurisprudence in the Modern World*. New Delhi: Taj Company. 1986

Qureshi, A.I. *The Economic and Social System of Islam*. Lahore: Islamic Book Service. 1979.

al-Rafi'i, M. *Islamuna*. Middlesex: The Muhammadi Research Trust. 1987.

Rahman, A. *Economic Doctrines of Islam*, Vol. IV. Lahore: Islamic Publications Ltd. n.d.

Rahnema, A., and F. Nomani. *The Secular Miracle: Religion, Politics and Economic Policy in Iran*. London: Zed Books. 1990.

Rodinson, M. *Islam and Capitalism*, London: Pelican Books. 1977.

Russell, B. *A History of Western Philosophy*. London: Unwin Paperbacks. 1979.

Sadowski, Y. "Arab Economies after the Gulf War". *Middle East Report*, vol. 21, no. 3, 1991.

Sadr, M. Baqir. *Iqtisaduna* (*Our Economics*). 2 vols. Tehran: World Organization for Islamic Services. 1982.

Sadr, M. Baqir. *Iqtisade Ma ya Barrasihae dar bareh Maktabe Iqtesade Islami*, Volume 1. Tehran: Entesharate Eslami. 1350. Volume 2. Tehran: Entesharat-e Islami. 1357.

Sadr, M. Baqir. *Our Philosophy*, London: The Muhammadi Trust, 1987.

Sadr, S. Mousa. *Iqtisade dar maktab-e Eslam*, Tehran: Jahan Ara. n.d.

Safa, F., and S. Mohsen, *Estesmar*, n.p. Anjoman-e Daneshjoyan-e Mosalman-e Faranceh. n.d.

"Saudi Arabia". *The Middle East and North Africa, 1988*. London: Europa Publications. 1989.

Sayigh, Y.A. *The Economics of the Arab World: Development since 1945*. London: Croom Helm. 1978.

Schacht, J. *An Introduction to Islamic Law*. Oxford: Clarendon Press. 1991.

Shad, A.R. *Zakat and 'Ushr*, Lahore: Kazi Publications. 1986.

al-Shafi'i. *Risala*. Cambridge: The Islamic Text Society. 1987.

Shariati, A. *On the Sociology of Islam*. Berekely: Mizan Press. 1979.

Shariati, A. *Hajj*, Houston: Free Islamic Literatures. 1980.

Shariati, A. *Islam-Shenasi*. Mashhad: Chape Tus. n.d.

Shariati, A. *Khodsazi-e Enqelabi*. n.p. n.d.

Shariati, A. *Shahadat*, Tehran: Abu Dharr Foundation. n.d.

Shariati, A. *Collected Works*, Vol. 2. Entesharat-e Niloufar. n.d.

Shariati, A. *Collected Works*, Vol. 26. Entesharat-e Niloufar. 1362.

Siddiqi, M.N. *The Economic Enterprise in Islam*. Lahore: Islamic Publications. 1979.

Siddiqi, M.N. *Partnership and Profit-Sharing in Islamic Law*. Leicester: The Islamic Foundation. 1985.

Siddiqi, M.N. *Muslim Economic Thinking*. Leicester: The Islamic Foundation. 1988.

Taleqani, M. *Partovi az Qur'an*, Vol. 3. Tehran: Sherkat-e Enteshar. 1358.

Taleqani, M. *Society and Economics in Islam*. Berkeley: Mizan Press. 1982.

Taleqani, M. *Islam and Ownership*. Lexington: Mazda Press. 1983.

Taqavi-Damghani, R. *Chehel Hadith*, Vol. 3, Tehran: Sazeman-e Tabliqat-e Eslami. 1369.

Taskhiri, M.A. *Darshay' az Iqtesad-e Eslami*. Tehran: Markaz-e Chap va Nashr-e Sazeman-e Tabliqat-e Eslami. 1368.

Tavanayanfard, H. *Tarikh Andishehay-e Iqtesadi dar Jahan-e Islam*. n.p. 1361.

Third Pakistan–France Colloquium. *Islamic Law and Social and Economic Development*. Islamabad. 1998

Va'ezzadeh Khorasani, M. *Majmou'eh Maqalat-e Farsi Avalin Majma' Barrasihay-e Iqtesad-e Eslami.* Vols 1–3. Mashhad: Astan Quds Razavi. 1369.

Vandewalle, D. "Qadhafi's Perestroika: Economic and Political Liberalization in Libya. *The Middle East Journal*, vol. 45, no.2, 1991.

Warnock, M. (ed.) *Utilitarianism*. London: The Fontana Library. 1970.

Wells, D.A. *Saudi Arabian Development Strategy*. Washington D.C.: American Enterprise Institute for Public Policy Research. 1976.

Wilson, P.W. *A Question of Interest: The Paralysis of Saudi Banking*. Boulder: Westview Press. 1991.

World Bank. *World Development Report 1987*. New York: Oxford University Press. 1987.

Zarinkoob, A.H. *Tarikh-e Iran Ba'd az Eslam*. Tehran: Amir-Kabir. 1363.

## Journals, periodicals and newspapers

*Bayan*, nos 3, 4.

*Howzeh*, nos 4, 27, 37–38.

*International Herald Tribune*, 7 August 1990.

*Keyhan*, 11 Aban 1364.

*Keyhan-e Hava'ie* (weekly airmail edition). Issues: 6 Azar 1364; 5 Mordad 1367; 24 Khordad 1368; 3, 30 Aban 1369; 10 Bahman 1369; 22 Farvardin 1370; 5, 12, 26 Tir 1370; 2, 23, 30 Mordad 1370.

*Le Monde, Bilan Economique et Social: 1985*. 1986.
*Le Monde, Bilan Economique et Social: 1987*. 1988.
*Le Monde, Bilan Economique et Social: 1988*. 1989.
*Le Monde, Bilan Economique et Social: 1990*. 1991.
*Le Monde, Bilan Economique et Social: 1991*. 1992.
*Newsweek*, 6 August 1990.
*OPEC Bulletin*, vol. XVIII, no. 7, September 1987.
*Pasdar-e Eslam*, nos 1, 10, 35, 39, 110.
*Payam-e Engelab*, nos 81, 82.
*Resalat*, 29 Shahrivar 1366; 20 Khordad 1370; 17 Mordad 1370.

# Index